P9-CEA-091

POLITICAL THINKING

LONGMAN CLASSICS in POLITICAL SCIENCE

POLITICAL THINKING

THE PERENNIAL QUESTIONS

SIXTH EDITION

GLENN TINDER

University of Massachusetts, Boston

With new foreword by
Steven M. DeLue

Miami University, Ohio

PEARSON
Longman

New York   San Francisco   Boston
London   Toronto   Sydney   Tokyo   Singapore   Madrid
Mexico City   Munich   Paris   Cape Town   Hong Kong   Montreal

To Galen, son and independent thinker

Vice President and Publisher: Priscilla McGeehon
Executive Editor: Eric Stano
Senior Marketing Manager: Megan Galvin-Fak
Production Coordinator: Shafiena Ghani
Cover Designer/Manager: Wendy Ann Fredericks
Cover Art: Auguste Rodin (1840-1917). *The Thinker*, 1906. Musée
    Rodin, Paris, France. Vanni/Art Resource, NY.
Senior Media Production Specialist: Jeffrey Streber
Publishing Services Manager: Alfred Dorsey
Printer and Binder: RR Donnelley & Sons, Inc.
Cover Printer: Lehigh Press, Inc.

Library of Congress Cataloging-in-Publication Data

Tinder, Glenn E.
    Political Thinking : the perennial questions / Glenn Tinder.—
    6th ed.
        p. cm.
    Includes bibliographical references and index.
    ISBN 0-673-99389-2
    1. Political science—History.   I.   Title.
    JA81.T56   1995   94-18671
    320'.09—dc20   CIP

Copyright © 2004 by Pearson Education, Inc.

All rights reserved. No part of this publication may be reproduced,
stored in a retrieval system, or transmitted, in any form or by any
means, electronic, mechanical, photocopying, recording, or otherwise, without the prior written permission of the publisher. Printed
in the United States.

Please visit our website at http://www.ablongman.com

ISBN 0-321-00527-9

    45678910—DOC—06

*F*OREWORD

Tinder's Contribution to Political Thinking

G lenn Tinder's *Political Thinking: The Perennial Questions,*
which first appeared more than thirty years ago, demonstrates better than any other work of its type that the
activity referred to as "political thinking" contributes mightily
to making possible decent societies in which people thrive and
prosper. Understanding how this is possible requires an expla-
nation of the symbiotic relationship between Western political
theory and political thinking.

For Tinder, Western political theory is far more than just writers' responding to the issues of their times. Political theory is a tradition that consists of the concepts and ideas arising from the body
of writing that makes up the history of political theory. Concepts
found within the tradition of political theory include ideas such as
power, authority, and rights.[1] Concepts common to the tradition
of political theory are used in political thinking to reflect on and
to discuss the problems of achieving a decent society.

Scores of difficult questions must be addressed well if a
decent society is to be realized. However, because no single
individual can successfully deal with these questions solely
from his or her intelligence and experience, the search for
answers must take place within a community dedicated to this
purpose. Still, the community of discourse on behalf of creating
a decent society will not materialize unless there is a common
language that allows people to engage in discussions designed
to make reasoned, political judgments. The tradition of Western
political theory, with its many concepts and ideas, makes available a common language that satisfies this need and thus places
political thinking on a solid footing.

Many writers have helped fashion Western political theory
into a common language that provides the foundation for polit-

---

[1] Many other concepts could be cited, such as the nature of citizen obligation, the role of the state
and offices in the state, the concept of a constitution, and so on.

v

ical thinking. In this regard, there are two types of political theorists. First there is the *historian* who discusses theorists in the history of Western political theory from the classical period to the present. Among the historians of political theory are George Sabine, Mulford Sibley, and William and Alan Ebenstein.[2] Each of these writers helps his readers to understand political ideas in terms of their historical contexts, thus clarifying not only how various concepts emerged, but how they were revised over time. The historians of political theory, by focusing on the environments in which concepts arise and are modified, encourage political thinkers to be sensitive to the fact that as the contexts in which concepts are used change, so too might the significance of those concepts change.

The second type of political theorist is the *intellectual* who investigates political ideas central to Western political theory and of supreme importance for creating and nurturing an environment in which people can thrive and flourish. In general, intellectuals seek to preserve a cultural setting in which political ideas and the ways of life they represent can be preserved in spite of the social or political forces that threaten them.

Among the intellectuals are Sheldon Wolin, Leo Strauss, Karl Popper, and Jean Bethke Elshtain.[3] Wolin read the history of Western political theory as the tradition that promotes a public, political realm in which public issues, among diverse groups, could be resolved in the interest of securing shared solutions. Wolin worried that the contemporary setting is filled with the efforts of various groups to undermine the political realm by imposing a particular group perspective on the whole of society. Strauss hoped to defend a conception of natural right by which he meant enduring truths that were not the product of social convention but of reasoned inquiry, and these truths would serve as the standards with which to make distinctions

---

[2] George H. Sabine, *A History of Political Theory*, third edition, first published 1937 (New York: Holt, Rinehart and Winston, 1961); Mulford Q. Sibley, *Political Ideas and Ideologies: A History of Political Thought* (New York: Harper and Row, 1970); William Ebenstein and Alan Ebenstein, *Great Political Thinkers: Plato to the Present*, sixth edition, first published 1951 (New York: Harcourt, 2000).

[3] Sheldon Wolin, *Politics and Vision: Continuity and Innovation in Western Political Thought* (Boston: Little, Brown, 1960); Leo Strauss, *Natural Right and History* (Chicago: University of

between real needs that politics should support and false ones that politics should resist. Popper saw the history of Western political theory in terms of his hope to ensure the triumph of an open over a closed society. In an open society, critical discussion of all issues—including those involved with science and politics—is fostered. But in a closed society, the kind of setting Popper argued that Plato advocated, the reverse is the case. Popper claimed that Platonic support for a closed society was repeated by various writers throughout the history of political theory. Elshtain demonstrated the way in which the idea of the public realm, so often advanced in the tradition of Western political theory as the setting for defining the foundations for achieving a decent society for all citizens, ends up denying any place to women. Instead, women are cast into the private realm where they are subordinated to men and denied their dignity. As a result, a fundamental idea of the modern public realm—the idea of equal respect for all people—rings hollow.

Glenn Tinder, as a political thinker, embraces the roles of both historian and intellectual in undertaking a philosophical exploration of significant political questions. In doing this, Tinder uses the central ideas and concepts in the history of political theory to address issues peculiar to making possible a decent society in the contemporary world. His treatment of these issues presumes an audience—his readers—whom he engages in reflective discourse, making use of the common language arising from the tradition of political thought. Indeed, a reader can easily imagine being part of a discussion that includes not just Tinder and his views, but those other viewpoints that Tinder brings to bear. And Tinder's list of questions is comprehensive, as the reader of this book will quickly see. He includes the big questions: the relationship between inequality and equality; the nature, limits, and ends of power; and the relationship between history and politics. And within each of these questions lies a multitude of no less important questions,

Chicago Press, 1953); Karl R. Popper, *The Open Society and Its Enemies: The Spell of Plato*, vol. I, (Princeton: Princeton University Press, 1966) and *The Open Society and Its Enemies: The High Tide of Prophecy: Hegel, Marx, and the Aftermath*, vol. II, (Princeton: Princeton University Press, 1966); Jean Bethke Elshtain, *Public Man Private Woman: Women in Social and Political Thought* (Princeton: Princeton University Press, 1981).

such as who should rule, why people should obey their government, what moral limits governments should observe, how the principle of equality should be applied to men and women, the nature of the relationship between liberty and equality, and many others.

Tinder Writes the Book That Socrates Would Have Written

Tinder's extraordinary contribution to the development of political thinking is that he models for his audience the sharp philosophical intelligence with which one should approach political issues. His *Political Thinking: The Perennial Questions* is viewed as the model for today's world of Socrates's declaration that "an unexamined life is not worth living."[4] In this regard, Tinder's work takes us on a journey of philosophical reflection oriented toward the attainment of a decent society. Along the way, we become fully acquainted with the characteristics, challenges, and circumstances of the thinking self that uses the tradition of political theory as the foundation for its reflective, reasoned activity.

To impart an understanding of the thinking self, Tinder writes the book for today's readers that Socrates would have written. The activities of political thinking—reflection and discussion—are best characterized by many turns and angles, by an array of arguments and counterarguments, and often by the absence of a definitive conclusion satisfactory to all. Indeed, political thinking is *not* an enterprise akin to using a political concept as a measuring standard to assess the validity of a proposition or a proposed action. Were this possible, all political thinking could be reduced to deductive statements such as "A is true, and given that B is an instance of A, then B is true."

As Tinder shows, however, the concepts in the tradition of political thinking serve only as guides to a deeper, more enhanced understanding of the issues. The role of political concepts in political thinking often involves puzzling through para-

---

[4] Plato, "The Apology," in *Euthyphron, Apology, Crito, Plato: The Last Days of Socrates*, translated by F. J. Church (Indianapolis: Bobbs-Merrill, 1956), p. 45.

doxes—statements that appear "self-contradictory" (19, 242). Paradoxes establish a strong linkage between rationally defensible, if mutually contradictory, concepts. One important paradox in political thinking is Rousseau's contention that human beings must be forced to be free (19). Rousseau suggests that force and freedom, which are mutually contradictory concepts, are connected in a reciprocal relationship. Finding ways to explain how each of these concepts contributes to the other is the starting point and the thrust of political thinking.

This undertaking always takes place in relation to a concrete issue or problem that a society faces. With respect to Rousseau's paradox, there will have to be laws that protect people from interference with the exercise of their personal freedom. These laws will carry penalties for those who violate them, which suggests that a degree of coercion is needed for the sake of freedom. But how much coercion can a society tolerate on behalf of freedom? Some might say that the more coercion a government invokes to protect freedom, the more unchecked a government is likely to become, and this could lead to the abuse of the freedom that government is supposed to safeguard. The implication of this view is that freedom is best protected when citizens voluntarily respect the freedom of others, thus minimizing if not making completely unnecessary the coercive power of government. People who argue against this view might say that this position is naïve, and claim in contrast that the best protection for freedom is a vigorous government empowered to enforce a host of laws. This approach might result in severe penalties being inflicted on a great many people for the sake of ensuring the greatest possible freedom in society.

Which approach is best? Often the only way to resolve such matters is to assess the circumstances in which an issue arises. Perhaps, in a society with a strong and pervasive presence of civic friendship, people will abide freely by the laws that protect freedom, thereby minimizing the need for government coercion. Where there is a high level of mistrust, if not dislike, among people, a government exercising large doses of coercion to enforce laws that defend freedom may be the most reasonable course, at least until civic friendship can be established.

Another familiar paradox in political thinking is that there is no liberty without equality (78–83). For many, this proposition links two rationally defensible yet contradictory concepts. To explain how this might be the case, let's assume that by the term "freedom" we mean that people have the wherewithal to make their own choices about matters such as career and religion and the opportunity to take a meaningful role in affecting public policies. This view of freedom is linked to equality when society's concept of justice requires that the freedom afforded to any one person should be accorded equally to all others. But in order to ensure equal freedom in this sense, it is necessary to provide each person with sufficient quantities of certain basic goods. Included in this list of goods are fundamental rights, the freedoms of speech, conscience, religion, association, and political participation. Also to be included are basic opportunities for things such as education and health care. Only when people have these things can they make personal choices and take part fully and effectively in the political system. Consider education, for example. People will be incapable of realizing their potential, and thus the freedom to choose their career, unless they are well educated. But where should the money to support education come from? Some say it should come primarily from the wealthy, yet the wealthy might claim that this approach threatens their liberty. Ironically, then, the quest for equal degrees of freedom may impose on some people constraints that limit their liberty.

Should the conflict between liberty and equality manifested in this example cause concern? Some would say no, that to achieve equal freedom may require some degree of redistribution of the wealth in society. Of course, a decent society will have some policies for the redistribution of wealth, but what is a fair policy for redistributing wealth in society, and at what point does such a policy cease to be fair? With these questions, the discussion now turns to questions of fairness and how best to achieve it with respect to the relationship between liberty and equality.

These paradoxes—only two of the many to be found throughout this book—demonstrate how Tinder makes the thinking self a replica of Socratic reasoning. Like Socrates,

Tinder constantly challenges his readers to test the answers provided by people defending a given perspective against the answers provided by people holding competing viewpoints. Throughout, Tinder demonstrates that key political concepts enable people to take part in political argumentation and reflection in which the parties learn both to understand fully and to contest with reasoned intelligence the opinions and views of others. During argumentation it becomes clear that the concepts are instrumental to people's having fruitful, reflective discussions of important political issues, even when the discussions made possible by these concepts may never reach outcomes acceptable to all reasonable parties.

Political thinking would lead people to arrive at some conclusive answers on some issues. Rational political thinkers would conclude that tyranny is always wrong and that crimes against humanity must be prevented and punished when they occur. But for so many other issues, the best that can be achieved is a reasonable compromise in which none of the parties is completely happy with the outcome. More problematic for the thinking self, however, is the demand that issues be resolved in keeping with a particular ideological framework. Indeed, the thinking self is always watchful and suspicious of those who promise easy solutions to complex problems that require ongoing reflection and discussion. For Tinder, political "thinking provides no certain and unequivocal answers but nevertheless opens the way to understanding" (242).

That there are conclusive and overwhelmingly important benefits to individuals and societies from political thinking is made clear throughout this book. As a result of political thinking, people not only become autonomous thinkers, demanding from themselves and others convincing reasons for any position, but they contribute to a public realm in which matters of importance are decided by reasoned argument. In this way, people engaged in politics replace the slash-and-burn rhetoric, so common in contemporary political life, with reasoned thought and discourse. This is the only path available for those seeking a decent society.

In acquainting his audience with the thinking self, Tinder helps his readers to understand that the purpose of politics, in making possible a decent society, is to ensure not just that people—to paraphrase Socrates—live, but that they live well.[5] To achieve this end, it is necessary to provide what satisfies people's basic needs for food, shelter, and safety. In addition, it is indispensable for a society to provide the goods that make life worthwhile and meaningful: community, liberty, democracy, justice, art, science, religion.

Estrangement and "Humane Uncertainty"

Despite the benefits of political thinking, Tinder lamented that the American public placed little emphasis on thought embodying "philosophical breath and seriousness" (12). He blamed this problem on a variety of factors (12–13). His hope in addressing this matter is to convince the reader of the importance to society of the way of life represented by the thinking self. In arguing for this position, Tinder does not in any sense sugar-coat the reality in which political thinking occurs. Indeed, Tinder paints a sobering picture of the arena that any person who engages in political thinking must enter, a world in which estrangement is the norm.

For Tinder, "estrangement" signifies the continuing "disunity among human beings" (23). Estrangement arises from the absence of enduring friendship and community among fellow citizens, from the reality of injustice and war, and from the horrific experiences of totalitarian regimes (23, 250). These realities, and many like them, cause people to experience the searing emotions of the alienated self, such as hatred and loneliness, emotions that make it impossible for people to feel fully at home in their own society. People in the face of this experience naturally hope to terminate estrangement and the pain it causes them. And it is precisely this quest that makes political thinking necessary. As Tinder says, "if human beings were not estranged, whether in quiet loneliness or in active conflict, political thinking would not occur" (23).

---

[5] Plato, "The Crito," in *Euthyphron, Apology, Crito, Plato: The Last Days of Socrates*, p. 57.

Political thinking, then, must confront the estrangement that shrouds human life. One of the most serious consequences in this regard is the uncertainty that accompanies estrangement. In a society marked by estrangement, there is an intense awareness that people are subject to many misery-creating factors beyond the control of anyone, even government. Further, people may respond to uncertainty in different ways, some with fear or hate, but in most cases with a strong desire to escape to a place where uncertainty no longer exists. Worse, some end up believing that the best escape route is a form of government that Tinder, like all people who prize liberty, most fear: totalitarianism (250).

In this circumstance, an ideological mindset that justifies the annihilation of political thinking becomes pervasive. After all, political thinking never promises that doubt and uncertainty will be erased from the human condition. As Tinder says, "to think is to be uncertain," and moreover the path to "wisdom lies in uncertainty" (243). Political thinking, in embracing these views, acknowledges that people must find a way to achieve a decent society despite the ever presence of uncertainty. In contrast, totalitarian ideologies promise an end to uncertainty so long as the society jettisons political thinking and any hope of achieving a democratic, rights-based society. These events, taken together, open the door to a totalitarian state's vicious assault on human dignity (250). And when this happens, political murder, which mandates killing others merely for their cultural or philosophical views, becomes commonplace.

In response, Tinder advocates what he calls "humane uncertainty." The moral outlook promoted by this doctrine is that we should uphold freedom, equality, and community in the face of the ambiguity of contemporary life (243). Freedom is secured when citizens maintain the reflective qualities of the thinking, questioning self against monolithic group domination that, not unlike the spirit of a totalitarian society, stifles independent reflection and thought. Equality exists when individuals of differing talent and ability recognize that, to address well the perennial political questions for which there are no definitive answers, each person must consider carefully the views of all others. And a community, which helps all persons realize their socially creative and useful potential, arises when there is a shared affirmation to sustain the thinking self, especially against those whose ideological disposition encourages its diminished significance—or its destruction.

Political Thinking: The Perennial Questions is a classic because it helps us to understand the high significance of political thinking in the quest for decent societies the world over.

RECOMMENDED READINGS

Berman, Paul. 2003. *Terror and Liberalism*. New York: Norton. Discusses the reality of modern totalitarianism, with its sources in the West and its spread to other areas of the world, including the Middle East.

Buber, Martin. 1958. *I and Thou*. New York: Scribner Library. Speaks to the way that estrangement can be overcome among people engaged in a discussion based on the quest for authentic human relationships.

DeLue, Steven M. 2002. *Political Thinking, Political Theory and Civil Society*, second edition. New York: Longman. Seeks to use the tradition of political theory as the basis for political thinking by imagining conversations among many past and present writers on enduring questions of politics.

Ignatieff, Michael. 2001. *Human Rights as Politics and Idolatry*. Edited and introduced by Amy Gutmann. Princeton: Princeton University Press. Discusses human rights in terms of the need to strike a balance between international human rights commitments and the particular needs of state sovereignty.

Kant, Immanuel. 1956. *Groundwork of the Metaphysic of Morals*. Translated by H. J. Paton. New York: Harper. Discusses both the paradoxes that ground morality and the way by which morality can be reconstituted in the face of them.

Margalit, Avishai. 2002. *The Ethics of Memory*. Cambridge: Harvard University Press. Discusses the moral obligations arising from the memory of crimes against humanity.

Plato. 1956. "The Euthyphron." "The Apology." "The Crito." in *Euthyphron, Apology, Crito, Plato: The Last Days of Socrates*. Translated by F. J. Church. Indianapolis: Bobbs-Merrill. These dialogues between Socrates and others are the classic statements that describe, in the tradition of Western political theory, the nature of political thinking.

Shklar, Judith N. 1990. *The Faces of Injustice*. New Haven: Yale University Press. Discusses injustice in all its varieties and how this continuing problem hinders the hope of achieving a decent society.

Walzer, Michael. 1997. *On Toleration*. New Haven: Yale University Press. Discusses the quest for toleration, an essential virtue in a decent society.

STUDY QUESTIONS

1. Discuss the two paradoxes—Rousseau's view that people must be forced to be free and the notion that liberty and equality are inextricable even if contradictory ideas—in the context of such major issues as affirmative action and privacy rights.

2. In what ways do you think estrangement continues in today's society? Or do you think that estrangement is no longer a problem? Provide a reasoned argument for your position.

3. If political thinking is based on a tradition of shared concepts and ideas emanating from Western political theory, how do you engage in political thinking when the people with whom you are talking do not share these concepts or even have knowledge of them? What are the implications of this question for political thinking and for the quest for a decent society?

4. Is engaging in political thinking a worthwhile activity? Explain your position in light of the arguments presented above.

STEVEN M. DeLUE
Miami University, Ohio

The paradox is the source of the thinker's passion and the thinker without a paradox is like a lover without feeling: a paltry mediocrity.   .   . . The supreme paradox of all thought is the attempt to discover something that thought cannot think.

Søren Kierkegaard

Contents

*P*REFACE

The present edition of *Political Thinking* is not a substantially different book than the preceding edition. I think it is quite definitely a better book, however. I have carried out revisions of three different kinds. To begin with, I have entirely rewritten the discussions connected with three different questions. In doing this, I have not only strengthened the presentation of issues, but have brought in arguments from recent debates among political theorists. Further, I have rewritten fifteen passages, ranging in length from a short paragraph to two-and-a-half pages. With these new passages I think I have effected improvements both in style and in substance. Also, I have been able to remove or rephrase references to events current when the earlier edition was published but now past and thus creating a slightly anachronistic atmosphere. Finally, I have combed through the whole manuscript looking for places where I could make improvements of detail. I found many such places, typically two or three on each page. The improvements were not only in style and clarity but also in theoretical precision. I have greatly improved the wording of two of the questions as well.

The cumulative result of these changes, I believe, is a book that reads better, is more provocative, and lays a more solid basis for discussion and exposition than did the earlier edition. I suspect that instructors will find the present edition more interesting.

Two people who have contributed greatly to *Political Thinking* need to be mentioned. One is Ruby Riemer, of New Jersey, a feminist writer and teacher, and a good friend. Ruby was engaged by the publisher (at my suggestion) to try to keep me from missteps when I undertook the perilous task, in preparing the preceding edition, of discussing feminist concerns. She accompanied me at every step, from recommending reading at the outset to checking the final draft. As a male, I no doubt blundered at times, but not so badly that any cries of outrage have reached my ears. This is due above all to Ruby's criticism and advice.

I also want to mention Jack Beatty, an old friend, now senior editor of *The Atlantic*. Jack helped me with two or three of the earlier editions, not only providing valuable suggestions concerning content but also helping me to remove many infelicities of style. Jack's mark (like Ruby's) is still on the book.

—Glenn Tinder

POLITICAL THINKING

*I*NTRODUCTION

This book may prove difficult and trying for some readers, perhaps especially for careful and probing readers. It is made up wholly of questions. Not only do I give no indication of the answers I accept, I am often as unsure of them as the reader is likely to be. As a result, *Political Thinking* has none of the satisfying finality characteristic of most books on political theory.

This is a warning, not an apology. The lack of finality is connected with the primary intent of the book. My purpose is to provide an introduction to political thinking, and I have tried to do this not by describing the great political philosophies of the past, but rather by helping each reader to engage in the activity of political thinking. This has necessitated asking questions but refraining from any effort to provide answers. Even when I could have—and this was not often—I have not offered any positions of repose.

It has been said that anyone who gives people the illusion that they are thinking will be loved by them, whereas anyone who actually prompts them to think will be hated. If so, some exasperation on the part of the reader (although I have tried not to cause more exasperation than is intellectually fruitful) will be a sign of this book's success.

Perhaps too much is said in universities about how exciting it is to think. Thinking undoubtedly has its excitements and satisfactions, but these feelings do not disclose its general character, and there is something very much wrong with the idea that they should. We do not think in order to enjoy ourselves but in order to understand life, which is troubling and problematic. We think because we are compelled to. And while thinking occasionally brings exciting discoveries, the periods in between these discoveries are likely to place heavy demands on the thinker's energy and patience. When thinking, we should not need to tell ourselves we are having an exhilarating experience; it should be enough to realize that we are behaving with the seriousness, rationality, and self-discipline that the human situation requires of us.

Such gravity is particularly applicable to *political* thinking in so tragic a time as the twentieth century. Should we find it enjoyable to ponder dilemmas that have cost uncounted millions of lives? The following pages are not supposed to be easy or uplifting. They are intended, rather, to introduce the reader to the trials of political thinking in an age of turmoil and doubt.

Once on the high seas of thought, however, a reader may feel that this book does not give enough instruction on how to navigate and remain afloat. How does a person go about thinking? I shall offer a few suggestions in this introduction. Help of this kind, however, is necessarily of limited value. The trying nature of thought results largely from the impossibility of thinking according to teachable techniques. Although much is said about "teaching students to think," a teacher can do little more than offer encouragement and criticism. The appearance of an idea is a mysterious occurrence, and it is doubtful that anyone does, or ever will, understand just how it happens.

But a student can *learn* to think. My reason for saying that no one can be *taught* to think is to focus at the onset on the dependence of the entire process on the student's own solitary efforts. It is both the glory and the burden of thought that it is an exceedingly personal undertaking. The solitude of the mature thinker must be entered into immediately by the beginner. As the mature thinker thinks all alone, the beginner must *learn* to think all alone. Occasionally one may receive a gift of encouragement or useful criticism, but nothing is decided by these gifts. Everything depends on the capacity for solitary effort.

It follows that little instruction in the art of thinking can be offered beyond suggestions such as the following.

1. Do not try to arrive at ideas no one has ever thought of before. Even the greatest thinkers have rarely done that. The aim of thinking is to discover ideas that pull together one's world, and thus one's being, not to give birth to unprecedented conceptions. An idea is your own if it has grown by your own efforts and is rooted in your own emotions and experiences even though you may have received the seeds from someone else and even though the idea may be very much like ideas held by many others.

2. Be open. Ideas cannot be deliberately produced, like industrial products. They appear uncommanded; they occur, as we recognize when we say, "It occurred to me that. . . " You place yourself in a fundamentally wrong relationship with ideas if you assume you can control their appearance. You can only be open to them.

3. Do not hurry. Initial efforts to think about a problem are often completely frustrating. They may best be regarded as a tilling of the ground; time is required before anything can be expected to grow.

4. Make plenty of notes. It is easier to work with your mind if you are doing some corresponding work with your hands. It is often helpful to make notes on large pads where there is room for sketching out patterns of ideas. It can also be helpful to make notes on cards and then to cut up the cards so that each idea is on a small piece of card. These can then be laid out on a desk and rearranged. Often this process suggests new connections among your thoughts.

5. Beware of substituting reading for thinking. Reading about the thoughts of others is not the same as having thoughts of your own. To be sure, to engage in thinking you need some acquaintance with the thoughts of others. The great thinkers inspire, provoke, confirm, and in other ways help you do your own thinking. But to think you must at some point lay down the book and strike out on your own.

I have a final suggestion that I do not number with the five above because it must take the form, not of a briefly stated tip, but of a somewhat extended comment on the structure of political thought.

Most political ideas, perhaps all of them, are based on some particular conception of human nature. The conservative idea that political authority should be strong and highly centralized, for example, is apt to be based on a conception of human beings as selfish and competitive; the liberal notion that extensive social changes can ordinarily be brought about peacefully may arise from the premise that human beings are for the most part reasonable. These examples are very simple, and in an actual political philosophy the relations between the underlying conception of human nature and the superstructure of political ideas may be far more complex; they do, however, illustrate the general logic that is implicitly or explicitly present in almost every political theory.

What is the bearing of this observation on the question of how you should go about thinking? Simply this: you will probably find that your mind is clarified and stimulated through articulating this logic in your own thought. In the course of political thinking you should occasionally pause to ask yourself how you view human nature and what implications this view has for your political ideas.

You may feel that to ask in this way about human nature is to face a mystery even darker than those encountered on the level of political reflection. There are, however, two overriding issues in this area, despite the infinite complexities of human nature; you may initiate the process of thought by trying to respond to these issues. One issue concerns the extent and origins of evil in human beings: are we deeply and incurably evil, or is evil a superficial and removable aspect of our character? The second issue—less universally recognized nowadays than the first—concerns the import of death: is an individual totally extinguished by death? Does the term *eternal life* correspond to anything we may actually experience?

Your response to the first issue will very largely determine your ideas on such matters as how much freedom people should have, to what extent historical progress is possible, and the degree of violence necessary to bring about change. Your response to the second issue decides in a general way your whole conception of the purpose of life. If you believe that death is complete extinction, you must somehow call on people (using Nietzsche's words) to "be true to the earth"; if you do not believe that death is extinction, you must see earthly politics as significant only insofar as it helps or hinders people in working out their relations with eternity.

Perhaps it is in order to say here that these ethical and metaphysical areas contain many pitfalls and surprises, and that we should be wary both of offhand answers and of facile inferences. For example, it is often assumed today that affirming the goodness of humankind, if an error, is a generous and harmless error. Hence political discussions are often punctuated with complacent expressions of trust in human nature. But this trust can have some paradoxical results. If people are fundamentally good, then how does there happen to be so much evil in human affairs? It is hard to avoid concluding that it must be because some people are exceptions to the general human norm. Thus Communists have tended to blame all the evil in the world on capitalists, and vice versa. It is apparent how sinister a line of thought this is, for the next step is deciding that to free the world of evil it is necessary only to eradicate the few who are the sources of evil. Through so natural a logic as this, a benign and generous judgment becomes murderous.

On the other hand, we should not lightly judge people to be evil, for if we believe that people are evil, how can we avoid being dominated by hatred and by hopelessness?

The issue of death also has its pitfalls. It has often been noted that to deny the finality of death can imperil freedom. This is simply because such a denial can only be based on religious faith, and religious faith readily takes the form of a dogma forcibly imposed on everyone.

It does not follow, however, that accepting the finality of death is safe and sets up no dangerous reverberations in the area of political thought. For example, it is doubtful that the idea that every individual is a repository of unique and measureless dignity would ever have arisen apart from the idea that every individual is immortal. The idea of personal immortality disentangled the human being from natural realities and set each of us above the whole natural world. That is why a person could not be regarded as a mere means, but had to be regarded as an end. A being that is not immortal, however, tends to sink back into nature and in some circumstances may be regarded, like any other natural reality, as a means rather than an end.

You may feel that you cannot possibly decide issues so vast. And of course you cannot, if deciding them means finding answers that are exact and sure, answers that are never altered and never doubted. But these vast issues do not concern something far away but rather the most immediate and intimate of realities—one's own self. Are we not in a position at least to hazard some guesses concerning the nature and destiny of persons, when we ourselves are persons? Can we live without making some assumptions concerning these matters? And if we are to make some assumptions, is it not best to bring them into the open and use reason to examine them?

But how are we to judge the truth of our ideas? This question can be asked not only about ideas concerning human nature but about political ideas in general. How can we test the validity of an idea that strongly appeals to us?

There are some standard and well-known tests: the idea must be consistent with other ideas we hold at the same time, and it should explain, or at the least be compatible with, all established, relevant facts. But even the most conscientious and dispassionate application of these criteria does not carry us very far. It can never, in the field of political theory, lead to proof; it probably will not lead even to a useful and stirring—if unprovable—insight. A set of ideas may be internally consistent and compatible with all known facts and still be dead and useless. In learning to identify the truth one needs to look beyond these standard criteria—but not toward another criterion so much as toward the idea of wholeness and integration that is implicit in the standard criteria.

An idea is living and important only so far as it brings us into relationship with ourselves and with reality, so far as it pulls ourselves and our worlds together. What is implied by the standards of logical consistency and factual accuracy is that nothing be suppressed and nothing ignored. An idea has the function of extending and integrating relationships. Hence, an idea that calls on us to ignore things we know or deeply believe to be true must be judged false or at least inadequate—it has a disintegrating effect on experience and being. A true idea is one that makes for inclusiveness and unity.

Feeling necessarily plays a large part in searching for the truth. Much that must be pulled together does not have the definite and conscious form of a fact or belief. A great idea is one that symbolizes and unifies not only facts and beliefs that are clearly present to consciousness but also intuitions and impulses that have not been focused on and given form. The idea that does this is exciting. This may seem an invitation to believe whatever is pleasant or interesting. It must therefore be added that thinking tries one's depth and honesty. We are thinking deeply and well when we acknowledge and draw together into a single pattern all that emerges from our experience and emotions. Our search must be without sentimentality or carelessness or fear.

As for the best way of using the present volume, the kind of reading appropriate for most other books—that is, without long pauses for reflection, discussion, and writing—should prove of some value. Although the questions are posed without being resolved, they are linked together in a way that makes them a wandering pathway over the terrain of political thought. Through an ordinary reading you should gain some sense of the intellectual state in which political thinking originates.

This book is designed, however, not just to be read but to be used—through discussion, writing, and prolonged reflection. The questions are set forth not simply to inform you of the dilemmas of others but to draw you into dilemmas of your own. This will happen only if, in addition to reading the book as a whole, you dwell on at least a few of the questions and try to answer them. The questions are stated and arranged to facilitate being used in these ways.

While I believe that reflection on politics is an end in itself, this book may also provide help in studying the history of political thought. To understand the great thinkers requires getting some sense of the interior of their minds, and doing this depends on feeling on your own the doubts and anxieties that provoked them to think. Only a rare and profound intellectual sympathy, brought to the analysis of a particular thinker, can make this possible. What *Political Thinking* can do, I believe, is help readers gain a vantage point from which such sympathy, gained from their own insight, or from a teacher or a biographer, will become possible.

But are the questions we reflect on in the twentieth century really the same as those that people reflected on in past ages? Are there, in fact, any "perennial questions"? To ask this is to raise the most serious doubt that political theorists are apt to feel about the way ideas are dealt with in the following pages. Most intellectuals today are deeply imbued with a sense of history. This means that they see ways of life and thought as continually changing and as differing from one historical period to the next. They are keenly sensitive to the uniqueness of generations and centuries. Hence, in studying ideas they are inclined to say not merely that every era formulates its own particular answers, but also that every era asks its own particular questions. If that is so, it is an illusion to think that our questions are the same as Plato's or even as Locke's, and *Political Thinking* rests on a mistaken premise.

No one, of course, would deny that questions as well as answers do change with time. Every generation has certain unique concerns and perspectives and also certain unique ways of speaking and thinking; every generation asks some questions that were not asked by the preceding generation, and it asks old questions in new ways. This is very far from saying, however, that there are no enduring or recurrent questions. The complete denial of perennial questions is not at all implied by the mere fact of intellectual change and is, for several reasons, highly dubious.

If it were true, the ideas of the past would have no deep and compelling interest for us. They would not answer any of the questions we are asking. They would be mere relics, like the tools or weapons of a former age that we glance at with idle curiosity in museums. They would be unusable. But the truth is that civilized people do not contemplate political ideas of the past in a mood of detachment. The rediscovery of Aristotle, for example, was one of the great events of the Middle Ages; and Plato's presence in Victorian England may have been as consequential as his presence in post-Periclean Athens—his own historical period. The idea that there are perennial questions—questions grappled with in former ages that engage us vitally today—is not a mere assumption; it is a vivid experience.

One may go further and ask: if there were no perennial questions, would the ideas of the past even be comprehensible to us? In some formal sense, of course they would be; we could repeat the words in which they were cast. To comprehend an idea, however, it is not enough simply to think it; one must be moved by it, for ideas have emotional power and this power is part of their essence. This is why they are important in history. But can we be moved by an idea that answers a question we have not asked and feel no inclination to ask? If there are no perennial questions, then past ideas are not merely like ancient tools that we have improved upon; they are like tools designed to do something we no longer care to do.

Perhaps the greatest weakness of the idea that there are no enduring or recurrent questions, however, is that it ignores our common humanity and thereby flies in the face of common sense. Were not those who lived in ancient Greece finite, as we are, and subject to emotion and equipped with reason? Were not the inhabitants of the Middle Ages, like us, often in error intellectually and at fault morally? Did not human beings of the Renaissance and the Enlightenment encounter threats of disorder and the necessity of organizing a governing power? And do we not share with every age one profound similarity, bursting with implications concerning our common humanity: that we live in history? Conditions such as finitude, fallibility, and temporality occasion some of the most pressing questions that we ask. If those conditions are enduring, it is hard to avoid the inference that there are enduring questions.

While I believe that there are perennial questions, however, I certainly do not believe that I have perfectly identified and formulated them. The most that I would like to claim for *Political Thinking* is that it provides an impulse and sense of direction that will help a reader think about the political dilemmas of human existence and hence of all times rather than of our time alone. This caveat has a practical implication: the reader should feel free to ask new questions. Since the following set of questions does not purport to be definitive, one may appropriately respond to them not only by trying to answer them but by pursuing further any line of questions they suggest. The aim of this book is to engage the reader in intellectual movement, and asking questions is at the origin of all such movement.

Chapter 1

WHY ENGAGE IN POLITICAL THINKING?

One reason for asking this question is that thinking is a peculiarly arduous and discouraging undertaking. Of course, it is often remarked that thinking is hard work. However, one who enters fully into the process of questioning set forth in the following chapters will discover that the difficulties of thinking are far more subtle and exasperating than those of mere hard work. You will probably find, for example, that the effort of thought at first is completely fruitless; to admit uncertainty, as you must do in order to think, may seem to leave you in a kind of void with no horizons in the distance and no solid ground underneath. Further, you will find yourself annoyingly given to daydreaming and persistently inclined to think about other things than the question at hand. Finally, you will discover that the products of thought are intangible and often fragile. Ideas that have taken hours to develop may evaporate owing to a few remarks by a friend.

A thinking person is exceedingly vulnerable. Such a person must appear before others, not behind the armor and shield of books read and of ideas formulated by others, but in the nakedness of purely personal thoughts and doubts.

Nor are the long-range results of this nerve-racking effort likely to be unarguably good. It is not obvious that thinking is the way to moral elevation, or happiness, or even wisdom. More than two thousand years of philosophical doubt and disagreement have proved that thinking is not the way to unshakable and enduring knowledge. Undoubtedly, something tells many of us that it would be ignoble to refrain deliberately from thinking. But not everyone feels this qualm; as great a writer as Rousseau believed that through thinking we alienate ourselves from reality and from our own being.

Contemporary American culture reinforces our natural reluctance to think. Granted, verbal tributes are frequently paid to articles or speeches that supposedly "provide food for thought" or that "make people stop and think." But Americans today do not seem to assign much importance to thought possessed of philosophical breadth and seriousness. This is indicated by how rarely a philosophical work is found on the best-seller lists. The political books that become widely known are mostly factual works, often written by journalists and concerned with immediate issues in domestic and foreign policy. Books addressing personal concerns are ordinarily designed to provide encouragement and guidance rather than understanding of the universal realities of personal existence. Signs of a society biased against serious thinking are found even in universities, where one might expect philosophy to flourish; here there are diverse intellectual currents, such as behaviorism and deconstructionism, which are subtly if not overtly antiphilosophical. But perhaps the most conclusive evidence of a prevailing disinclination to think is simply the devotion among Americans of hours of daily time to television entertainment.

Any society probably has an inherent bias against original thought. Social order depends heavily on tradition and habit, and these are apt to be weakened by genuine thinking. The execution of Socrates in Athens exemplifies this antagonism. Nevertheless, today in America two forces, both stronger than they have been in many times and places, intensify the normal antiphilosophical cast of society and deepen the reluctance of individuals to subject themselves to the uneasiness and labor of thought.

One of these forces is a strong propensity toward action. Americans have probably always had this propensity, which our environment necessitated and rewarded. Today this traditional American inclination has been reinforced by the multitude and gravity of the problems confronting us—problems such as urban disintegration and persisting racial injustice. Politically conscious Americans are intensely preoccupied with all the things that demand doing and are ordinarily confident of our power to do these things successfully. This dynamic spirit is in many ways advantageous; despondency is avoided and great tasks are often accomplished. But people in consequence are impatient with reflection and disinclined to entertain questions that do not have immediate practical urgency. They seek programs of action.

Another antiphilosophical force particularly strong in present-day America is a thirst for facts, which, at least partially, is a result of the bias toward action. Most Americans want to know what is actually going on—in the schools, in the ghettos, in the nonindustrial countries. If asked, for example, whether human beings are essentially estranged (the first question considered in the following pages), they may wonder what that has to do with the deterioration of the inner city or the poverty of Africa and Asia and dismiss the question as irrelevant. This thirst for facts is no more inherently reprehensible than is the bias toward action. Facts can be verified and often put to practical use, which cannot be said of most philosophical theories. But perhaps philosophical theories are important in other ways, a possibility not likely to be of much interest to those who are avid for information.

In sum, the paths of thought are not altogether inviting. Following them leads inevitably to toil and insecurity but not necessarily to solid answers or inner rest. Also, thinking goes against the grain of our culture, which continually presses on us the urgency of action and the need for reliable information.

Then why—to recur to the title of this chapter—engage in political thinking?

For one thing, some questions cannot be answered by any other means. For example, when does a person have the right to disobey the government? Can a government legitimately break moral laws if the welfare of the nation seems to require it? Should all social and economic inequalities be abolished? Questions of this kind cannot be answered without thought. Information bearing on them may come from social sciences, personal experience, history, or other sources. But only thought can determine what information is relevant and then use it in answering the questions.

But, many Americans might ask, must such questions be answered? Would we not be better off concentrating on the concrete problems at hand? The answer to both questions is that to adopt any attitude at all toward reality, even one of concentrating on practical matters and spurning philosophical reflection, is implicitly to adopt a philosophical position. The very idea that practical problems should have priority over philosophical problems is philosophical—it can be formulated and defended only through philosophical reflection. Questions of the kind Americans are inclined to dismiss impatiently are imposed on us by our lives. We have no choice but to answer them. Our only alternative is how we answer them: either reflectively and carefully or thoughtlessly and irresponsibly.

To put the matter in another way, only through ideas can we discern reality and enter fully into relations with it. An idea is a kind of light. If it were not for the great political ideas, our collective lives would be immersed in darkness.

For example, it is apparent to most of us that Nazism was fundamentally wrong. This would not be apparent, however, were it not for ideas like the dignity of law and the evil of tyranny; and these are not innate ideas of the human mind but were formed by philosophers such as Aristotle, Cicero, and Locke. As another example, it is plain to nearly everyone today that the discrimination suffered by blacks in America is unjust. But why is this so plain? Drastic inequalities have prevailed in most societies for thousands of years and have been taken for granted by most of the members of those societies; one can cite, as an example, Aristotle's casual acceptance of slavery. The light in which we view America's racial situation comes from the idea of equality—an idea we probably would not possess had it not been for thinkers such as Locke, Rousseau, and Marx. Perhaps eight or ten ideas—these not innate in the human mind, but rather products of reflection—are the lanterns of political civilization; they enable us to discern the realities of collective life.

Both the action and the facts prized today by American culture presuppose ideas and the thinking that forms them. In order to act intelligently, we must have ends we are seeking to effect. What are ends, however, but ideas of a certain kind—conceptions of a desirable state of affairs? For example, during the last two centuries people have often protested and rebelled in order to gain self-government. But for several millennia most people acquiesced in the rule of highly exclusive elites. The demand for self-government does not arise directly from human nature, but from an idea. Activist Americans, impatient of thought, stand on a groundwork of ideas that has been built by reflection. If that groundwork were removed, they and all their plans would fall into a void in which intelligent action would be impossible.

Something similar can be said of the thirst for facts. This thirst is not satisfied by indiscriminately gathering in every fact that happens to be noticed. Such research would only create a chaos of insignificant and unrelated atoms of information. Indeed, without ideas that tell us what is real and what is significant, it is doubtful that any such thing as a fact could be discovered, for facts do not just lie about like pebbles; their very existence depends on the power of mind to distinguish and relate. An interest in facts that deserves any respect at all is an interest in organized and significant knowledge, and such an interest cannot exist in a mind without ideas. Consider, for example, the amount of knowledge we possess about poverty. Would we possess this knowledge if the ideas of Marx and other social reformers had not inspired and directed its accumulation?

Of course, only a few great thinkers create the ideas that illuminate reality and thus guide action and research. But the fact that the most influential thinking is done by only a few does not mean that the rest of us need not think at all. For one thing, the great thinkers do not agree. They offer different and often mutually contradictory ideas. How can we decide which ideas to accept without doing some thinking of our own?

Further, even if we were willing to commit ourselves to certain ideas instinctively and uncritically, we probably could not understand them without having experienced some of the labor and doubt that have gone into creating them. What is meant, for instance, by the idea that human beings are equal? Clearly they are not equal in any measurable quality, such as intelligence or health or emotional balance. One may say that they are equal only in their rights before the law. But why should they be accorded equal rights before the law if they are in no respect equal in fact? The question need not be pursued. It is plain that for someone who has never reflected on the matter, the concept of equality can hardly have any intelligible content.

Thus, despite the emphasis in this book on questions rather than answers, my first response to the query, "Why engage in political thinking?" is that we do so to reach answers that cannot be reached in any other way.

This response, however, ignores one of the weightiest and oldest objections to philosophical thought—that the ideas it reaches must always be undemonstrable and uncertain. It follows that to engage in thinking is to entertain doubts that can never, through thought, be wholly overcome.

This objection is far from baseless. Few, if any, of the main political ideas held by a typical American or European at the present time can be proved; most of them can be severely shaken. Substantial arguments, for example, can be brought against even so seemingly unassailable an idea as the rule of law. As Plato argued, the rule of law inhibits the full application of intelligence to social problems; further, it may restrict the initiative and energy of the police and thus may enhance the difficulty of protecting property and persons. The reader will perhaps think of answers to these arguments but none that conclusively refutes them. Every important idea is attended by inseparable counter-ideas; the idea of freedom, for example, calls to mind and can never altogether destroy or subordinate to itself the idea of authority. In reaching the "answers" referred to above, a number of counter-ideas must be more or less subdued; but they will prove recurrently troublesome and refractory to those who refuse to turn their "answers" into iron-clad dogmas.

The history of political thought shows how doubt continually pursues thought and frequently overtakes it. There is no more agreement concerning political truth now than there was twenty-five hundred years ago, when political thinking began. There may indeed be less. This divergence of opinion sharpens our original question. Why engage in inquiry of a kind that can only lead to uncertain and disputable conclusions?

This is an exceedingly important question, for it asks whether it is worthwhile trying to reason about the ultimate ends and fundamental assumptions governing our lives in common. This, after all, is the business of political thinking. Clearly, your position on this issue will have a great deal to do with your whole conception of how life in society should be organized and carried on. At the same time, the question is very difficult. Like the other questions with which political thinking deals, this one, having to do with the value of political thinking itself, has no incontrovertible answer. I shall suggest three provisional answers that may enable us to ponder the perennial questions with some confidence that we are not wasting our time.

First, while political ideas and political philosophies contain subjective elements (like a work of art, a political philosophy is emphatically and thoroughly the creation of a particular person, lacking the impersonal authority of a body of scientific laws), they are not wholly subjective. Very simply, we cannot believe whatever we choose. We must take into account evidence and observe the rules of logical consistency. Granted, no great idea or philosophy is demonstrably true. But it would be easy to formulate an idea or a philosophy that is demonstrably false, either because it is contrary to unquestionable facts or because it is self-contradictory. The uncertainty of political ideas should not be exaggerated.

Further, however disputable the conclusions of thought may be, we cannot live as human beings without them. Ideas enable us to live by understanding rather than by instinct. Of course they also can cause us to live by illusions, but they do not compel us to; and even a false idea can be a step in the direction of truth. While it may seem unsatisfactory that our ideas are so vulnerable to doubt, it is far better to have doubtful ideas than to have none at all. The former state is uncomfortable but civilized, the latter barbarous.

The final reason why it is worth thinking politically is the most important but also the most puzzling; hence it requires more discussion than the two reasons already cited. Regardless of any conclusions that are reached, thinking in itself helps us gain a humanity not available in any other way. We are thinking beings, and even through inconclusive thinking, we can gain access to our humanity. Our yearning for action and facts, although often expressing a strong civic conscience, threatens us with a brutalization inherent in thoughtlessness.

How is humanity gained through thought?

First of all, questioning and reflecting enable one to realize one's own being in its freedom and distinctness. "All deep, earnest thinking," Herman Melville wrote, "is but the intrepid effort of the soul to keep the open independence of her sea." Speaking again of the soul, or self, he added that "the wildest winds of heaven and earth conspire to cast her on the treacherous, slavish shore."[1] Today, we may think "the wildest winds of heaven and earth" to be fear, bigotry, and fanaticism, and we may see the "treacherous, slavish shore" as the ideologies, bureaucracies, and totalitarian states that abound in the twentieth century. To think is to stand apart and

[1]Herman Melville, *Moby Dick, or The Whale* (New York: Modern Library, 1930), p. 153.

affirm one's own irreducible reality. Those who regard political thinking as futile should remember that the totalitarian regimes of our time agree; they have done everything possible to stifle such thinking. This is partly because they have wished to stifle individuality.

Thinking is not only the realization of the self through denial and doubt, but also a way of gathering together and tentatively defining the self. To reflect on a problem of philosophical scope is to call your strongest impressions and convictions into consciousness, to relate them to one another, and to test them. It is to think back on all you have read and experienced, trying to fathom its significance. Thinking is a summoning of the self. Hence the subjective character of philosophical thought, which makes it unverifiable, is not altogether a drawback. It may deprive philosophy of the universally compelling force of scientific law, but it reflects its personal nature. Struggling with and living with doubt has a role in the formation of individual identity.

Moreover, thinking not only summons the self, it puts us in touch with others. If all serious and candid reflection is an admission that I may be mistaken, it is by the same token an admission that others may be right. In this sense, thinking is a communal state. It means breaking down the walls of dogmatic self-assurance and trying to enter into the minds of others. Strong convictions have undoubtedly had a part in the development of political philosophies, and convictions of some kind may be necessary for personal stability. Convictions that go unquestioned, however, divide human beings from one another. Those holding them become hard and self-enclosed. To think, we must question our convictions and overcome the contempt we often feel for those whose convictions differ from our own. In sum, if thinking sets the individual apart from others in their conformity and slavishness, it also places the individual in the company of others in the incertitude and mystery of their existence.

Finally, some philosophers have held that thinking is a pathway to the consciousness of transcendence or of God. For atheists and agnostics, of course, this would make thinking a pathway to illusions, not humanity. Even those who believe in God may be surprised and perhaps offended by the idea that an activity destructive of certainty and leading to no definite conclusions can bring us into contact with God. Is not religious faith a state of absolute certainty, in which all doubts and questions are definitely set aside? Thinkers of great stature have held that it is not.[2] The things we are certain of are usually idols: God cannot be contained in a doctrine.

It can be argued that encouraging religious openness and awareness is one of the main ways in which thinking contributes to our humanity. There is no tension between God and the kind of independent personal being cultivated by thinking; rather there is a mysterious unity. The great German philosopher Karl Jaspers (1883–1969), one of the founders of modern existentialism, asserted flatly that "freedom and God are inseparable." And he added, in one of his typically difficult but provocative utterances, that "where I am authentically myself, I am certain that I am not through myself. The highest freedom is experienced in freedom from the world, and this freedom is a profound bond with transcendence."[3]

Through thinking, then, a person may enter into the mystery of being—the being of the self, of others, perhaps of transcendence. If this is so, fixed and definite conclusions are not only unnecessary, they are undesirable. One is nearer the truth when thinking—keeping the open independence of one's sea—than when securely housed in conclusions built on "the treacherous, slavish shore."

It is because a thinker is searching for truths of a kind that cannot be put into words that, as stated in the epigraph chosen for this volume, "the paradox is the source of the thinker's passion." A paradox is a statement that appears to be, whether or not it actually is, self-contradictory. For example, Rousseau's assertion that a human being can be forced to be free is a paradox, since we usually assume that being forced and being free are opposite states.

Not every paradox, of course, has value. The assertion that Julius Caesar was assassinated in 44 B.C. and in A.D. 1865 is formally a paradox. It is valueless, however, because it cannot in any way be true. It is simply senseless. A paradox worthy of a thinker's passion must contain a possible truth, as does the idea of being forced to be free. The nature of force and freedom, and the relationships be-

---

[2]Among the major thinkers who have taken this position are Martin Buber, Gabriel Marcel, and Karl Jaspers, all of whom lived and wrote in the twentieth century.

[3]Karl Jaspers, *Way to Wisdom: An Introduction to Philosophy,* trans. Ralph Manheim (New Haven: Yale University Press, 1951), p. 45.

tween them, are highly uncertain. Hence the idea of being forced to be free, as startling as it is on first encounter, is not a palpable absurdity.

Aside from containing a possible truth, however, the value of a paradox lies in the very fact that it is unacceptable. It compels us to keep thinking, to remain open to the mystery of being. A person cannot settle down and live comfortably with it. While Rousseau's statement makes us aware that force and freedom may not be as contradictory as they at first appear, it is not something we can accept, file away in memory, and never question. Again and again it forces us to think.

Handling paradoxes properly is a difficult and puzzling task. It is also a somewhat perilous task, for paradoxes can be used irresponsibly. They can be used as rhetorical devices, lacking serious meaning, intended only to impress listeners and to avoid significant communication. But this simply says that understanding reality—the self, others, and encompassing being—is a difficult and puzzling as well as a perilous task. And there is no need for being relentless and extreme in seeking paradoxical formulations; there is no need, for example, to go as far as a recent French thinker, Simone Weil, has urged. When thinking of something, she asserted, we should as a regular method of investigation immediately try to see in what way the contrary is true. While such a method might be effectively used by a person of genius—like Simone Weil herself—for most of us it would be hopelessly confusing. What is called for is only a kind of tenderness toward reality—a willingness to apply ideas gently, an openness to those who take issue with our ideas, and a resolve to keep thinking.

Readers of this book must be ready to suffer the yeses and the nos that will crowd about as soon as they read a question, that will solicit support from one side or the other, and that will not quickly disperse and leave them in peace. The great questions of political theory are perennial precisely because intelligent people through the ages have not found it possible all to side with the yeses or with the nos. To approach the ultimate realities to which these questions point, one must be prepared to put up with mixed feelings and a divided mind—to struggle against contradictions but to remember, as the epigraph states, that "all thought is the attempt to discover something that thought cannot think," and to keep in mind that understanding will not come in the form of an unequivocal answer.

One must realize that the most important questions we can ask cannot be settled once and for all. One must be willing to entertain paradoxes, and that means being willing to put up with uncertainty. In this state of mind it may be found, unexpectedly, that uncertainty is illuminating.

In other words, a reader should not be discouraged by finding it impossible, in struggling with any of the questions that follow, to settle on a single answer. If two mutually exclusive answers appear in some sense both to be true, then thought has achieved a kind of success. It has found a paradox. Rather than being discouraged, one should look about and see whether the truth is near at hand.

Today we possess awesome powers of action, as is manifest in our command of nuclear energy, our exploration of space, and our industrial productivity. We also possess highly developed skills in accumulating and interpreting facts, as is dramatically evident in the scope and refinement of the physical sciences and in the vast quantities of data accumulated by the social sciences. But it is doubtful that we possess wisdom. Our lives are therefore carried on under an ineffaceable question: can we make our powers of action and our skills in research serve any valid ultimate purpose? The fear that pervades our time—fear of war, of poverty, of despotism, and of numberless other evils—shows how far we are from being able confidently to respond to this simple question in the affirmative.

I suggest that the wisdom demanded by our powers of action and research does not lie in knowing something beyond all doubt, as we feel we do when we adhere unwaveringly to a set of clear-cut and perfectly consistent principles, but in a certain kind of not-knowing—in an uncertainty that expresses both independent selfhood and openness to others. We all long for absolute assurance concerning what is true and right; we feel that our selfhood and our relationships are imperilled when that assurance is lacking. But the selfhood and relationships thus imperilled are bound to be false. They necessarily depend on an illusory certitude rather than on thought. This book is based on the premise that we humans are thinking beings. Only through thought do we affirm our rationality, our freedom, and our loyalty to being. Hence, if we learn to consider questions with clarity and determination and an open mind, we learn something that is irreducible to objective answers—the wisdom and poise of humane uncertainty.

Chapter 2

ESTRANGEMENT AND UNITY

The word *estrangement* is used here to signify every kind of disunity among human beings. War among nations, conflict among classes, and personal alienation are manifestations of estrangement; hatred, indifference, and loneliness are emotions of estrangement.

Without estrangement, there would be no politics. The antonym of *estrange*, according to *Webster's Dictionary*, is *reconcile*. Following this lead, it may be said that politics is the art of reconciliation and that the need for this art always arises from some kind of estrangement. When the leaders of one nation covet territory held by another nation or when one class resents the privileges of another class, demands are placed on political leadership. Of course, not every kind of estrangement necessarily gives rise to political demands; it is not clear, for example, whether the personal alienation so acutely felt in advanced industrial societies at the present time constitutes a political problem. The point, however, is that while not every situation of estrangement produces political problems, all political problems are rooted in situations of estrangement.

If estrangement is the fundamental condition for politics, it is also the fundamental condition for political thinking. If human beings were not estranged, whether in quiet loneliness or in active conflict, political thinking would not occur. We are impelled to ask about the ultimate forces and standards governing human relations only when those relations are strained or destroyed. The greatest achievements of political thought have for the most part been responses to social disintegration. Plato's *Republic* can be read as a meditation on the Peloponnesian War, in which the Greek cities not only fought one another for several decades but were also torn within by ferocious factional conflicts; Saint Augustine's *City of God* is an explicit commentary on the fall of the Roman Empire; Thomas Hobbes's *Leviathan* was called forth by the civil wars of seventeenth-century England, and Rousseau's essays were inspired by the degeneration of *l'ancien régime*, as manifest in the artificiality and loneliness of Parisian intellectual life and in the autocracy of royal officials.

Hence, we must begin our questioning by probing the nature of estrangement—by inquiring, for example, whether it is inherent in human nature and whether it can be counteracted or overcome.

The cardinal question about estrangement concerns its origin. Do such conditions as loneliness and conflict derive from the very nature of human beings, so that as long as the human species endures people will be estranged from one another? Or is estrangement caused by circumstances that can be altered or by human characteristics that can be eliminated without destroying anything intrinsically human?

1   *Are Human Beings Estranged in Essence?*

Today this question presses on us from various sides, although we do not often recognize it. For example, can we hope ever to achieve harmony and understanding among all the nations of the world? If human beings are not estranged in essence, perhaps we can. However, if we are thus estranged—if, for example, we have ineradicable aggressive impulses—a wise leader will not aim at anything so far-reaching as global understanding and unity. If human nature is such that our deepest satisfactions are experienced in war and conflict, then there is little use in dreaming of universal concord; much will have been accomplished if we can moderate hatreds and confine wars to limited areas and to the less destructive weapons.

The importance of this question is exemplified in the conflict not only of nations but also of races. Can we someday achieve complete racial harmony and integration? Probably so, if human beings are, as it were, made for harmony and integration. It may be, however, that they are essentially uneasy and suspicious creatures, offended even by superficial differences in others (differences like skin color), and inclined in their innermost nature toward aggression and combat. If so, it would be senseless to dream of racial harmony and integration. The utmost we could reasonably hope for would be uniform justice, decent conditions of life for all races, and absence of violent conflict.

As Nazism shows, however, it is possible to envision human nature in a way that invalidates even goals like moderating conflict. Racial war and racial imperialism become conditions under which men supposedly realize themselves fully. Such a vision is no doubt contrary to reason, and for most people today has a bizarre appearance. But European history in our century shows that it is possible for highly educated peoples to repudiate reason and assert—more through violence than through argument—that racial differences set people apart in their very essence. Nazism makes it plain that the question of our essential relations with one another is not a matter of mere idle curiosity.

The question also presses on us through the alienation pervading contemporary middle-class life. Many people today feel that although their lives are superficially harmonious, they lack relationships that are substantial and significant. Such conditions as the disintegration of families and the mobility entailed by many jobs tend to make all personal links tenuous and impermanent. But is it perhaps written into our nature that our relationships be tenuous and impermanent? Would the many people who bewail the lack of community find, once they entered a community, that it has little value or even is oppressive? Is defiant individuality perhaps of greater value than community, and should we cherish solitude rather than merely endure it? Those who celebrate community also celebrate public life, for that is supposedly where community is realized. Could it be, however, that private life is far more precious to us than public life? Such questions can be answered only by determining whether human beings are estranged in essence.

It might help us in thinking about this question to investigate briefly the meaning of the two main terms making it up—"estrange" and "essence." As the preceding comments suggest, estrangement can be manifest in many different forms. A shooting, an angry argument, and a quiet and harmless life devoid of friends, all exemplify estrangement. Often estrangement is manifest in the feeling that other persons are strangers. It would probably be unsafe to reduce the concept to feeling, however, since our deepest attitudes may be hidden from us, so that we scarcely are aware of them; hence the fact that people who care little for one another may display a jovial and momentarily sincere friendliness in their mutual relations. Perhaps the best word for characterizing estrangement is one which refers to actualities whether these are registered in feelings or not. The word is "distance." People are estranged in essence if, when it comes down to what is deepest and most enduring in them, they are at a distance from one another. Another way to put the same point is to say that people are estranged if they can live apart and alone with more joy and more real fulfillment than they can live together.

Let us consider the term "essence." An example may help. It often happens that someone drinks excessively and behaves foolishly and shamefully. The next morning there is deep chagrin and embarrassment, and the person who behaved foolishly and shamefully tries to tell his friends that they did not see him the night before as he *really is*. That person is referring to his essence and is urging his friends to think of him, not as he *happened* to be, on one occasion, but as he is on a deeper level of his being. One's essence is one's "innermost" or "basic" self. Is *your* essence the same as *mine?* This is a large question and cannot be dealt with here. To answer briefly, however, it is in some ways if there is such a thing as human essence and if both of us are human. This points to the fact that the human essence is universal. It would not make sense to say that some people are estranged in essence and others aren't. To ask what we are in essence, then, is to try to see beneath ephemeral and misleading appearances. It is to look for what distinguishes us from dogs and horses, and from trees and mountains.

To think of "estrange" and "essence" together may enable us to see why it makes sense to ask right at the beginning of any effort to think politically whether we are estranged in essence. It is to ask about the primal character of our relationships with one another. It is a highly practical question, for our essence determines our possibilities. If we are estranged in essence, it would be fatuous to think that we can ever create a paradise on earth—to dream of a commonwealth where all nations and races and classes live together in a state of perfect understanding. On the other hand, if we are communal in essence, there is no telling what earthly possibilities lie before us.

There are always more than two opposite answers to fundamental questions like the one we are discussing. However, in order to delineate sharply and concisely the issues involved in these questions, it will sometimes be convenient to discuss only two polar positions. This procedure will be followed here.

No one has so masterfully argued that people are essentially estranged as Thomas Hobbes (1588–1679), the mordant and witty English philosopher. The natural human state, Hobbes maintained, is one of war "of every man, against every man." Where there is no strong central government "to overawe them all," then "men have no pleasure, but on the contrary a great deal of grief, in keeping company." Life in such a state, Hobbes asserted in one of the most famous phrases in the literature of political theory, is "solitary, poor, nasty, brutish, and short."[1]

There are, so to speak, two levels of estrangement in Hobbes's philosophy. The surface level is psychological. People are estranged because they are essentially egotistical. One is concerned above all with the preservation of one's own life; one also seeks such things as wealth and prestige. None of these benefits can be gained without power. Thus Hobbes attributed to human beings "a perpetual and restless desire of power after power, that ceaseth only in death."[2] We care nothing about others except as they can help or hinder us in reaching our private goals. Such self-centeredness is not perverse, nor is it avoidable; it is our true nature. To be human is to be concerned exclusively with personal interests and personal power.

---

[1]Thomas Hobbes, *Leviathan, or the Matter, Forme and Power of a Commonwealth Ecclesiastical and Civil*, ed. with an introduction by Michael Oakeshott (Oxford: Basil Blackwell, n.d.), pp. 81–82.

[2]*Leviathan*, p. 64.

Beneath the psychological level of estrangement is what can be called the ontological level. Ontology is the study of being; *ontological* refers to Hobbes's conception of the nature of being. Hobbes was a materialist, meaning that he saw every reality as wholly definable in terms of space, time, and the laws of causation. The universe is composed of objects in motion. A human being is simply one of the objects making up the universe, more complex than such things as rocks and trees, but not essentially different. What concerns us now is only one consequence of this view: unity among human beings, as we usually understand it, is impossible. Material objects are essentially external to one another; they cannot be united by bonds such as compassion, empathy, or common purpose. They can be united only in the sense of being put in the same place or forcibly joined together, as stones are in building a wall. Because Hobbes saw human beings as material objects, he concluded that they could be united only by the power of an absolute government.

Many thinkers have argued the opposing view: that human beings are essentially united. Probably the most influential of these was Aristotle (384–322 B.C.), the founder of political science. Aristotle came from outside the world of the Greek city-states (he was from Macedonia) and witnessed the fall of that world. But from his vantage point he saw deeply into the prevailing political ethos and gave powerful expression to the ancient Greek feeling for the primary and pervasive significance of the city-state. For Aristotle, just as a leaf in its innermost nature is part of a tree, so a person by virtue of the human essence is a member of a city. "The man who is isolated—who is unable to share in the benefits of political association, or has no need to share because he is self-sufficient—is no part of the *polis* [the city-state], and must therefore be either a beast or a god."[3]

Aristotle did not carry the concept of unity to its logical extreme, the ideal of a global and completely egalitarian polity. People could not unite on any larger scale, Aristotle believed, than that of the city-state; moreover, even within the city-state only a few could

---

[3]Aristotle, *Politics*, trans. Ernest Barker (Oxford: Clarendon Press, 1946), p. 6.

attain the full unity of common citizenship, most people being fitted only to be artisans, laborers, or even slaves. Despite these qualifications, however, Aristotle's political thought is a sober and powerful denial that human beings are essentially estranged. Perhaps his most famous utterance is that "man is a political being," meaning that we cannot realize our essence in solitude and privacy but only in the company of fellow citizens.

Facing the task of deciding between Hobbes and Aristotle—of deciding whether human beings are estranged in essence—readers may be forgiven for feeling at an absolute standstill. How can such a question be resolved? How can it even be approached? Probably the best way is by looking into yourself, examining your own conduct and motives. To *be* a human being, after all, should provide some pretty fundamental insights into what sort of thing a human being fundamentally is. Nevertheless, looking into yourself deeply and honestly is not easy. Ways of checking on the conclusions of introspection are needed. One of the most obvious of these ways is simply that of observing the people around you. Friends and acquaintances may reveal a lot about human nature. People you read about also may offer instruction concerning human nature. One of the deepest students of human nature, the Russian novelist Fyodor Dostoevsky, apparently gained, or at least confirmed, many of his insights by reading newspapers. One of the shrewdest of American Presidents, Harry Truman, spent much time reading history. And one of the richest resources for studying human nature lies in fictional literature. A good novel contains the distilled observations of someone who is apt to be a genius in the art of observation.

In the final analysis, however, there can be no scientific answer to the question of whether human beings are estranged in essence. This is simply because a human being is not an object, like a rock or a planet, which can be objectively studied and understood. Hence choosing between Hobbes and Aristotle depends finally on faith. This does not mean one's choice is blind. It may be shaped and guided by daily newspapers and other kinds of empirical evidence, by great literature, by the Bible, or by all of these. But finally, to speak somewhat summarily, you must choose sides. You must pick the view of human nature which you feel you can live with. More will be said on these matters in connection with ensuing questions.

In the meantime, let us move on to a question which may shed some light on the issue of whether we are estranged in essence. If, as Aristotle argued, human beings are not estranged by their nature, why have peace and harmony always been so impermanent and elusive?

2   If Human Beings Are Not Estranged in Essence, Why Are There So Many Divisions and Conflicts Among Them?

This question presents a simple (although not easily resolved) issue: if human beings are not estranged in essence, the divisions and conflicts among them must proceed either from human beings themselves or from circumstances external to them. Let us consider first the former alternative—that human beings cause estrangement even though they are not in essence estranged.

What could this mean? The answer is delineated as sharply as anywhere in the writings of Saint Augustine (354–430), a brilliant churchman and thinker, and author of one of the classics of Christian thought, *The City of God*. Augustine held that God did not intend us to live in a state of division and conflict, hence these conditions were not attributable to the human essence, which was created by God. There is estrangement because we have betrayed the human essence. This betrayal was broadly what Augustine and many other Christians meant by "original sin." We have carried out a tragic rebellion against the order of God's creation. In doing this we have rejected our nature as received from God and have become different in actuality than we are in essence. The unity of divine creation has been lost. Neither God nor the human essence created by God can be blamed for this dreadful derangement, but only human beings in their universal perversity.

As Augustine envisioned it, sin is not merely a *tendency* of the will; it is a settled and—humanly—unchangeable configuration of the will. We not only commit particular wrongs; we do so out of a confirmed disorientation of soul. But we are still responsible not only for the particular wrongs we commit but also for the state of will from which these wrongs arise. This primal responsibility is symbolized by the concept of original sin. Each of us is an alien within creation, divided from both Creator and fellow creatures. So far as human powers go, this condition is irreparable; at the same time it is our own fault. There is hope only in the grace of God.

Dark and censorious theology of this sort repels many people today. But Augustine's view is not just dogma; it conforms with a strange but common experience. We sometimes feel unable to resist doing things for which we nevertheless blame ourselves; we feel helplessly estranged (assuming that the acts for which we blame ourselves in some way separate us from others), and at the same time we feel guilty of producing our estrangement.

Augustine's is an awesome and impressive philosophy, with its picture of humanity as a ruined race toiling in a world with little light aside from the gleams of God's mercy. Equally powerful philosophies, however, have been founded on the idea of human innocence. This idea is old because it is not only possibly true, it is pleasant. Augustine devoted much time and effort to attacking Pelagius, a monk who argued that we have it within our power to turn away from sin. But perhaps the most eloquent claims for human innocence are found in the writings of Jean Jacques Rousseau (1712–1778), a tormented genius who suffered almost unbearably from loneliness and was acutely conscious of the disorders of modern society.

Let us, then, ask of Rousseau: if human beings are essentially united and have never betrayed their essence, how has history come to be filled with so much hatred and turmoil? The only possible answer is that they have in some way accidentally (and not from grave, inherent defects) become entangled in circumstances that have estranged them from one another. It was Rousseau's conviction that such a misfortune had occurred in the distant past. Early in the human career on earth, property and power came to be concentrated in the hands of a few. This did not happen because people were extremely evil, but it did subvert the natural decency of human beings and the natural harmony of human relations. Rousseau's confidence in humankind did not lead him to palliate the evils of society; on the contrary, he was one of the most bitter social critics of modern times. But he did not blame the dislocations of society on human beings—at least, not on the human essence or on a humanly irreversible repudiation of that essence.

Augustinian and Rousseauean views of estrangement have had powerful reverberations in other spheres of political thought. For example, conceptions of the value of established institutions are determined largely by the alternative chosen. According to Augustinian philosophy, a human being is a dangerous creature; existing social and political institutions may be imperfect, but insofar as they assure some kind of order, even if only through the pressures of habit and fear, they have some value. From a Rousseauean point of view, however, order alone is worth very little, for people are capable of far greater things; they can attain justice and happiness.

This is not to say that Augustine always and Rousseau never approved of established institutions. For Augustine, institutions are made by sinful humanity and are bound to have much evil in them; and Rousseau thought that the original virtue in the human will had occasionally, as in the ancient Roman republic, escaped corruption and gained sovereign power. But for Augustine, heaven on earth is impossible and any order of life precluding the chaos implicit in human nature deserves appreciation. For Rousseau, on the other hand, because human innocence is not irretrievably lost, there is hope of earthly paradise or at least of earthly justice; but by this standard few actual societies can be seen as anything but mean and degraded.

Another way of stating the issue between Augustine and Rousseau is by asking whether the primary source of evil is human nature or human institutions. For Augustine, the evil in institutions is a result of the evil in human nature; Rousseau maintains the opposite, that the evil in human nature is a consequence of the evil in institutions. Thus for an Augustinian, the idea that humans might escape the influence of institutions and recreate civilization is unthinkable, whereas for a follower of Rousseau, such a possibility is real.

This polarity suggests another. An Augustinian is apt to be conservative—not in the sense of revering the prevailing order but in the sense of fearing any effort to change it. To tamper with restraints grounded in personal habits and long-standing customs might unleash the disorder inherent in sinful human nature. A follower of Rousseau, on the other hand, can readily take revolutionary pathways. Our original innocence provides possibilities of historical reconstruction. For such reconstruction to occur, of course, humankind in its primal decency must somehow throw off the influence of oppressive and corrupting institutions. But nothing in Rousseau's thought forbids the hypothesis that this liberation is possible through an act of revolutionary destruction. As it happens, Rousseau himself was not so carefree about revolution, and he did not in fact assume that any act of institutional destruction was an act of liberation. The explosive effect of his thought in history, however, derived primarily from the revolutionary implications of his psychology—implications Rousseau drew out cautiously, but his posterity exuberantly.

In America, students have sometimes adopted a revolutionary attitude or at least employed a revolutionary rhetoric. The established order perhaps contains enough evil, such as poverty and racial injustice, to warrant such an attitude. But is there enough goodness in human nature to warrant it? If Augustine is nearer the truth than Rousseau, then this radicalism, often infused with intolerance and self-righteousness, might lead to evils greater than those it attacks.

We have now considered the origin of estrangement—whether it lies in our essence, in a tragic rejection of our essence, or merely in accidental historical circumstances. This discussion puts us in a position to ask how estrangement can be overcome, or, if human beings are estranged in essence, how the conflicts among them can be moderated. In considering this question it may help to focus on a human faculty that political philosophers throughout history have seen as the primary source of unity and order, that is, reason.

3   Can Estrangement Be Overcome Through Reason?

There is no doubt concerning the consensus of the West on this question: it is strongly affirmative. Granted, in ancient Israel, one of the two major roots of Western culture, there was relatively little respect for reason, our overriding duty being to obey the commands of God. But God and human beings sometimes engaged in reasonable discourse; the Hebraic God was a God who listened and spoke. And in ancient Greece, the other source of our culture, the most powerful and prevalent theme of political thought was probably the idea that people can overcome conflict through reason. The Greek view won the day, and even Christianity became markedly rationalistic in the Middle Ages. The modern world thus inherited a strongly rationalistic tradition, which has been carried on most spectacularly in science and technology. While there have been some powerful revolts against the reigning rationalism, they have not so far succeeded. Western society might still take as its motto the biblical injunction "Come, let us reason together."

This consensus rests, however, on the assumption that human beings in essence are united or at least that their interests at some point coincide. If they were essentially estranged and their interests altogether in conflict, then, of course, there would be little that reason could do. Far from drawing human beings together, reason would enable the most cunning and ruthless to gain advantage over others. No great political thinker (not even Machiavelli) has argued in favor of using reason in this fashion. But according to Plato, at least two intellectual figures well known in his own time, Thrasymachus and Callicles, did so. For these two men, as Plato depicts them, reason was a solvent of the irrational customs and baseless scruples that sometimes lured superior people into subordinating their own interests to the interests of others.

If at some point individual interests do coincide, however, then even if human beings are essentially estranged and care nothing about one another except as means to individual satisfaction, reason might draw them together by disclosing the underlying identity of their interests. Such an idea enters into one of the most enduring concepts in Western political thought, the idea that government is based on a "social contract." This concept is illustrated by the views of Hobbes. As we have seen, Hobbes regarded human beings as estranged in essence. Yet he did believe that everyone has an interest in peace and thus in effective government. Reason, he thought, could make this congruence of individual interests indisputably clear, thus saving people from the "war of all against all" into which they otherwise would plunge owing to their essential estrangement. For Hobbes, each person is concerned only with personal safety; but reason shows that the safety of each one necessitates obeying a government that secures the safety of all.

The Western faith in reason reaches its height with the denial of essential estrangement. The idea that through reason we can discern our common essence and from this source derive the laws that unite us is among the oldest and most durable principles of our heritage. In Plato it was the first principle of an elitist political philosophy built around the city-state; in Stoicism it became the basis of an egalitarian and universalist outlook; in the Middle Ages it retained its authority, although combined with the principles of orthodox Christianity; and in modern times it has been the theoretical foundation both of international law (limiting state power in its external application) and of constitutional government (limiting state power in its internal application). By using our reason, according to this view, we become members of a community that is not destroyed by the conflicts among nations and among classes. Our common membership in this universal society of reason enables us to subject power, with its ceaseless tendency to become brutal and limitless, to rationally certain and morally unchallengeable standards. These standards constitute what is usually called "natural law." If there is a single indispensable idea in our past, it is this one.

Nevertheless, several thinkers have viewed this idea either with reservations or with hostility. An indication of the power of the idea of natural law is that probably no great thinker has repudiated it altogether. But one who came near to doing so, and thus serves as a convenient example of the antirationalist position, is Edmund Burke (1729–1797), an Irish-born philosopher and statesman whose *Reflections on the French Revolution* is a manifesto of modern conservatism. Burke candidly defended prejudice in place of reason. His writings show a belief in the essential unity of human beings that is as emphatic and unqualified as Aristotle's. But Burke did not trust reason to disclose the human essence. He thought that established customs and traditions reflected human nature far more accurately than did the abstract conclusions of reason; these customs and traditions, enthroned in the human mind, he called "prejudice."

We are not only too deep and complex to be adequately guided by reason, according to Burke; we are too dangerous as well. Burke had an Augustinian view of human nature. Order needs the support of habit and emotion, and thus it depends on institutions and traditions that are old, hallowed, and unquestioned. Prejudice is not only wiser than reason, it is also more powerful. For Burke, then, estrangement is overcome only through allegiance to venerable and awesome institutions. The claim to understand human nature imperils the mutual understanding and respect found only in humble submission to the traditions, customs, and institutions inherited from the past.

The aim of this book is to mark out the main pathways of political thought, not every possible pathway. I do not mean to suggest that there are only a few alternative routes that a reflective person logically can follow. Thought is (and should be) ingenious in finding untraveled ways. Nevertheless, the terrain of thought does impose certain common tendencies on all who start from the same basic principles. Accordingly, the rationalist and the Burkean positions divide philosophers into two broad groups, and these, despite differences within them, reflect two different ways of looking at the social and political world. The following polarities, in their typical forms, derive from this distinction.

1. *Moral absolutism* versus *moral relativism*. Moral absolutism is the theory that there are moral standards independent of the interests of individuals and societies and also of the standards that happen to prevail in any particular time and place. The main form of moral absolutism in Western history is the idea of natural law, of a universal and eternal law based on the human essence and discernible by reason. Plainly this idea expresses the conviction that reason does draw people together. Relativism has various forms, which vary according to what is held to determine morality, and thus what morality is held to be relative to. One of its main forms is the principle that good and evil are defined by each society. Burke was not an extreme relativist, for he believed that certain standards are incumbent on human beings regardless of the rules prevailing in their societies. But his regard for custom and tradition led him naturally to accept moral variations among times and places that a rationalist might condemn.

2. *Uniformity* versus *organic unity*. Reason can discover only the general—that which is common to many particulars; consequently, rationalism readily gives rise to a conception of unity hard to distin-

guish from uniformity. In contrast, thinkers like Burke are likely to be particularly open not only to the societal differences that are sanctioned by moral relativism but also to those individual differences—for example, in character, talent, and vocation—that are coordinated in the organic unity of the group. A clear expression of this polarity can be seen in Aristotle's protest that Plato erased crucial differences among persons in order to unite them. "It is," Aristotle complains, "as if you were to turn harmony into mere unison, or to reduce a theme to a single beat."[4]

3. *Radicalism* versus *conservatism.* To believe that we can comprehend human nature rationally may lead to the notion that we can and should destroy all those ancient institutions that rest on mere prejudice and rebuild them in accordance with rational designs. Rationalism in this way gives rise to radicalism. Such pride before the majestic, enigmatic past infuriated Burke. He set against it the conservatism that necessarily follows from the principle that the human essence is disclosed only through custom and tradition. The kind of order built through generations of prudent statecraft and spontaneous life cannot be deliberately and swiftly constructed according to the counsels of reason, as Burke saw it. If you are fortunate enough to live within such an order, all you can do—and this is your overriding duty—is to respect and preserve it.

To guard against oversimplification, however, it seems appropriate to take note of one of the "untraveled ways" that, as I remarked earlier, human thought is ingenious in finding. Contemporary feminists are apt to shy away from both the rationalism running through the Western political tradition and the irrationalism inherent in subordinating critical judgment to established customs and ancient traditions. It is easy to see why feminists are not inclined toward the latter, toward reverence for old customs and traditions; these have practically always sanctioned the subordination, if not the outright oppression, of women. The use of critical judgment in relation to the past and present order of society is vital to the social changes that feminists seek. Still, critical judgment is

---

[4]*Politics,* p. 51.

based on reason. Why, then, it may be asked, should feminists shy away from rationalism, which means simply emphasis on reason?

The answer seems apparent. A faculty—reason—that from the time of Aristotle to the present seems to have lent itself readily to defining and justifying what feminists see as rank injustice is almost bound to be questioned. The purported universality of male generalizations and rules strikes feminists in many cases as specious. Traditional rationalism appears one-sided and in its one-sidedness inhuman and unjust.

But what would feminists put in place of rationalism? Not irrationalism, ordinarily. It is not reason itself that is apt to be rejected by feminist writers but what they believe is undue reliance on reason. Many of them see this imbalance as characteristic of male-dominated culture and envision a broader form of discernment, sensitive not only to the features common to many situations—features it is the function of reason to grasp—but also to features that are unique and thus beyond the scope of reason.

The feminist critique of rationalism has been reinforced by psychological studies indicating that female perceptions of reality differ significantly from male perceptions. Females of all ages are apt to be attuned to the possibilities inherent in particular situations, regardless of what those situations have in common with other situations, whereas males are inclined to appeal to general rules. Faced with a moral problem, females typically are responsive to the unique and concrete character of the problem, while males search for a universal standard in accordance with which the problem can be resolved. Females display empathy, males logic; females try to elicit harmony, males to do justice.

Perhaps no single word is adequate to designate the quality that feminists would add to reason, but words like "intuition" and "sensitivity" suggest what they seemingly have in mind. The point, at any rate, is that feminists often attribute to women an insight into the particularities of time and place and personality, an ability to enter imaginatively into situations and sympathetically into the lives of individual persons, that men either do not possess or have allowed to atrophy. They believe that such insight, brought fully into the public realm, might enable us to right the imbalances seen in traditional rationalism. In answer to the question before us, then—can reason overcome estrangement?—feminists often answer that alone it cannot; it needs to be fused with, or in some other way supplemented by, another kind of discernment, a kind more fully developed—in present-day societies at least—among women than among men.

To reflect on the power of reason in relation to estrangement may lead one to an even broader question. Can human powers of any kind overcome estrangement, or are we dependent on something beyond humanity? Asking this brings us to an issue that people today generally ignore. The spiritual atmosphere of our time seems to be one of religious doubt along with human self-confidence. It is widely assumed that we neither need to, nor can, call on anything beyond our own faculties for resolving our tensions and discords. But is this assumption so plainly true that it cannot be questioned? In the past, one of the most persistent and widespread convictions has been that a stable and decent society must be built on some kind of religious foundation. Numberless generations in all parts of the globe have assumed that people can be properly related to one another only if they are properly related to the divine.

We must ask whether this is so.

4 Is Religion in Some Form Needed for Overcoming Estrangement?

Three general positions in relation to this question can be conveniently distinguished. The first is the self-confident humanism of modern times, based on atheism or agnosticism, and ordinarily accompanied by a dislike of organized religion. The term humanism is intended here to designate the belief that human powers are adequate for achieving all reasonable human ends; religion has little, if any, role to play. Americans by and large profess, when interviewed by pollsters, to be religious believers. However, it seems likely that most American intellectuals—university professors, journalists, writers—are humanists. And a great many people, whether intellectuals or not, are suspicious of organized religion. No historical lesson has sunk more deeply into the American mind, it seems, than that drawn from the religious wars of Europe and the Puritan theocracy in Massachusetts: religious faith can be divisive and despotic. This conviction has been reinforced in the minds of many by the secularism of Marx and other social critics and reformers. For Marx, religion was "the opium of the people," and socialists have traditionally dismissed anticipations of another life as "pie in the sky." The serious allegation behind such rhetoric is that religion makes people indifferent to worldly suffering—the suffering of others, and even of themselves—and in that way inhibits social reform and the conquest of estrangement here on earth.

Humanists today often believe that the energies once devoted to religious worship should now be devoted to meeting the needs of the downtrodden and disadvantaged. For millennia the vast majority of human beings have lived in squalor and ignorance. But at last we have the powers of industrial production and human organization necessary for meeting the material and educational needs of everyone. Poverty and illiteracy have thus become intolerable. Most of those sharing such feelings make the crucial assumption that bringing everyone together on a level of material prosperity once enjoyed by only a few need not be hindered, and may even be helped, by the decline of religious faith which seems to have occurred in recent centuries. After all, when people felt closely united with the divine, they were very imperfectly united with one another; often they were horrifyingly cruel to one another. Now, perhaps, the love and devotion we once bestowed upon God, we can bestow instead on our fellow human beings. And perhaps the paradise hoped for in another world can be at least approximated in this world.

The humanist vision can be a moving one. In its light we see ourselves inhabiting a vast, indifferent universe and overcoming our cosmic loneliness in a purely human community. We see ourselves rising above the weakness and sinfulness humans had in religious eyes and affirming the immense power and goodness inherent in liberated humanity. Many even among those who still believe in God probably feel that such a vision is unobjectionable and will suffice, in the absence of a common religious faith, to undergird out common life.

In view of this humanist consensus, it is striking that the political thinkers of antiquity and the Middle Ages for the most part believed that unity among human beings depends on unity with the divine. The first great political philosophy set forth in the West, that enunciated by Plato (427?–347 B.C) in *The Republic,* exemplifies this viewpoint. Plato is among the greatest figures in the world's spiritual history, standing with such teachers as Confucius and Buddha, and his philosophy is marked by a dramatic consciousness of our dependence on transcendent realities. If the injunction implicit in much twentieth-century social commentary is "Forget the transcendent and concentrate on one another," the injunction implicit in *The Republic* is "Know first the transcendent, then consider one another."

Beyond all the things we can see and touch, Plato believed, there is a source from which these things draw their reality and value. He called this simply "the Good." He likened the Good to the sun, which makes it possible for living things to grow and be seen, thus suggesting that the Good makes it possible for all the realities constituting the universe to exist and be known. Human beings are seen in similar fashion. They can be fully understood, and their deepest needs identified, only in the light shed by the Good. Accordingly, a major theme of *The Republic* is that organizing a society worthy of authentic humanity is possible only through that supreme knowledge in which human beings (or a few of them) apprehend the Good. Thus politics is properly centered on the transcendent. Those who are separated from this ultimate principle of life, value, and truth cannot possibly attain true unity. Plato probably would find the twentieth-century notion that we should ignore ultimate realities and concentrate on building a good society as no less absurd than we would find the suggestion that we disregard the laws of physics in order to expedite the exploration of space.

Not long after the time of Plato, Stoic philosophers began to develop a far more ecumenical and egalitarian concept of unity than Plato's; all human beings, without regard to nation or class, were seen as essentially united. More will be said about this concept further along. The point that concerns us here is that this new concept of unity still rested on religious foundations. For the Stoics, the entire universe was divine (a view usually referred to as "pantheism"). The duties that bind human beings to one another are prescribed by the divine order they inhabit. It might be said that unity among human beings is inherent in the omnipresence of the divine.

The Platonic-Stoic conception of the dependence of society on religion is the second general position relating to the question we are discussing (the first being the humanistic outlook). What distinguishes it from the third position is its reliance on human initiative. The divine is thought of as entirely unmoved, tranquil, and self-contained. It is accessible to humans but does not seek them out. It is up to humans to seek out the divine. For adherents of the third position, that of orthodox Christianity, humans are too deeply immersed in qualities like selfishness and greed to be capable of finding God. It is God who must act, and does.

The two positions agree in regarding unity among human beings as dependent on unity with the divine. In the Christian view, a person is a worthy object of love owing to a wholeness and splendor that comes from God. Each one is created in the image of God; that image is ravaged and dimmed by sin; but through the life, death, and resurrection of Christ, the original image is restored in all of its primeval glory. Hence humans can and ought to love one another, for love is simply our recognition in one another of our original glory. God, manifestly, is at the center of the picture. Were there no God, human estrangement would be unconquerable and everlasting—inherent in the human condition. It would have been as unthinkable to Paul as to Plato that human beings should love one another, or even respect one another, simply for what they are in themselves rather than for the divine splendor they reflect. The only authentic unity, borrowing Augustine's phrase, is that of "the City of God."

While the second and third positions agree in seeing religion in some form as needed for overcoming estrangment, however, they disagree radically in their views of the relationship of the divine and the human. For the pagan thinkers, a human being—at least a very intelligent and highly educated one—can ascend to God. This is a power inherent in reason. For Christian thinkers, however, the idea of humans ascending to God is foolishly and sinfully unrealistic—expressive of the illusory confidence in human powers often called "pride." The distance between the human race and God is far too vast for humans on their own to be able to cross it. Through sin they have separated themselves from God and crippled themselves as spiritual beings. Only God can traverse the no man's land lying between the divine and the human. This God did in the life and death of Christ.

In sum, the ascent of humanity was replaced, in the Christian vision, by the descent of God. As a result, the conquest of human discord came to be viewed very differently from the way it was viewed in the philosophy of the Greeks. For Plato and the Stoics it was sufficient that the divine was real and that humans, through reason, could comprehend the divine. By virtue of this power they could find their way to the high plateaus of divine reality and build their cities there. Even for those Greeks who emphasized the dependence of human harmony on divine harmony, all cities were in their origins thoroughly human. Christians necessarily disagreed. No authentic community, no real unity of humans with humans, could be built by human beings alone. Only God could break the chains cast by human wickedness and enable us to rediscover in one another the glory and harmony of God's original universe. Thus true unity originates, not merely in the serene accessibility, but in the merciful action, of the divine. This is why any city worthy of human habitation must be a "City of God."

Today many people find it hard to take concepts like sin and salvation seriously. But for many centuries they were taken very seriously indeed. What has changed? Have we become more profound, hence able to see through illusions that captivated earlier ages? Or have we become more shallow, so that the insights of more spiritual centuries than ours have become incomprehensible to us? In the interests of fair inquiry we ought to hesitate before choosing the more flattering of these alternatives.

Are we more dependent on religion than we realize? What do we mean, for example, when we speak of the dignity of the individual? This is perhaps the key phrase for expressing the modern ideal of community. Every human being, according to this ideal, has a mysterious and immeasurable worth and therefore deserves respect and fair treatment, regardless of race, gender, or class. To exclude anyone whatever from this community of respect and fair treatment would be a denial of dignity. Few today would reject this line of reasoning. Due either to its elemental and self-evident truth, or to cultural conditioning, it has immense authority. Does it make sense, however, on the basis of humanism? It does on the basis of

Biblical faith, whether or not that faith is valid. According to the Bible, "God created man in his own image."[5] Moreover, man is not created and then abandoned. God is concerned with the eternal destiny of each individual. One may find such beliefs incomprehensible or implausible, but they did give meaning to the concept of the dignity of the individual.

If God is nowhere on the scene, however, what qualities entitle every individual to the deep respect that is called for when we speak of dignity? If there is no Platonic sun of being, no God, can there still be glory in every human being? People today readily say there can. Is this glory discernible by the dispassionate eye of observation and reason? Is it a plain empirical fact that we can perceive in human beings as we do the color of their hair? Then why was it unseen by Plato, Aristotle, Thucydides, or any of the great minds of ancient Greece at the peak of its brilliance? Does anyone claim to be able to see with the naked eye, so to speak—the eye unaided by religious presuppositions of any sort—the dignity (that is, the glory; we are not speaking of qualities that may arouse compassion) in each of the filthy and ruined figures making up the homeless population of America? If the dignity of every individual cannot be derived from any principle concerning the transcendent, and is not an ordinary worldly fact, manifest to the senses, then is it anything at all? Is it real?

There are perhaps no questions of greater importance before us in the twentieth century than these, for the individual is threatened from all sides. "The organization man," "the lonely crowd," "the revolt of the masses," and like phrases are well-known signals of alarm in which writers have expressed the pervasive sense that the individual is being engulfed by society and lost. In shocking spectacles of homelessness and urban squalor, in the hatred of race for race, and in violence so uncontrolled that many children in American cities now arm themselves before setting out for school, we see evidence that the individual has become like a waste product, to be discarded or casually destroyed. But how can we save the individual

---

[5]Genesis 1:27. Except where noted otherwise, Biblical quotations are from the Authorized (King James) Version.

if we really do not know what we mean when we speak of "the dignity of the individual"?

Nowhere is this question posed more dramatically than in the writings of Fyodor Dostoevsky (1821–1881), the great Russian novelist of the nineteenth century, who was one of the few who foresaw our troubled times. For Dostoevsky the issue lay between two radically antagonistic visions—that of the "man-god" and that of the "God-man." The former envisions men and women as having thrown off the thralldom of religious faith and as having through their own achievements—in art, politics, war, business, science—taken on the glory of gods. Dostoevsky held that the image of the man-god was a logical and inevitable outgrowth of atheism. Human beings aspire toward the infinite and must, refusing to bow down to God, try to become gods themselves. The results, however, will be far from the global love and compassion invoked by the humanitarian atheists and agnostics of the twentieth century. Dostoevsky believed that the denial of God was, in effect, also a denial of the dignity of individuals and of all moral laws. The man-god consequently would become a criminal, a tyrant, or a nihilistic revolutionary.

Not only did Dostoevsky reject the atheism and agnosticism so common at present; he also rejected the widespread sentiment—shared even by many believers—that whether a person is an atheist or a believer is a purely private matter. What happens in the "secret hearts" of people will find expression in the public world, and loss of faith among private individuals imperils civilization. Sooner or later the man-god will issue forth from the quiet homes in which he may have been born and begin to create havoc on the earth.

The God-man, in Dostoevsky's mind, was an entirely different matter. Christ is the original God-man. The ideal delineated in Christ is that of men and women exalted to divine status through the mercy of God rather than through their own powers and actions. The ideal can be realized only through Christianity. Christ is in effect an offer of divine companionship, and whoever accepts that offer steps into the light of divine glory. But whoever rejects that offer steps into everlasting darkness. There all dignity is lost. Hence the decline of Christianity—more pronounced probably in the twentieth century than in Dostoevsky's time—was in his eyes an all-engulfing catastrophe.

The four questions so far discussed have enabled us to consider human relations in their most basic character. We have asked about the source of estrangement: does it derive from deep and inalterable human traits? If not, why has it so persistently afflicted human relations? We have also asked about the possibilities of healing estrangement: can reason unite us or is something beyond reason, that is, religion, needed?

It might be well to pause for a moment and recall that we can't think about such questions without thinking about the human essence—what we really are, as distinguished from what we just happen to be. It might be well also to recall that in thinking about the human essence we are dealing with something that can't be totally and finally summed in any literal statement. A human being is fundamentally and everlastingly mysterious. More simply, as Karl Jaspers has written, we are always more than we can know about ourselves.[6] What does this mean for our efforts to think?

It means mainly that we must be tentative. If human beings are always more than they can know about themselves, then any statement about human nature can be added to. In speaking of the individual and society, therefore, we must stay clear of any suggestion that what we are saying comprises the whole, unchangeable truth of the matter. Even though we are given in our daily lives to voicing fervent opinions about other people, when we start philosophizing about them we have to be wary of the conclusive yes and the conclusive no. In short, we have to remember, as the epigraph states, that in trying to understand what constitutes our essential humanity we are striving "to discover something that thought cannot think"—not, at least, comprehensively and unquestioningly.

Being tentative is not easy, for we love to make statements with an air of finality and absolute assurance. Even so, it does not suffice merely to be tentative. We must develop a certain tolerance of contradictions. This is to allude to something we have already discussed—the role of paradoxes in our thinking. If we are always more than we can know about ourselves, any statement about human nature can be added to; but what is added to it may not fit

---

[6]Karl Jaspers, *The Perennial Scope of Philosophy,* trans. Ralph Manheim (New York: Philosophical Library, 1949), p. 60.

with it comfortably. If, when this happens, we feel quite sure of what we have said, and if what is added to it (but does not fit comfortably with it) seems to have some foundation, then we are faced with a paradox—an apparent contradiction. And if Kierkegaard, as quoted in the epigraph, is right, the paradox may in some mysterious sense represent the truth. This is bound to seem confusing. But one thing it means is that you should not be greatly discouraged if seemingly irresolvable inner conflicts develop in the course of your thinking. These conflicts may signal an approach to the truth. It may be, for example, that human beings are not unequivocally either estranged or united in essence. The words we use for discussing and thinking about such matters seem better suited for dealing with things like stones and bricks than with human beings, and it may be that they do not allow us to express the truth unambiguously. (It would make sense to say that to be truly united, people must be *freely* united. But does *freedom* connote individual separateness, and does it thus necessarily introduce into the heart of any freely created community an element of estrangement?)

It does not follow that you should be unworried about apparent contradictions in your thinking. A paradox will not yield its truth unless it is vigorously attacked and if possible resolved. It must be battered and shaken, so to speak. Philosophers for the most part do choose sides in facing the great issues of human thought, and doing this forcefully and rationally is what makes them impressive. A beginning thinker should follow their example. In trying to choose one side over the other you strike at the paradox and try to see the truth which is hidden behind it.

It follows from all I have said, however, that choosing one side should never mean closing your mind to the other side. Readiness to reconsider arguments you disagree with is a way of being open to the paradoxes in which truth is often concealed. Openness to the other side was at least one of the reasons why Plato ordinarily cast his responses to the perennial questions in the form of dialogues, or conversations, and why he often did not permit these conversations to reach any definite conclusions.

It would not be illogical for the present chapter to end at this point. Some of the ideas discussed may become more alive, however, if we see how they apply to the most serious divisions among

humans. Over the centuries, the two most profound and unbridge-
able divisions have been those among peoples (city-states, empires,
and nations) and those among classes. These will be the subjects of
the final two questions of this chapter.

5   *Should All Peoples Be United in a Single Global Society?*

The history of thought discloses two extreme and opposed responses to this question. Both are old and enduring; both appear in
ancient as well as in modern times.

Greeks in the age of Socrates and Plato believed that a political
order as large as the modern nation-state was incompatible with a
fully human life. Aristotle's assertion that "man is a political being"
expressed a widely shared conviction; it was commonly assumed,
however, that people can live according to their political nature
only in states that are small. To live in a large state or an empire is to
be governed from a distant center and thus to be a subject rather
than a citizen. In Aristotle's vision, people are united by a universal
essence, yet only a parochial state, the *polis,* enables them to realize
that essence and the unity it implies.

This is plainly a vision in which the idea of a global society is
threatening and antihuman. Such a vision has recurred with increasing frequency in modern times, as people have sought ways of
escaping the impersonality and inhuman scale of industrial civilization. Rousseau reaffirmed the basic standard of ancient democracy—that a state should be small enough for the citizens to meet
regularly in a single assembly. Since his time, some of the most idealistic thinkers have felt that only through breaking up the vast
states and organizations of the modern world could community be
saved. And in contemporary America most radicals seem to believe
that the only way to a new humanity is through drastic decentralization. Indeed, the ideas of community and face-to-face association
have become virtually equivalent in many minds. From this point
of view, for all humans to be collected together in a single society
and live under a single government would be ruinous.

Another kind of idealism, however, is inspired by a very different vision: one of all human beings, with no peoples or races ex-

cluded, living in common humanity in a global polity. This conception, like its opposite, that of face-to-face democracy, arose in ancient times. It was developed by the Stoics after the city-states had been incorporated in empires. The *polis* is replaced in the thought of the Stoics by the *cosmopolis*—the cosmic *polis*. As we know, Stoics saw the universe as a divine order; this order is present in laws that can be apprehended by reason; we are all therefore citizens of a universal city. Here the principle that there is a universal human essence takes a very logical political form, the ideal of a universal human community. Not surprisingly, Stoicism was the principal philosophy embraced by the most effective strategists of universal order that the world has known—those who administered the Roman Empire and shaped the Roman law.

Christian thinkers during antiquity and the Middle Ages were even more universalist than the Stoics; typically they envisioned humankind as united not only by natural law but also by a divine plan of redemption. These two forms of unity, they thought, should be recognized and acted upon both through some kind of universal political order and through the Catholic (that is, world-embracing) Church.

The Roman ideal of universal and eternal peace and the Christian ideal of one global faith linger as a bitter longing in the twentieth century. These ideals glimmer faintly in international law and in the United Nations. They deepen the horror that we feel before the maelstrom of nationalism, fanaticism, and war that has filled the history of our times.

One of the most powerful restatements of the universalist outlook is found in the philosophy of Marx. Nations are held by Marxists to be organizations of a doomed class; the workers will establish the lasting and all-encompassing unity that eluded both the Roman Empire and the Roman Church. But how far we are from realizing this ancient dream is indicated by the contributions of Marxism itself to the passions pitting nations against one another.

Which do we really want, associations so small and personal that they might, as Aristotle believed, be bound together by friendship, or a peace so inclusive and just that in its compass all humankind is one community? Is our ideal Athens or Rome? These two visions have been invested with such splendor by their idealistic defenders that we may feel let down when reminded that many prefer what we now have, the nation-state, a social form that crystallized early in the modern era, about five hundred years ago. The nation-state, it might be said, is the alternative offered by the modern world to the face-to-face polity of ancient times and the global society idealized by Rome and the Middle Ages.

It may seem puzzling that anyone would prefer the nation-state. Isn't it just the wrong size—too large for personal relations and too small for global concord? Most people prior to the Reformation would have said that it is, and many today would agree. The nation-state is vast and impersonal; individuals and their intimate, spontaneous relations seem of little account alongside the hulking mass of the nation, with its demands for money, soldiers, technicians, and submissive workers. The antipathy some students have felt toward "the Establishment," the draft, the Pentagon, and so forth, probably arises in part from their sense of the vulnerability of personal life in confrontation with the overwhelming and omnipresent power of the nation. At the same time, however, no single nation can guarantee global peace, and thus national might is dedicated above all to war; nations bring the impersonality of the global state, but not its security and peace. Professors and students seem to have felt these defects keenly; in universities today the nation-state has few warm friends.

During the past two centuries, however, it has been one of the chief objects of human devotion, and not only on the part of the worst human beings. People of intelligence and high ideals have been nationalists, among them the great German philosopher Georg W. F. Hegel (1770–1831), whose ideas had an impact on Marxism, liberalism, and practically every other major strain of modern political thought.

Hegel believed that for a community to have any real life it must have some significance in history, it must play a part in the affairs of the human race. In the past, it is true, small associations had been able to do this; Athens is the outstanding example. Hegel believed, however, that life now had to be conducted on a larger scale. The nation-state could attain a degree of power and inner diversification beyond the reach of smaller associations. At the same time, however, a community should not be coextensive with that vast and miscellaneous collection of people we call "humankind." It would then have no identity as a particular community. To have this identity, it must be distinct from other communities—in a position to define itself through its differences from them and to test itself against them in war. On these grounds, Hegel looked on Athens and Rome—the small and the universal—as stages that have been left behind in the progressive development of humanity. The climax of history, he thought, would occur in the era of nation-states.

These political bodies took on religious grandeur in Hegel's thought. A nation is of greater reality and value, he held, than any individual human being. And in one of the most notorious propositions in the literature of political thought, he referred to the nation-state as "the Divine Idea as it exists on earth."[7] Hegel has been condemned and derided for such statements, but he was only saying explicitly and philosophically what many modern nationalists have felt.

Hegel was more extreme, however, than it is necessary to be in order to defend the nation-state. It is possible to feel that polities no larger than the ancient city-state are in most circumstances too small to be economically viable, militarily defensible, or culturally profound and diversified, and yet also to feel that it would be presumptuous and oppressive to place the entire globe under one set of institutions. These polar attitudes might lead one to favor something on the order of the present nation-state—a polity that is large but less than global.

From this point of view, the nation, with all its flaws, may seem an indispensable medium for uniting the individual with others. Only as a member of a nation can a person enter into the full range of human relationships—those involved in family, vocation, military responsibilities, and so forth. You can hold this view while admitting that your nation is very imperfect and that your fellow citizens (and presumably you yourself with them) have much to be forgiven. There is, in short, a sober and repentant nationalism that rejects not only the ideal of a single, global society but also the national self-glorification expressed by Hegel.

[7]Georg Wilhelm Friedrich Hegel, *The Philosophy of History*, rev. ed., trans. J. Sibree (New York: Wiley, 1900), p. 39.

Who is most nearly right—the Athenian citizen, the Roman-Christian universalist, or the modern nationalist? Each one speaks for an indispensable condition of unity and life. Each makes a reasonable argument.

Let us now, by means of a final question, reflect on unity among classes.

6   *Should All Class Distinctions Be Abolished?*

If we assume that unity is good and our end is to overcome estrangement, this question presents us with two subordinate questions. The first is whether class distinctions necessarily stand in the way of unity. It is possible to argue, after all, that unity depends on the coordination of differences; if that is so, a properly arranged set of class distinctions might be a prerequisite rather than an obstacle to unity.

The second subordinate question we confront is whether it is possible to abolish all class distinctions. There is a dilemma here. If no unity can be achieved without abolishing classes, and if unity is good, it follows not only that classes should be abolished, but also that this has to be done through violence, for classes that are in no way united would be unable to agree peacefully to their own abolition. But the use of violence itself promotes class distinctions by advancing those who employ the violence into a separate and dominant class. This dilemma, perhaps, is the contradiction—as fatal as any that Marx saw in capitalism—that wrecked the promise of the Russian Revolution.

As we consider the question of abolishing classes, then, keep in mind both the relationship that class distinctions bear to unity and the possibility that the very project of abolishing classes is self-defeating.

The call for the abolition of classes contained in the research and thought of Karl Marx (1818–1883), the major intellectual source of socialism and communism, has shaken Western institutions more profoundly than any utterance since the Reformation. The key to Marx's attitude lay in the importance he attributed to economic conditions. Marx held that our ideas and feelings—in truth our whole nature—are shaped by our economic situation.

What people think and feel is decisively influenced by what they do for a living. A person must work in order to live, but in order to work must accept a place in the economic system. That place will determine a person's entire situation in life. It is manifest from history and from anthropological and sociological studies that human nature is not fixed but is malleable. We may infer that the character of human beings will be shaped by circumstances inherent in their work.

This view may at first glance seem innocuous and sensible. It implies, however, that classes must be composed of completely different kinds of people and that they cannot possibly be united in a single community. Marx identified classes in economic terms because his emphasis on the formative power of economic circumstances allowed no other differentia to be of primary significance. The main class division is between people who own nothing and thus have to work and people who own property and thus command the resources on which the lives of all others depend. Between these two groups there is not simply a divergence of interests or ways of life. One is tempted to say there is a divergence of species, for their different economic situations make them entirely dissimilar in character.

Reverting to the concepts we have been discussing in this chapter, this differentiation amounts to a denial (1) that there is a common human essence uniting people and (2) that there are common faculties, such as reason, by which this essence can be discerned.

As for the first point, according to Marx a human being cannot be identified with any abstract, changeless concept of human nature. Rather, we *are* what we *do;* hence our nature is defined by our work. Those who do different kinds of work, therefore, such as wage laborers and capitalists, must be fundamentally different in nature and have little or nothing in common. As for the second point, even if there is some very general human essence by virtue of which both laborers and capitalists are human, there are no common, impartial faculties powerful enough to define this essence accurately and to bring everyone to respect it. Our ideas and feelings about life as a whole are products of our economic situation; this must also be true of our ideas and feelings about our own essence. Thus not only are owners and workers basically different in nature, they have different conceptions of themselves.

It is apparent that for Marx there could be no unity among the classes even if there were no serious conflict of interest dividing them. As a matter of fact, however, Marx believed that there was such a conflict. Owners of the means of production (primarily factories, in the era of industrialism) are compelled by the system of production to oppress the workers. In other words, all systems of production, aside from communism, are essentially exploitative. It follows that the exploited cannot remain satisfied with moderate reforms but are driven to attack the entire economic order within which they live and work. The owners are, of course, the custodians and beneficiaries of the established order. Thus the two classes are not only different; they are antagonists in a deadly war.

Any social order claiming to unite all classes is, therefore, basically fraudulent. Ruling classes always claim that the populace accepts their governance and the ideology behind it; but this is no better than an effort to disguise the despotism they impose. The liberal democracies, in Marx's eyes, were covert dictatorships run by capitalists. They cannot, as they pretend to, establish the rule of the people, inasmuch as the interests of those being ruled are in fundamental and ineradicable opposition to the interests of their rulers.

Thus Marx provided one answer to the question of whether class divisions are an obstacle to unity. What about the question of abolishing these distinctions? How can this be done without using violence in such a way that new distinctions arise while the old are being suppressed?

Here Marx appealed to what he saw as the natural course of events. History was moving irresistibly, he believed, toward the abolition of private ownership and toward a society without classes. This movement does not depend primarily on deliberate human planning, but arises from tensions inherent in the capitalist system. Thus a group using force to abolish classes, when the time is ripe, would only serve as a midwife assisting in the birth of the emergent community and would not need to embark on the kind of sustained and systematic violence that might create a new class. And since Marx thought that economic circumstances form human beings, common ownership of the means of production would give rise to a cooperative human type and bar the rise of a new governing class.

Among the philosophies opposed to Marxism in the matter of class relations, two principal kinds can be distinguished: the conservative and the liberal.

In the conservatism of Edmund Burke, class divisions are assumed to be just and necessary. Societies need ruling groups, and some people, because of innate ability, education, and other advantages that cannot in the nature of things be enjoyed by everyone, are particularly well fitted to be members of these ruling groups. Not only are class distinctions justified, but the lower classes can see that they are justified. Thus the conservative idea is that of unity *through* class distinctions, which is the possibility noted at the outset of this discussion: class distinctions are a prerequisite, rather than an obstacle, to unity. Class lines required by a sense of justice shared by all classes are not lines of estrangement but rather articulations of the structure giving unity to the whole.

To put this in terms of the central concepts of this chapter, through loyalty to common traditions and customs, all classes participate in the "prejudice" that unites them. This prejudice discloses the human essence, on which unity is based. Here the human essence is realized not through the absolute uniformity and equality envisioned by some radicals, but by the simultaneous diversity and unity of classes.

In this view, there is no point in asking how to abolish these classes, for they should not be abolished but preserved. Conservatives point to the apparent impossibility of abolishing one class system without creating a new one as evidence that class distinctions are natural and inevitable and that it is vain to oppose such necessities with will and violence.

The most effective opposition to Marxism has probably come from those who hold that while justice does not sanction the division of society into separate and unequal classes, all classes can perceive the requirements of justice and can be brought to cooperate in eradicating, or at least mitigating, class distinctions. This is the central idea in liberalism of the sort represented by Franklin D. Roosevelt and John F. Kennedy. In answering the question of whether class distinctions necessarily stand in the way of unity, liberals tend to agree more nearly with Marx than with Burke. Granted, many liberals would be satisfied with moderating class distinctions rather than totally doing away with them. Nevertheless, liberalism is generally on the side of equality and is not easily reconciled with the Burkean idea that class differences contribute to social unity.

As for the possibility of attaining this goal—the possibility of abolishing class distinctions—liberals generally differ from both

Marx and Burke. They feel that class distinctions cannot be abolished (or moderated) by force, but that nevertheless they must be abolished (or greatly moderated). The means of doing this is the community of reason that transcends class divisions. The classes should unite not in accepting society but in reforming it. All classes should come together in a single community, as called for by conservatives, but not in one that remains what it has always been; they should come together rather in a reforming community, a community that is imperfect but gradually perfects itself.

Two ideas we have discussed are at the core of the liberal outlook: that people are essentially at one, and that reason enables them peacefully to realize their unity. A common essence and common rationality have greater force than the economic system. Owners may not gladly give up unfair privileges, but reason and legal pressure can bring them peacefully to do so. Marx's basic premises—that people are made by their economic situation and that the classes are in mortal conflict—rule out the possibility of any such understanding between owners and workers. This is why Marx was a revolutionary rather than a reformer; unity would normally have to be created through violent destruction of the owning class. Liberalism, in contrast, rests on the idea that economic estrangement is not total estrangement; a common human essence dictating harmony, and common rational powers making this harmony accessible, remain in spite of class divisions.

This faith has been of immense historical importance. It has been professed in one way or another by most of the governing parties in the Western democracies during the present century and has provided the main ground on which the totalitarian extremes of fascism and communism have been opposed. But is it valid?

For those of us who are not hungry and cold, liberalism is a more *appealing* faith than Marxism. It does not tell us that we live in a doomed society or that we are obliged to take on the burdens and perils of revolutionary action. It regards all persons with affection and hope.

But is liberalism a *truer* faith than Marxism? It requires some complacency to say without hesitation that it is. We see more and more clearly how skillfully, through the several decades of social reform that began with the New Deal in 1933, the owning classes have preserved their wealth and privileges. Further, we see now that under the governance of these classes, our cities have decayed, nature has been debauched, and the wealth of the nation has been spent in a futile and barbarous war (Vietnam) and in deadly nuclear competition. It is no longer easy to count on peaceful reform or to regard all human beings with liberal affection and hope.

But most of us can't side with Marxism either, at least not without serious misgivings. Our misgivings may come in part from the fact that the most conspicuous and determined effort to apply Marxism in practice—in the Soviet Union—has ended in failure. It might be an error, however, to infer simply from the collapse of the Soviet Union that Marxism is fundamentally false. It is possible to argue that it was misapplied. It is therefore worth noting that misgivings about Marxism may have other grounds. These lie mainly, perhaps, in Marx's vision of the warfare of classes. Soberly considered, if capitalists and workers are irreconcilable enemies, is there any prospect before us but despotism and terror? Marx after all presented a somber picture of the human situation. He did not succumb to despair because he shared the typical nineteenth-century faith in the common people and in historical progress. But today our faith in the common people has been shaken by such phenomena as the popularity of crude and superficial television programs; our faith in progress has been ravaged by the catastrophic events of our time. In these circumstances, Marx can prompt despair.

Such considerations have affected the outlook of many twentieth-century Marxists. The workers are no long relied on to usher in a new society; hope has been placed in some cases on oppressed and revolutionary groups such as Third World peasants, in other cases on intellectual critics of capitalist culture. Historical progress is seen, not as assured by natural economic evolution, but as dependent on changes in popular consciousness, changes affected at least in part by dissident writers, professors, and students. Calling forth such revisions is the realization of contemporary Marxists that workers and capitalists are not as sharply differentiated and opposed as Marx had thought, and the recognition that capitalism and its culture have been accepted by most workers about as emphatically as by the owners and managers of capitalist enterprises.

Such realism and flexibility on the part of his followers has gained for Marx what may turn out—in spite of the debacle of Soviet Communism—to be an enduring vitality. He represents an alternative to liberalism, with its highly questionable optimism, even in circumstances at odds with expectations arising from his original

views. Is it really Marx, however, who lives in the thought of followers who have largely lost his vision of the radical estrangement
and the world-mission of the working class? Has Marx inspired a
view of things that, however worthy of consideration, he would
neither recognize as his own nor look on with sympathy? Indeed,
one can ask whether Marx would see his inventive followers as
having brought into being, in his name, a new form of liberalism.
When all is said and done, these followers count very heavily on
reason, as do liberals; and like liberals they count on reason, particularly through cultural criticism, to lead everyone—workers and
owners together—toward the classless society.

In concluding this chapter, it should be pointed out that all the
doubts arising from this question and the preceding one are expressions of the simple issues set forth in the first four questions. Let
these be restated. Are the rampant hatred and violence of our times
mirrors in which we see ourselves as we basically and inescapably
are? If not, what has caused such turmoil, and how can we probe
beneath it and discern, and found our lives upon, the more pacific
human essence underneath? Will human faculties such as reason
suffice? And can we safely assume that God is dead—and un-
needed?

SUGGESTED READINGS

*(This list, like possible readings listed at the end of other chapters in this book, is in-
tended merely to be suggestive—to help instructors think creatively about suitable
reading. As the slightest perusal will show, it is far from comprehensive. Titles are
listed chronologically, and most are available in paperback or other inexpensive editions.)*

Plato. *The Symposium*
———. *The Republic*, Books I–IV
Aristotle. *Politics*, Books I–III, VII–VIII
Saint Augustine. *The City of God*, Chapters 11–14
Saint Thomas Aquinas on Politics and Ethics. Ed. and trans. Paul E. Sigmund
Dante Alighieri. *On World-Government (De Monarchia)*
Hobbes, Thomas. *Leviathan*, First Part
Rousseau, Jean Jacques. *The Social Contract*
Kant, Immanuel. *The Fundamental Principles of the Metaphysic of Ethics*
Burke, Edmund. *Reflections on the French Revolution*

Paine, Thomas. *The Rights of Man*
Marx, Karl. *Economic and Philosophical Manuscripts*
Dostoevsky, Fyodor. *The Brothers Karamazov*
Durkheim, Emile. *Suicide*
Buber, Martin. *I and Thou*
Freud, Sigmund. *Civilization and Its Discontents*
Bergson, Henri. *The Two Sources of Morality and Religion*
Silone, Ignazio. *Bread and Wine*
Berdyaev, Nicolas. *Slavery and Freedom*
Fromm, Erich. *Escape from Freedom*
Niebuhr, Reinhold. *The Nature and Destiny of Man,* Vol. I
Weil, Simone. *The Need for Roots*
Arendt, Hannah. *The Human Condition*
Marcuse, Herbert. *Eros and Civilization*

Chapter 3

INEQUALITY AND EQUALITY

The problem of inequality carries us into the center of modern political conflicts. The history of recent times could be told largely in terms of the rebellion against privilege and power that began with the French Revolution in 1789. Socialism and communism have both been deliberate, sustained assaults on inequality; twentieth-century upheavals in Asia and Africa have been inspired by a determination that wealth and power shall not be monopolized by white people. In America, the black rebellion against white supremacy has been perhaps the most significant event since World War II. And pervading the Western nations, the feminist movement has brought under attack not only institutions that for millennia have confined women to subordinate and restricted roles in society but also the philosophical principles buttressing those institutions.

Granted, changes have occurred in the last two centuries. Inequality is a less flagrant fact of life than it has usually been in the past. Traditional aristocracies have largely disappeared; the physical lives of most people, in the industrial nations, have become considerably more comfortable and secure than in earlier ages; governments in most Western countries have come to depend for their power on the votes of the populace at large; and the predominant styles and values in many societies have become those of the common people. Even within recent decades, discrimination based on race and gender has been reduced in fact and rendered almost indefensible in theory.

Although we do not yet understand the full significance of these changes, it would be impossible to claim that they are meaningless; and they may be leading us into—or already have led us into—a new era of history. Nevertheless, marked inequalities of wealth, power, and status remain in every nation; the lives people lead are shaped throughout by where they stand within established economic, political, and social hierarchies; and where they stand, in turn, is heavily influenced, and often determined, by such accidents as whether they were born white or black, male or female.

Thus, inequality and equality are not merely abstractions that can be safely and responsibly ignored, even if one prefers not to think about them. They have so much to do with the history of our times and with the circumstances in which each of us lives that we are compelled to think about them.

The logical starting point for this undertaking is a question that parallels Question 1, which asked whether it is in the fundamental nature of things or the result merely of historical accident that human beings are estranged. Here it must be asked whether, beneath all the inequalities incorporated in the social and political order, human beings are really—in nature and not just in custom and tradition—unequal.

7 *Are Human Beings Unequal in Essence?*

Certainly, human beings are unequal in most physical and psychological characteristics. They are unequal in health and intelligence and emotional balance and in so many other ways that it would be tedious to try to list them. It is easy to see, however, that these unassailable facts are far from deciding the issue.

To start with, we must ask whether such apparently *natural* inequalities are in reality merely the result of *social* inequalities. May not poor health, for example, derive from the inadequate nutrition that often accompanies poverty, and may not low intelligence merely reflect the illiteracy of an impoverished household? In some cases, the answer clearly is yes. It does not seem, however, that all inequalities can be traced to social causes. After all, inequalities are manifest among people who have been shaped by the same conditions. Among those who have been raised in the most favorable physical circumstances, some are healthier than others, and among those who have had the greatest educational advantages, some manifest greater intelligence than others. There seems to be no escaping the fact of natural inequality.

Still, a shadow of doubt remains. No two people ever grow up within *exactly* the same circumstances, and differences that appear minor to an outside observer may be decisive for those molded by them.

Concerning another aspect of the matter, the doubt is greater. Do inequalities we can measure pertain to the essence of the human being measured? For example, in gauging intelligence are we gauging the entire capacity of consciousness or only the ability to carry on intellectual operations that happen to be emphasized in our culture? Our doubts about judgments of inequality may go deeper than this. Let us assume that an absolute standard of intelligence has been discovered, so that when we measure intelligence we are truly measuring the entire capacity of consciousness. Does even a measurement of this kind pertain to the essence of the human being measured? Is intelligence—or any other particular quality—part of the essence of a human being?

The question may be put in this way: is it possible that someone markedly and demonstrably inferior to most others in health, intelligence, emotional balance, and other qualities is yet *in essence* equal to everyone else? The idea sounds strange. But we seem to be saying something of this kind when we say that there is an inherent dignity in every individual or that each person should be treated as an end and not merely as a means.

In our age it may seem that idealism is on the side of equality and that there is something cynical in the idea that human beings are essentially unequal, for to say that they are essentially unequal is to say that they are unequally human. Nevertheless, some of the most exalted figures in Western intellectual history have been willing to say this. Aristotle is a good example. He envisioned the human race as a great natural hierarchy, with the main determinant of rank being the degree and kind of reason a person possesses. At the summit of this hierarchy are those preeminent in their powers of general understanding, such as scientists and philosophers. Beneath them are natural citizens, who are rational enough to manage political affairs in company with many others of their kind, and yet further down are natural artisans and workers, who should be excluded from political affairs. At the base of the hierarchy are people who have only enough reason to perform services for others; these by nature are slaves. Aristotle defined humanity in terms of reason; hence, to have only enough reason to be an artisan or worker is to be deficient in humanity, and to be a natural slave is to be hardly human at all. Aristotle would have regarded as a dangerous absurdity the Christian notion that a person unfit for science, philosophy, or political activity may nevertheless be equal in essential humanity to the greatest scientists, thinkers, and political leaders.

Aristotle would also have regarded as a dangerous absurdity the modern suspicion that no such hierarchy of the kind he envisioned in fact exists; that being an able physicist, for example, is not inherently nobler than being an able carpenter, and that the life of a philosopher may embody disabilities, such as habituation to abstractions, that prevent it from being unambiguously superior to the life of a farmer or laborer. And he would most certainly have been disconcerted by the notion that many scientists might find equal fulfillment as artisans, that many artisans may possess scientific talents and proclivities, and that whether one is a scientist or an artisan, a philosopher or a farmer, may depend more on the chances of life (particularly by such chances as skin color and sex) than on one's natural level. Aristotle would have been particularly offended by the idea that women are not at all inferior to men in either their intellectual or their practical abilities. It was manifest to Aristotle that women were in the same general category as slaves and children.

But if Aristotle oversimplified, exaggerated, and in some cases grossly misunderstood the inequalities distinguishing human beings, it does not follow that he was in principle wrong. It does not follow that human beings are simply equal or that a society that treated them as equal would work. Hence the matter must be pursued. To do this, let us begin by noting that views affirming essential inequality usually assume one of two main forms. For some, the superiority of the few consists in their relationship with a sacred and transcendent reality—with the Good or with God. This relationship shapes their mind and character. It may be said, consequently, that the superior few are superior in sanctity. One of the greatest proponents of this outlook was Plato. In Plato's vision a few stood above all others in their capacity for philosophical understanding (these might be women as well as men; it was not from Plato that Aristotle, who learned much else from Plato, learned his disdain for women). The preeminence of philosophers lay, however, not in philosophical ability in itself but in that which philosophical ability enabled them to attain: knowledge of the divine. In other words, the glory of the philosopher was not the intrinsic glory of a superior mind but rather the reflected glory of the paradisal heart of all reality—the Good.

For other thinkers the excellence of superior people is purely worldly. It consists in such qualities as political genius, artistic mastery, and military prowess. Excellence does not depend on any sort of transcendental relationship but is entirely within the person. It might be said to consist, at least for some thinkers, not in being *related* to the divine but in *being* divine.

The works of Friedrich Nietzsche (1844–1900), a writer and thinker of exceptional power, tormented by a prophetic vision to which hardly anyone in his time paid any attention, constitute an extreme and moving statement of this belief. Nietzsche was convinced that one event alone, an event occurring in human consciousness, determined the spiritual atmosphere of his time and the duty of serious people: an awakening to the unreality of God. His melodramatic proclamation of this event—"God is dead"—is by now a familiar phrase. The death of God compels us to cast off the self-destructive humility into which Christianity has seduced us and to affirm our full worldly being. What does this mean? What is the nature of our worldly being? According to Nietzsche, it is "the will to power." Being is power, and power is mastery—over all things around us and, above all, over our own selves. We are impelled ceaselessly to transcend the established order of things, and the established self as well, and to strive for greater and greater power. Hence, if we are now to affirm ourselves, taking up the cosmic room, so to speak, that once was filled by God, we must unapologetically dedicate ourselves to the enhancement of our mastery and our greatness. For Nietzsche, this did not necessarily mean political activity and war; a great artist, Nietzsche thought, might be more powerful—in better command of the materials being worked with—than a Roman emperor. But it did mean inequality.

Nietzsche repeatedly and with utmost bitterness attacked the idea of equality, which he saw as one of the devices by which the masses, in their pettiness and rancor, crush human greatness. The average person is weak, and the grandeur of humanity thus depends on those with the daring and strength to raise themselves far above the vast herds of common people. Now that God is dead, human existence depends for its splendor and significance on the few who, rather than worshipping transcendent gods, become gods themselves. These few would not necessarily be white or racially pure. Human superiority was a matter of culture and spirit, not race. It is worth noting, however, that the superior few would always be men; Nietzsche unapologetically, even stridently, called for male mastery and female subservience. In many ways, Nietzsche was exhilaratingly free of ancient prejudices; in his views of women, however, he clearly exposed himself to the charge that he failed in what he was above all trying to do, to think anew. At any rate, Nietzsche's philosophy as a whole amounts to a repudiation of the idea of equality. A concept that was for ages a basic—if largely unobserved—principle of Western thought is cast aside. Human relations must once more, as in ancient times, be shaped by domination and rank.

Plato and Nietzsche, both maintaining that human beings in essence are unequal, are among the greatest names in the history of the Western spirit. Despite their authority, however, one of the most irrepressible and potent ideas ever conceived is that all inequalities are insignificant; in essence, human beings are equal. Without this idea the modern attack on inequality would not have occurred. There probably would have been no French Revolution; socialism and communism would perhaps not have arisen, nor the revolutions in Russia and China have occurred; blacks in America and Africa, landless peasants in Asia and the Philippines and Latin America, might not have set out to transform their situations. Without the idea of equality, there perhaps would have been no feminist rebellion against the ways in which established institutions discriminate—much to the disadvantage of women, feminists believe—between the sexes. Of course, what might have happened in history, but did not, can never be surely known. It is quite certain, however, that if the idea that human beings, regardless of all external features, are equal had never entered anyone's mind, the face of the civilized earth would look very different than it does today. What is the basis of this idea?

Nietzsche was right in associating belief in equality with belief in God. The first philosophical defense of equality seems to have come from the later Stoics, with their religious reverence for cosmic order. Human beings were held to be equal in that every person could understand the demands of the moral law, demands implicit in the divine harmony of the cosmos. In this way, human beings were equal in their relationships with the divine. Moreover, if the idea of equality was planted in the Western mind by the Stoics, it deepened its roots and grew under the care of Christians. Here, too, equality was grounded, not on the claim that human beings are similar in character or intelligence or some other worldly quality, but on their relationships with transcendence. For Christians, transcendence meant God, and God was merciful toward all persons, regardless of worldly excellences and distinctions. Every person was formed by God, and every person, having betrayed these divine origins, was offered redemption. In the face of the glory and hope surrounding God's descent into the world, all natural and social distinctions—health, intelligence, and beauty no less than rank, power, gender, and wealth—faded into irrelevance.

Transcendentalism remained in the concept of equality that helped inspire the rise of modern liberalism and democracy. John Locke (1632–1704), for example, who defended the establishment of constitutional (that is, lawful or limited) government in England and who influenced the framers of the American Constitution, clearly did not believe people to be equal in their observable qualities. They were, for Locke, equal only in the rights received from God. In like fashion, Thomas Jefferson (1743–1826) asserted that human beings were *created* equal and that they were endowed *by their Creator* with inalienable rights. Thus the idea of a sanctity received through a relationship with the divine is the basis not only of a certain conception of essential rank and inequality, as in Plato, but also of the traditional idea of essential equality.

Among the great political thinkers only one, Thomas Hobbes, maintained that in their purely worldly qualities people are essentially equal. However, his argument is not likely to appeal to those who, without believing in God, believe in the dignity of the individual, for in Hobbes's view people are less deserving of equal respect than of equal disdain. Our equality lies in our common subjection to human limitations and desires and, above all, in our common subjection to death. Hobbes sardonically pointed to the equalizing power of death with the observation that anyone can kill anyone else (a point tragically illustrated in the assassination of President Kennedy, apparently the attempt of a profoundly alienated young man to rise forcibly above obscurity and insignificance). And not only are we all mortal; we all are governed by the egotistical desire to postpone death as long as we possibly can. This is where the interests of human beings coincide, despite their essential estrangement, making it possible to organize a society that is advantageous for everyone. Hobbes's egalitarian outlook did not rest wholly on death; he looked skeptically on all the supposed virtues and merits in which people take pride and he deftly punctured human pretensions. He conveyed the impression, however, that death was the sovereign equalizer. While in the eyes of Christians all worldly rank and excellence melted into insignificance before God, before the glory of divine mercy and omnipotence, in the eyes of Hobbes this happened before inescapable death.

Hobbes's unusual view aside, the foundation of traditional egalitarianism is religion. Where does this leave contemporary humanity, which doubts the existence of God and the soul but is convinced of the dignity of the individual? Many people today assent to Nietzsche's declaration that the time has come for us to rely on our own intelligence and courage and not on God. But most of those people refuse to take seriously Nietzsche's insistence that when it comes to intelligence, courage, and other qualities we presumably need in order to take the place of God, we are drastically unequal. Instead, they continue, with Christians, to exalt the common person.

Does this make sense? Can one make a case, on empirical grounds, and without any reliance whatever on religious presuppositions, that all human beings are equal? *All* necessarily includes criminals and alcoholics, the retarded and the insane, the diseased and the aged; it includes those who are filthy and personally repellent and those who are unable or unwilling to fulfill any useful function in society. Counting every one of such persons and looking unsentimentally and irreligiously at the simple facts, can it be argued that all human beings are equal? The question is important partly because today the ancient religious foundations beneath the idea of equality have been largely abandoned. Socialism and communism, for example, are typically more or less irreligious (liberation theology being an exception); peasant uprisings have commonly been led by Marxists, who, as such, are atheists; feminist writers do not, for the most part, appeal to religious principles. How thin is the ice on which this great multitude of rebels is skating?

Perhaps it is not fair, however, to suggest that we stand in an either-or situation—either equal before God or unequal in a godless universe. A powerful strain in Western thought holds that human beings are equal by virtue of the fact that they are all rational beings. Those holding this view typically see reason as a moral rather than a practical faculty; it enables us to formulate laws governing our behavior. It is reason, for example, that leads us to insist that all persons in like circumstances be treated alike. Thus, admitting that people are unequal in some of the uses of reason—for instance, in writing books or playing chess—it may be argued that they are equal in their capacity for judging whether they and others have been treated fairly. If this is true, it is not necessary to choose between religious egalitarianism and agnostic, or atheistic, elitism. Whether God exists or not, all persons can discern with equal clarity and depth the requirements of justice and thus can make equal claims to take part in political affairs and share in the common life.

But again we face the recurrent question: is this true? Certainly it may be. It has been accepted by numerous distinguished philosophers, among them Immanuel Kant. Still, if reason were a moral faculty, one would expect all who are capable of reasoning to be moral. As we all know, however, they are not. And if moral inequalities occur among people able to reason (even though they should not, according to the original hypothesis), one would expect evil people to be deficient in reasoning ability and good people to be exceptionally rational. But again, we all know that some criminals are highly intelligent and that tyrants may be cunning and astute. On the other hand, we do not assume that saints will display intellectual brilliance or uncommon intelligence, although some of them have. It appears, then, that morality depends on something more, if not other, than reason—perhaps on certain emotional or character traits. But can that "more" be added without undermining the principle of equality?

The question, then, remains: does the idea of equality necessarily presuppose that of transcendence? Can we claim that all people are equal without appealing to something beyond the realities we can see and measure?

The issue of equality is involved in some of the most pressing concerns of our time. Despite centuries of equalization, inequality remains a stubborn reality. It is manifest in the acute poverty that persists even in a country as wealthy as the United States, in vast concentrations of private wealth, in the immense hierarchical organizations that dominate economic life in the industrial nations, and in the overwhelming power that has accumulated in the hands of governmental executives, exemplified strikingly by the American presidency. It is manifest also in the economic and educational deprivations still, in spite of all recent progress, suffered by blacks and Hispanics in America. Inequality is evident, finally, in a host of disabilities and inequities still suffered by women. The question is whether under these circumstances the cause of equality is doomed by the secularism of its defenders, that is, by their inability to appeal to any source of dignity beyond the plain empirical character of the average person, with all of its manifest limitations and faults.

However you respond to this issue, the position you take will shape your views of how society should be organized. Let us consider this aspect of the matter.

8 If Some Human Beings Are Essentially Superior to All Others, How and by Whom Can They Be Identified?

First, it must be asked whether the best human beings, if such there be, can be identified at all. We are strongly tempted to assume without thought that they can, for it is humbling and exasperating to think that, grounded in the depths of human nature and destiny, there may be a hierarchy of excellence but that we cannot bring it to light. Those I esteem most highly may stand very low in this hierarchy and those whom I ignore or condemn may be, in a manner of speaking, ontological princes. I myself may be far more base and contemptible (or, of course, far more admirable) than I realize. Such a view of things may seem strange, but—assuming that excellence can consist in a transcendental relationship—it has been held by many people, most of them Christians who accepted the doctrine of predestination. Only God, they believed, could determine one's true worth, and God's judgment would be handed down only at the end of time. The difficulty of living in the face of so dismaying an uncertainty, however, is indicated by the anguish of devout people at the thought that, if not they themselves, others whom they love—husbands, wives, friends—might be eternally condemned and lost. And aside from the personal anguish likely to arise from the idea of an invisible hierarchy of excellence, there is the political consternation: how can we reasonably arrange for the distribution of power if we cannot distinguish between the better and the worse?

Plato, Aristotle, and Nietzsche all provide a measure of reassurance. Granted, our casual judgments may be in error, and serious mistakes may thus be made—especially in democracies, where reliance is placed in masses of ordinary people, who lack the time, training, information, and all else needed for making accurate judgments. Nonetheless, the true rank of human beings can be humanly known and the order of society can be regulated accordingly.

Still, one must wonder. Even if excellence is entirely worldly, consisting in visible qualities, such as political sagacity and artistic genius, it seems that human beings may often fail to see it. Abraham Lincoln, ranked by most present-day historians as the greatest American President, was regarded by many of the best-informed people of his time as an oaf and a buffoon. Impressionist painters whose works now seem enchanting to most viewers were occasionally, while at their easels in the streets of Paris, spat upon by disgusted passersby.

If excellence consists not in visible, worldly qualities but in a relationship with transcendence, is not our fallibility magnified? How can we have reliable knowledge of any such relationship? Can one be sure even of one's own relationship with God or the Good? These questions are likely to be particularly persistent and sharp to those who believe, like orthodox Christians, that our relations with God depend not on our own intentions and powers, but on God's. Who among us can anticipate and announce the decisions of God? "Judge not, that ye be not judged."[1] The most dramatic symbol of God's nullification of human rank is the crucifixion of Jesus: one who died ignominiously with two thieves was, in the faith of Christians, the Lord of the human race.

In order to proceed with the discussion, however, let us set aside these doubts and assume that excellence can be recognized. By whom? There is much sense in the notion that if there are absolutely superior human beings, the only ones who can identify them are others of like superiority. To argue otherwise is to suggest an anomalous defect in the superior people—their lack of ability to recognize superiority—and an anomalous virtue in their inferiors—their possession of that ability. Thus, in Plato's plan for government by philosophers (those who have ascended to the Good), philosopher-rulers would be chosen by philosopher-rulers. This is partly

[1]Matthew 7:1.

because Plato conceived of the philosopher as not merely superior but virtually perfect; hence no electorate composed of those inferior in philosophical excellence could possibly have grounds for challenging a philosopher's judgment. But a similar logic works, although not quite so irresistibly, in an aristocracy where the leading class is conceived to be merely superior to other classes without being perfect; the superiority of the aristocrats disqualifies every competing electorate. In short, the idea of a self-chosen elite, given elitist premises, is natural and logical.

The paradoxical idea is that of an elite chosen by their inferiors, and it is a surprising fact in the history of thought that this idea has been supported by a number of distinguished thinkers. The main form of the idea is the principle that government is legitimate only with the consent of the governed. This principle was common both in ancient times and in the Middle Ages, long before the rise of modern democracy. It is true that it grew less out of confidence in popular judgment than out of the moral conviction that people cannot be rightfully subjected to power without their consent. But this conviction could not have been given practical effect without a measure of confidence in the good sense of the people. Thus a number of thinkers who believed in government by a superior few trusted sufficiently in the many to accord them the right of consent. The preeminent minority was to be identified, at least to the extent of being freely accepted, by the common majority.

The trouble with vesting electoral powers either in the few or the many is that neither is infallible or even nearly so. This fact makes it easy to understand the charm of an impersonal process. For example, one of the most alluring features of the doctrine of *laissez-faire,* or "free enterprise," is the idea (not insisted upon by sophisticated defenders of the doctrine, but arising spontaneously and inevitably) that those who succeed in a free market are those with personal qualities deserving of wealth, status, and power. Competition automatically sifts out the superior people. It can be objected, of course, that financial success is not a reliable indicator of general human excellence, and perhaps not even of economic acumen (since it can be caused by luck or trickery). It cannot be doubted, however, that the ideal of the free market has attracted support partly because it seems to some a reasonably accurate way—a way invulnerable to the hazards of human judgment—of singling out and empowering the best and most intelligent people.

It testifies to the charm of an impersonal process that opponents of market economics have devised their own system for evading human fallibility. This is the so-called merit system for appointing and promoting civil servants. The principal alternative to the free market is governmental intervention, and opponents of laissez-faire have generally favored larger and more efficient government. This could be achieved, it was often thought, by appointing people to official positions solely on the basis of examinations open to all aspirants to governmental service and by advancing people to higher rank on the basis of performance in office and without regard to party affiliation. The main cause of an incompetent officialdom is party favor and bias, and those would be largely eliminated by a well-designed merit system.

Faith in impersonal ways of elevating elites has been severely shaken—by economic crises and by the absence of clear cultural or spiritual distinction, or even political sagacity, among business leaders (in the case of laissez-faire) and by the rise of large, inefficient, and unwieldy bureaucracies (in the case of the merit system). Where does this leave us? The reigning democratic ethos tells us to trust the judgment of the people. Yet hardly anyone does, as is evident in the widespread contempt for those raised up by popular judgment—the politicians. Thus, contemporary uncertainties compel us again to ask: if there are superior people, how can we find them?

In order to think fully about this question one must ask not only who—or what process—will decide, but also what standards will be used. What are the surest manifestations and most reliable signs of human superiority?

The most common answer given in the past is hard for most people now to take seriously: the best are to be found among the wellborn. This belief was widespread during antiquity and the Middle Ages. Even John Locke, the principal theorist of modern liberalism, apparently assumed that government would generally be carried on by a hereditary aristocracy. The major reason people were able to accept birth as a reliable indicator of virtue and governing capacity for so long probably lies in their belief in "breeding." The connotations of this concept are both biological and cultural. A person with breeding supposedly has inherited superior psychological and physical potentialities and presumably has been disciplined and educated in ways that bring those potentialities to their fullest realization. A titled member of a traditional aristocracy thus might be looked upon as an embodiment of centuries of biological selection and cultural development.

The aristocratic ideal is not absurd. This is shown by its workability during many generations and in many civilizations. It is shown also by its acceptance in our own time by so intelligent and skeptical a man as Nietzsche. Few of us today, nevertheless, would willingly embrace it. We are too sensitive to its overtones of race and privilege; we are democratically unsentimental about titles and skeptical of inherited wealth and power.

But what better signs of superiority are there than birth?

The modern world has one large answer to this question, an answer very widely accepted, although it means different things to different people. This is performance. Superiority, it may be said, is defined by *action* rather than *being:* it is what one has done that counts. There are many types of performance—political, military, and academic, for example. Most esteemed in recent centuries, perhaps, has been business performance; it was regarded by early Calvinists as a sign even of the kind of excellence prized by God. The American people have occasionally taken military success as a sign of excellence; this is exemplified in General Eisenhower's two terms in the presidency. It must be said, however, that while virtually everyone agrees that superiority must be determined by performance, there is little agreement as to what kind of performance is decisive. It is a commentary on the fragmentation and uncertainty of modern civilization that no human activity has preeminence. This fact lessens the practical and political force of our esteem for performance.

Despite our uncertainties, however, there is a popular concept that sharply focuses such beliefs as the superiority of a few and the importance of empowering them. It is that of *meritocracy.* Gradations of excellence are assumed to exist and to constitute the only reasonable basis for social organization. The concept of meritocracy includes no precise specifications concerning the kind of performance determining excellence or the way it can best be judged. But meritocracy is commonly an ideal of technological and administrative efficiency. Excellence is thought of as scientific, industrial, and managerial rather than artistic, religious, or heroic. Competence is more important than inspiration. The concept tends toward ideological neutrality. A conservative and a reformer both might believe in the hierarchy of merit. But meritocracy is more apt to be favored by conservatives than by reformers for it is premised on a concept of justice in which equality means little but equality of opportunity. Thus the standards of meritocracy are often invoked against programs of racial justice that would compromise the apportionment of power and position strictly on the basis of competence.

The idea of meritocracy provides a timely focus for thought. By reflecting on it one might come to grips with all of the main issues touched on in the last few pages: Can superior people be identified? If so, by whom? Through what processes? And by what standards?

These are formidable questions, however, and the reader may begin to despair of finding answers to them. Let us, therefore, go back to the beginning and try another path. This path starts out with a rejection of the premise underlying this entire discussion, that some human beings are essentially superior to all others. On the contrary, human beings are essentially equal. This assumption requires us to consider an entirely different set of questions. To begin with, if human beings are essentially equal, must they be socially, economically, and politically equal?

9 If Human Beings Are Essentially Equal, Are All Conventional Inequalities Wrong?

Conventional is used here as an antonym for *natural*. All the inequalities resulting from the laws and customs of the social order are conventional; such inequalities include those of social status, power, wealth, and honor. Of course, it is possible to argue that in a good society the conventional inequalities would be natural as well, that is, based on natural inequalities. On the other hand, if human beings are essentially, or naturally, equal, then all inequalities are purely conventional.

The idea that human beings are essentially equal, strange to say, had been in the Western mind for over a thousand years before it motivated a serious attack on conventional inequalities. Neither Stoics nor Christians sought to abolish even slavery, let alone other established ranks. Their restraint came partly from their belief that nothing mattered except the state of a person's soul, which was not necessarily affected by rank in society. It stemmed also from their belief that the order of society was sanctioned by God and hence

was not to be attacked by human beings. The resulting social attitude was disrespectful yet submissive. Inequalities inherent in the
established order were at once condemned and tolerated—condemned because they clashed with the principle of equality and tolerated because of their ultimate insignificance and their dependence on divine permission.

However, once people began to feel that social conditions do affect the morals and the ultimate happiness of individuals, and that
these conditions are not sanctioned by God, the idea of equality began to shake the hierarchies of the established order. The idea was
like a volcano that had lain dormant so long people had forgotten
the fire and lava underneath and had built villages on its sides, but
that suddenly began to erupt, pouring destruction on all the habita-
tions around it.

Let me restate the logic of this upheaval. If human beings are
essentially equal, if the denial of their essential equality will not be
compensated on another plane of being but does grave and irreparable harm, and if the social order is a product of human will
rather than divine will, then privileges and power that cannot be
justified in terms of the public good are intolerable. About two hundred years ago, it began to seem that all of these conditions existed.
The idea of equality was no longer dormant.

In the eruption that followed, the two principal thinkers—the
volcanic figures of modern thought—were Rousseau and Marx.
Both expressed a new sense that the individual's whole life and nature are shaped by society; for beings without transcendental soul
or transcendental life the social order is an all-encompassing fate.
Both thinkers, moreover, reflected the loss of faith that society is
governed by God and the growing conviction that there is no heavenly order to compensate for worldly injustice or to ease our responsibility for correcting it. These attitudes, combined with the
idea of equality, moved both thinkers to challenge priests, aristocrats, kings, and (borrowing a phrase of Santayana's) all other
"dominations and powers." We live today amid institutional ruins
that Rousseau and Marx did much to produce, and we hear all
around us the continuing reverberations of their assault on established institutions.

It is hard not to share their outrage. It is by no means clear that
human beings are unequal in essence; at least it does not seem clear

enough to justify the inequalities in wealth, power, and privilege that have prevailed and still prevail in practically every society. Nor is it clear that religious faith obliges us to acquiese to injustice. From the standpoint of faith, the rectification of injustice is no doubt a matter of less desperate importance than it is from a purely worldly standpoint. Nevertheless, religion does not require—or, perhaps, even allow—writing off the world, and the idea that established injustice is always divinely sanctioned is the product of a particular religious culture, not a necessary inference from religion as such.

Thus, whether your basic stance is that of faith or worldliness, it is not farfetched to see the subjection and deprivation suffered by the masses throughout history as a continuing outrage perpetrated by the "respectable" classes commanding the social order.

All the same, people do seem to be unequal in important characteristics, such as intelligence and emotional balance, whether as a result of inequalities of essence or inequalities of social condition. Furthermore, the working of society seems dependent on inequalities of power and rank; planning can be done and action initiated only by a few. For these reasons, even while feeling the anger Rousseau and Marx felt over the inequalities relentlessly imposed on people throughout history, we may draw back from the project of establishing total equality.

Rousseau and major followers of Marx have manifested this ambivalence. Rousseau and Marx alike stood for the general principle of radical democracy, government carried on either directly by the people or by representatives held closely to the immediate will of the people. In drawing up actual governmental plans, however, as he once did for the government of Poland, Rousseau was willing to sanction inequalities of wealth, rank, and power. Some of Marx's followers have felt compelled to make even more far-reaching concessions of this kind, including the establishment and justification of a new kind of class dictatorship.

Hesitations about equalization are poignantly evident among women in our time. The experience of a great many women has revealed harsh discords between nature and convention. They have been conscious of potentialities stifled by the conventional specification that the home is the woman's sphere and raising children her proper vocation. Many have consequently been bitterly rebellious. Yet convention in this case has moorings of a sort that convention does not always have: distinctive biological capacities and social expediency. Many women have been strongly desirous of bearing children. But as most societies are presently organized, it is often difficult for mothers to arrange for the care, by anyone but themselves, of the children they have borne. In addition, some experts in child care have questioned whether it is possible for anyone but the mother to provide the kind of attention and love a young child needs. Hence, many women have felt compelled, either by existing social structures or by conscience, to conform in some measure with an order of things they find, if not flagrantly unjust, at least personally burdensome.

We shall return to this dilemma later in the present chapter, and in the following chapter we shall look again at the whole puzzle of equality from the vantage point of power. Meanwhile, we may reflect further on the ideal of equality by considering its relationship with two other ideals, those linked with it in the rallying cry of the French Revolution: "Liberty, Equality, Fraternity." We shall begin with liberty.

10 *If All Conventional Inequalities Were Abolished, Could Liberty Survive?*

Most of us spontaneously answer that it could, for liberty and equality have together been among the chief political goals in modern times. The minutemen of Lexington and Concord are heroic symbols of one of the first efforts to reach these goals. In 1789, only a few years after the end of the American Revolution, the French Revolution began. That revolution, in spite of the Reign of Terror and in spite of its denouement (the rule of Napoleon, followed by the restoration of the monarchy), has become a legend representing the human quest for both liberty and equality. A few have criticized this quest, to be sure, but they are a small minority, standing aside from—or occasionally in the path of—the major movement of modern thought and hope. Most of us, as part of this movement, assume that liberty and equality are fully harmonious.

Is it sensible, however, to assume that our political ideals in no way conflict with one another? Few of us have personal goals that are completely harmonious. In our private lives we often have to give up one thing we desire in order to gain something else. Why should we think public life is any different? The very fact that we are finite beings suggests that we cannot gain everything that we seek. We may, then, have to choose between liberty and equality; or if we choose both together, we may have to satisfy ourselves with a severely limited measure of each.

Such doubts do not arise merely from speculation, but are provoked by experience. The pursuit of equality seems to have been, in some ways at least, destructive of liberty. During the French Revolution, the attack on aristocratic privileges and powers led within a few years to the terrifying ascendancy of the Committee of Public Safety, under Robespierre, and, within a few years of the downfall of Robespierre, to other forms of authoritarianism. In the twentieth century we have seen the Communist drive toward equality eventuate, in the Soviet Union and elsewhere, in exceedingly cruel and repressive regimes.

Admittedly, the French and Soviet experiences do not conclusively demonstrate that liberty and equality are in conflict. While the quest for equality led in both cases to the suppression of liberty, the quest did not in either case succeed; equality was not achieved. To be sure, old inequalities were destroyed, but new ones were rapidly established. Thus, for example, it can be argued that liberty was always lacking in the Soviet Union primarily because equality was also lacking.

But another kind of experience in modern history also suggests the incompatibility of liberty and equality. This experience is found in societies that have come much nearer to equality than did those arising immediately from the French and Soviet revolutions. Some of the most careful and intelligent observers of society have been convinced that in places like America and Great Britain progress toward equality has seriously imperiled liberty. This has been seen as less a political than a social development. John Stuart Mill (1806–1873), a logician, economist, and political theorist, and one of the most highly respected minds of Victorian England, was alarmed by the way in which egalitarianism seemed to place an increasingly despotic power in the hands of the majority—a power exercised more often through public opinion than through government—and to draw ever narrower boundaries around individual liberty. Alexis de Tocqueville (1805–1859), the author of a great study of American democracy, developed views strikingly similar to Mill's from his observations of American society and politics. Tocqueville was on the whole sympathetic to the ideal of equality; moreover, he believed that the gradual advance of equality was historically inevitable. He studied America because he thought that America had come nearer to equality than had any other country and might therefore enable him to perceive the practical consequences of equality. Among these consequences, Tocqueville thought, was the weakening of liberty, owing not so much to governmental interference as to the censorious and ever-present eye of the populace. Tocqueville and Mill were among the first to note the appearance of a phenomenon many twentieth-century writers have seen as a dominant reality of our time, the despotism of the masses; here liberty is lost through social conformity.

While some have questioned whether liberty and equality go together, others have held that they cannot be separated. Wherever there is inequality, they maintain, it is at the expense of someone's liberty. Mill and Tocqueville were not the only ones in the nineteenth century to feel that in their time liberty was not as ample or secure as many assumed. Another was Karl Marx. The personal liberty enjoyed in the industrialized countries was, for Marx, little better than a hoax. People were legally free to do such things as work for whom they pleased and live where they liked. But most were lucky if they could work at all, even for wages that barely kept them alive and in dirty and dangerous manufacturing establishments. And their living quarters were almost always cramped and squalid. Legally free, they were actually enslaved. They were not enslaved, however, because equality had turned out to be unexpectedly antithetical to liberty, but, as Marx saw it, because there was no equality. The French Revolution had overthrown feudal rulers—kings, aristocrats, and bishops—but had replaced them with rulers whose despotism was colder and more relentless, although concealed behind governmental and legal forms ostensibly guaranteeing liberty. These new rulers were the industrial bourgeoisie.

Only by overthrowing the new tyrants of manufacturing and finance could the promise of the French Revolution—liberty and equality together—be realized.

Marx thus assumed liberty and equality to be interdependent. Many of his most determined opponents deny that this is so. One of the chief points of contention in this controversy is capitalism. Marx believed that capitalism created the kind of highly developed industrial order that would render both liberty and equality accessible but that capitalism had to be replaced by socialism before humankind could lay hold of these benefits. Capitalism could lead us to the gates of a truly liberal and egalitarian order, but only socialism could enable us to enter. Marx's opponents, many of them, assert that liberty and equality are in conflict, but that capitalism provides as large a measure of each as is practically attainable.

Which side you take—that of Marx or of capitalism—depends partly on how much you expect of the world. Can human potentialities be fully realized? Followers of Marx usually assume that with the abundance provided by advanced industrialism, they can. This will mean the enjoyment of both liberty and equality. Opponents of Marx often assume that even at best the world offers only limited chances for human fulfillment. We can gain liberty and equality only in part and only in an uneasy balance.

The overall question pertains not only to capitalism and the arguments of Marx, but also to the conformity feared by Tocqueville and Mill, and is not for sociologists and economists alone to answer. It is a question on which every individual can reflect. One can judge on the basis of daily personal experience whether the liberty one supposedly possesses is genuine and complete. One also can judge what threatens or infringes upon that liberty. Making these judgments is nothing less than trying to understand the character of one's own life and the forces that shape it.

Some people say that liberty and equality have been reconciled in the United States in equality of opportunity. They acknowledge that many inequalities still exist—inequalities of wealth, power, and social standing—but claim that the way to the top is open to everyone. Without creating the injustice that would be inherent in giving equal rewards for unequal performances, and without establishing the despotic government that would be necessary to achieve "equality of result" (actual equality in wealth, power, and social standing), American society provides everyone with opportunities for the fullest realization of personal potentialities. This, they argue, is the only kind of liberty or equality that matters. But is such an achievement possible even in principle? Can liberty and equality be genuinely reconciled in equality of opportunity?

It would be difficult to answer either question with a confident yes. Equality of opportunity is an appealing goal. This is partly because it seems at first glance that anyone who fails to use opportunities equal to those of everyone else does not deserve any other kind of equality. Equality of opportunity is appealing also because it seems to remove the tensions inherent in balancing liberty and equality. Each person will receive an initial grant of liberty, but if that liberty is squandered it is not the business of government or of anyone else to set things right. The trouble is that inequalities of result necessarily produce inequalities of opportunity. For example, people in business who start with no advantage over others and accumulate a fortune not only bestow an immense advantage on their children but personally enjoy enhanced opportunities in increasing degree as their fortunes grow. To assure complete equality of opportunity, it seems, it would be necessary to assure complete equality in every condition of life. Thus, equality of opportunity is an alluring phrase, but it does not clearly solve any problems. The United States may have produced as acceptable a mix of liberty and equality as is humanly possible. But has it produced a mix in which nothing of either component is lost?

The French Revolution celebrated not only liberty and equality but also "fraternity." Having considered the relations of equality and liberty, let us turn to those of equality and "fraternity." In doing this we shall reflect on the general place of equality in the context of modern ideals, and we shall also link the concerns of this chapter with those of the preceding one, for "fraternity" may conveniently be considered in terms of estrangement. "Fraternity" is community, the conquest of estrangement.

We shall not ask, as in the preceding question, whether equality and community are compatible. A better question is called forth by certain recent writings. Some thinkers say that inequality is the primary form of estrangement. According to them, the most drastic division among human beings is for some to have power over others, for some to be wealthy while others are poor, and for some to be continually honored and flattered while others live under an ever-lasting shadow of neglect and disdain. These views suggest that estrangement might be conquered by doing away with inequality. Is this possible?

11 *If All Conventional Inequalities Were Abolished, Would Estrangement Disappear?*

This is one of the most important questions of the present time because it bears closely on the problem of humanizing industrial society—of making a mechanical civilization considerate of the fragile, nonmechanical being of persons.

Radicals and reformers, such as English socialists and American liberals, have traditionally seen the solution to the problem of industrial inhumanity in the idea of equality. The sharp lines between classes seemed the most inhuman aspect of industrialism. Class lines separated people even more drastically than they had been separated under feudal and monarchical regimes. Class lines also seemed to delineate the basic situation that permitted industrialists to impose on workers such long hours and low wages that their lives may have reached greater depths of misery than those experienced by the serfs and slaves of earlier ages. It was easy to conclude that the abolition of inequality would, in effect, be the conquest of estrangement.

The advance of industrialization, however, has cast doubt on this conclusion. One of the most bitter and persistent complaints in highly industrialized societies has been over, not class distinctions and inequities, but personal alienation. Both the rich and the poor, it is said, make up a lonely crowd, and the rich are about as lonely as the poor. It is tempting to respond, and it may be true, that loneliness is far more bearable for the rich than for the poor. The fact remains that a major grievance of industrial life does not, on the face of it, concern the inequality that radicals and reformers have always taken to be the primary derangement of unreformed societies. This grievance concerns an estrangement that seems to affect the relations even of those who, economically, socially, and politically, are equal. Thus, middle-class suburbanites in America apparently feel estranged not so much from the lower classes or the upper classes but from one another (witness, for example, the typical suburb, with its separate, self-contained dwellings and its lack of public spaces).

These conditions explain why we must ask whether the estrangement suffered today is traceable to the inequality traditionally attacked by radicalism. As the preceding remarks suggest, there are two quite different views on this matter. These call for thorough examination, for the future of industrial civilization depends on our capacity to decide correctly between them.

Rousseau and Marx represent the side of traditional radicalism. Both were acutely aware that something in modern life was weakening and severing the relationships of people to one another and to the physical world. Rousseau's *Confessions* is a poignant account of a lifetime of personal alienation; Marx's *Capital* could be described as a detailed analysis of the fragmentation of life wrought by capitalism. But the root of the matter, for both thinkers, was inequality—an inequality that was merely conventional, that was not in accordance with the human essence. Beneath the many estrangements human beings suffer is one great estrangement from which all the others grow—that between the few who own most of the property and control the government and the many who own little or nothing and are the helpless subjects of an alien political power. As a consequence of this split, a communal and creative life is practically impossible—not only for the miserable multitudes but even for the rich and privileged, who are forced into a pampered and sterile defensiveness. The only way in which humankind can gain wholeness of life is by abolishing the distance between the few and the many.

In short, the conventional inequalities do not accord with the underlying human essence. They are in violation of the nature of human beings and disruptive of genuine relationships. Abolishing these inequalities, therefore, is essential for overcoming estrangement.

During the last century, however, some highly individual but profound and influential thinkers concluded the opposite: that by making people equal, we may deepen estrangement. One of the earliest and greatest of these thinkers was the Danish religious philosopher Søren Kierkegaard (1813–1855), who probably did more than anyone to implant in modern consciousness such ideas as commitment and "the leap of faith." The kind of estrangement that mattered most to Kierkegaard was estrangement from God. He thought this was likely to be reinforced by equality. His argument was directed against what is now called mass society, that is, society in which individuality is censured and suppressed not by government alone but by a bigoted and inquisitorial populace, by "the masses."

Kierkegaard was disturbed by what he saw as the disappearance of genuine individuals, persons capable of passion and decision. Only individuals can be Christians, he believed, for authentic Christianity depends on the decision, setting one apart from all others, to base one's whole life on the Christian hope of eternal happiness. To be a Christian merely because everyone else is a Christian is, in truth, not to be a Christian at all. For Kierkegaard the leveling that seemed to be occurring everywhere around him manifested the movement of the human race into a state in which everyone was merely a passive reflection of everyone else. This was necessarily a movement away from Christianity.

In this sense, equality meant estrangement from God. Does equality nevertheless unite human beings? Not for Kierkegaard and perhaps not for anyone adhering very seriously to a religious creed. A person's relationship with the transcendent must determine all other relationships. Its disruption propels a person into an isolation that is total, even though the resultant anguish may be partially relieved by behaving and thinking like everyone else. In Kierkegaard's case, authentic selfhood depends on religious faith. If faith is lacking, selfhood is lacking too, and unity among selves is necessarily precluded. The uniformity Kierkegaard abhorred was a sign not of unity but of deep estrangement.

The fading of the conventional inequalities inspired doubt or fear, rather than expectations of reunion, in other thinkers as well—thinkers who were quite different from Kierkegaard and also different from one another. For example, Tocqueville, whose observations on America we have already discussed, was interested primarily in the social and political consequences of equality; his interests were more historical than religious; and his style, in contrast with Kierkegaard's ardor and irony, was one of cool penetration. But Tocqueville saw in America things Kierkegaard too would probably have seen had he visited America: a dearth of bold and distinctive individuals, and attenuated human relationships. Nietzsche, too, belongs in this company. He was, as already noted, an atheist, and in this way very unlike Kierkegaard and Tocqueville, yet he felt a horror much like theirs before the rising tide of equality. Finally, in the twentieth century, José Ortega y Gasset (1883–1955), a cultivated Spanish philosopher who shared little of Kierkegaard's single-minded faith, Tocqueville's fascination with social and political institutions, or Nietzsche's hatred of Christianity, expressed the spirit of all three when he denounced "the revolt of the masses." Equalization, Ortega argued, threatened our very humanity. These thinkers, with all of their idiosyncracies, agreed that equality presses the individual into conformity with the masses and thus creates alienation from one's own real nature. Someone alienated from the self cannot help but be alienated from others, even though such a one may appear to be exactly like them. Paradoxically, then, as equality is attained, authentic unity is lost.

This view is not necessarily conservative. The critics of mass society have not ordinarily insisted on the preservation of traditional institutions or aristocratic rank. But all have refused to accept the common radical principle that doing away with conventional inequalities will end or even alleviate estrangement.

In what direction, then, should we move today? Radicals, although typically concentrating on class conflict, do not deny that estrangement has become more profound with the advance of industrialization. But they do deny, thereby separating themselves from the critics of mass society, that any real equalization has come about in the process of this development. Under the egalitarian surface of things, they see the same class warfare that Marx wrathfully delineated a century ago. Contemporary radicals therefore hold, with Rousseau and Marx, that we should move toward true equality.

Those on the other side, to their own disadvantage in public debate, do not agree among themselves on any single response to estrangement, nor do the various responses they suggest have the simplicity and clarity of the radical response. Many recommend that we treat inherited traditions and institutions with great care and respect, although, as noted earlier, the critics of mass society are by no means uniformly conservative. Others hope for the rise of new authorities and leaders. In general, however, their mood is strongly marked by historical resignation. They see no completely reliable solution to the problem of estrangement and do not pretend to provide us with one. What they try to do, rather, is to illuminate our situation. Thus they prepare one for carrying on a solitary life of resistance, in order both to salvage one's own humanity and to be open to a future that may be far better than the present even though beyond our foresight or control—a gift from destiny or God.

In concluding, let me suggest alternative lines of thought for those who would like to explore possibilities without following the usual pathways either of radicalism or of conservatism. One of these pathways will probably appeal primarily to those of radical temperament. It begins with the idea that what we need to overcome estrangement is not equality, pure and simple, but a particular kind of equality. What kind is the question. That there is such a question was indicated by no less an authority than Marx himself when he warned against a kind of communism in which "the role of *worker* is not abolished, but is extended to all men."[2] From this vantage point one can see the possibility of a more subtle radicalism than that of many radicals of the past. Such a radicalism might free its followers from the tiresome compulsion to show that the reality behind every undesirable situation is the exploitation of one class by another. It also might induce radicals to be less ready than they usually are to assume that any measure of equalization is bound to make life better.

The other line of thought begins with the idea that it is a particular kind of *inequality* that is needed to overcome estrangement. Starting with this idea, you might hold a course clear of both conservatism and resignation, affirming the future as uncompromisingly as do radicals. You would reflect on the future, however, in

---

[2]Karl Marx, *Economic and Philosophical Manuscripts*, trans. T. B. Bottomore, in Erich Fromm, *Marx's Concept of Man* (New York: Frederick Ungar, 1961), pp. 124–125. The italics are Marx's.

terms of a new aristocracy. What kind of aristocracy? This, like the earlier question—what kind of equality?—is the question demanding reflection. Are scientists qualified to form a new aristocracy? Philosophers of some particular persuasion? Professors and students? Is the progress of technology perhaps creating an aristocracy of technicians? There are a number of possibilities, all implying that our task is not equalization but the establishment of new dominations and powers.

The mystery of our nature—that we are always, as Jaspers says, more than we know about ourselves—is never more evident than when we discuss the idea of equality. That idea itself may be considered a paradox. Few would assert that it is literally true; human beings are conspicuously unequal by almost every standard of comparison. The claim that they are equal is hardly possible without invoking something incomparable in every person. In other words, egalitarianism is likely to admit that in what we know about ourselves we are unequal but to assert, with Jaspers, that we are more than we can know about ourselves; in that "more" we are equal. This implies the paradox that though in every observable and measurable quality we are unequal, in our ultimate being we are nevertheless equal. By contrast, those who oppose equality are likely to be more "realistic," and to maintain that it is neither just nor practical to ignore the manifest inequalities among people.

These are only tendencies, to be sure. To make out that egalitarianism spurns objective reality altogether, or that inegalitarianism is oblivious of the mystery of being, would be a great oversimplification. There are realistic arguments for equality, such as the waste a rigidly hierarchical society makes of the talents that turn up in the lower classes, or the arrogance and conformity that can destroy the spirit of a securely established aristocracy. On the other side, writers skeptical of equality sometimes see the mystery and grandeur of humankind as symbolized in an aristocracy of some sort (Nietzsche and Ortega write evocatively of the nobility of a hidden few, the natural rulers of human beings). Nevertheless, the tendencies remain—egalitarianism often appealing to what we are beyond all we can observe and prove about ourselves, with the other side insisting that neither practicality nor justice allows us to ignore actual inequalities.

Today, we are forced by a variety of conditions to think about equality—by throngs of homeless people in every American city, for example, and by the persistence of racial prejudice and injustice. There is one condition, however, that forces us to think more deeply than we probably otherwise would, and that is the position of women. Clearly, it is not a position of perfect equality with men. Should it be? To ponder this particular issue seems a fitting way of concluding our consideration of the general issue of inequality and equality.

12 *Should Men and Women Always and in All Ways Be Treated Equally?*

It may seem questionable to suggest that the position of women forces us to think more deeply than we otherwise would. How so? Should we not think deeply about the position of blacks, for example? In some ways, no doubt, we should. It is manifestly unjust and oppressive, yet it endures. Why is change so slow? What must be done? These clearly are serious questions. Still, it does not seem that the situation of blacks challenges political thinking quite so fundamentally as does the situation of women. This is because there are no arguments worth considering in support of the situation of blacks. As for the situation of women, however, there are intelligent and responsible people who see it as neither terribly unjust nor deeply in conflict with the interests of society and the interests of women. In other words, the subjection of blacks is in the nature of a structural *failure;* we do not consistently apply our principles. The position of women (whether the term *subjection* would be appropriate is a matter of dispute) is a structural *feature* of Western societies. Not only does it accord with principles that even now, although under serious attack, are widely accepted; to do away with it would require basic alterations in the social order—for example, in the way children are raised and the way work within and outside the home is compensated and divided.

Feminism might be defined summarily as the movement demanding that these alterations be made. The movement contains numerous and diverse currents of thought. These are fed by varying philosophical views, such as Marxism and existentialism, and flow toward varying goals, some highly radical and others relatively conservative. But all types of feminism call into question the institutional order determining the status of women in Western society today. What mainly concerns us here, engaged as we are in philosophical reflection, is the philosophical character of the feminist offensive. In this connection, one fact is particularly worthy of note: in questioning the basic institutional order, feminism challenges the whole Western tradition of political thought, from its beginnings in ancient Greece to the present day. Why is that?

The answer is simply that the tradition of thought has provided the institutional order with philosophical legitimacy. Feminists call attention, for example, to the views of Aristotle, perhaps the most influential of all political philosophers. Aristotle saw no place for women in activities like philosophy and politics, where human potentialities come to their fullest realization. In effect, women could not be fully human, and this seemed so obvious to Aristotle that the matter was not even discussed. Feminists call attention also to the persistence of such views among the great figures in the history of political thought, all of them men. Even so egalitarian a thinker as Rousseau accepted Aristotle's assumption that the most serious human affairs, those affecting nations and history, are to be handled exclusively by men. Not surprisingly, feminist thinkers wonder whether they should try to enter into the twenty-five hundred year philosophical conversation begun by the ancient Greeks; perhaps they should start a new conversation. In effect, they say, the status of women has *not* been among the perennial questions.

It really has, however, even though most political philosophers have neglected it, for Plato posed the question at the outset when he argued that women should be eligible for the supreme office in his ideal state, that of philosopher-ruler; and John Stuart Mill, in the nineteenth century, posed the question again in his book *The Subjection of Women*—a work still regarded with respect by feminists. So let us assume that men and women are in dialogue together. In challenging the Western tradition of political thought, feminism opens up some of the deepest issues facing human societies. People differ widely in their answers to these issues (and not simply in accordance with differences of gender). Few would deny, however, that feminism forces us to face the issues afresh. Let us try to do this here.

1. First of all is the issue of equality itself. What does equality mean? Presumably not uniformity, since it would manifestly be impossible to treat men and women always and in all ways precisely the same. But is it possible to treat people differently without favoring anyone? For example, if institutional changes could make it possible for women to bear children and tend young infants but to suffer no setback in their careers on account of the time thus taken, would that be unfair to men by providing women with a fuller and richer life experience than men can have? How can we distinguish between differential and prejudicial treatment?

Another issue here is social necessity. As already noted, some argue that the early years of a child's life require the full-time attention of the mother. This implies that, for women, a fairly prolonged withdrawal from the public world into the home is a social necessity. But is it? Can we know what is socially necessary without extensive experimentation? Have we any right to experiment with the well-being of children? Even with experimentation, can our judgments of social necessity ever attain a validity unaffected by cultural, economic, and social conditions that are constantly changing? But suppose it were demonstrated that, in all circumstances whatsoever, children are better off if cared for full-time by their mothers. How much better off must they be to justify the sacrifice of a mother's independent life? Even the most persuasive arguments for the advantages of slavery would not lead us to reinstitute slavery. Sometimes moral necessity transcends social necessity. Does that apply to the liberation of women from child care and housework?

Finally, feminism may prompt us to ask again what may be the hardest and deepest question of all: what makes the principle of equality so compelling? As we have seen, in ancient times highly civilized people often candidly thought of most human beings, women among them, much as we think today of machines—as things to be used and if not usable forgotten about or junked. Few today can think this way. Why not? Is this mere sentimentality? Or have we somehow keener eyes for human dignity than so preeminent a mind as Aristotle had? How could that be?

2. Feminism also forces us to think about the relative authority of nature and convention. It challenges customs and practices
sanctioned by centuries of social experience, thus assaulting convention in its most enduring, and for some people most precious,
parts. How much respect does convention (whether in the form of a
single custom or in the form of the whole network of customs
structuring a society) deserve? Does the fact that by definition it is
not natural condemn it? Or does its very existence, indicating that in
some sense it "works," entitle it to authority? If it has lasted for
many centuries does that add to its authority, showing that many
generations have tried it and found it of value, or does it show simply that it has never been rationally examined? If convention is destroyed, what remains? Nature? Is there such a thing, or is nature—
human nature—merely what convention makes it? If there is such a
thing as nature, can it be known? In pondering questions of this
kind, it may help to be more specific. Is the family natural, or
merely conventional? And what about the traditional roles of men
and women: do those accord with masculine and feminine nature,
or are they merely habitual and convenient? Here we reach an exceptionally fundamental and fascinating question: are masculinity
and femininity—concepts charged with subtlety and emotional
power—natural, or only conventional? The question deserves separate treatment, for it concerns that foundation stone of political theory—human nature.

3. Earlier I referred to psychological studies indicating that
men and women, and indeed boys and girls, perceive human situations differently—men legalistically, women intuitively; men typically look for relevant rules, women for the possibilities inherent in
particular situations. This difference goes with others. For example,
men are greatly concerned with personal autonomy and tend to regard relationships as threatening; women are apt to think of themselves as involved in relationships by virtue of their essential being.
When conflict arises, accordingly, men think first of their rights and
women (although feminism heavily stresses women's rights) of
their responsibilities. The highest standard for women may be that
of helping, for men that of not interfering. Such differences, of
course, vary among individuals, and they represent tendencies
rather than absolute laws. Nevertheless, it seems hardly excessive to

say that men and women differ in character—a hypothesis to which common experience, as well as psychological research, lends credence.

Thus arises an absolutely fundamental question for political thinking: are there any universal qualities defining a human being? If so, what are they? I pointed out earlier that political ideas almost always rest on concepts of human nature. But the feminist critique of traditional society forces us to think about human nature anew. If such a thing as human nature exists, is it roughly the same as masculine nature (implying either that women can never become fully human, and equal with men, or if they can, that to do so they must become like men)? Or if human nature exists, is it the same as feminine nature (suggesting that full equality for women would dramatically improve the character of society)? Or is human nature something that has been buried and forgotten, with men and women so far representing mere fragments of humanity?

4. One of the main characteristics of modern Western society is the division between public and private life; activities like politics and business are carried on in the world and are in various ways and degrees open to all, while the home is closed to all but those its inhabitants choose to admit. Feminism requires us to examine this division. Today, and traditionally, women have primary responsibility for the private sphere, with the public sphere reserved mainly for men. But this strikes many people as highly prejudicial to women. The public sphere, many assume, is the sphere of full participation in the affairs of the human race, whereas the private sphere is constricting and demeaning. But, one can wonder whether this is true in view of the fact that such significant elements of life as personal love, religious devotion, and reasoned conversation seem to be centered in (although not confined to) the private sphere.

For the ancient Greeks, public life and life in essence were largely synonymous; subsequent developments, such as the rise of Christianity, have made it possible to doubt this equation. But assuming the equation is accepted, what can be done? Must the division between public and private be abolished? One hesitates to say that it must, for that would mean doing away with private life and, one fears, with liberty itself. On the other hand, to say (given a desire to respond to feminist demands) that we need only open both spheres fully to men and women alike sounds too easy. For men and women to have absolutely equal access to the public realm, there would have to be absolutely equal sharing in the duties of the private realm. But in view of the possibility that women possess maternal capacities that men—regardless of their willingness to take on the tasks of child-rearing and home care—do not have, such sharing is not clearly desirable. Nor is it clearly practical. It would require for both partners time away from work, which the exigencies of business and professional life may make it hard to arrange; it would require as well a degree of mutual cooperation in the home that, current divorce statistics suggest, is anything but common. These are rather mundane matters, but they concern a philosophically sweeping issue: the proper structure of the social order.

5. The basis of the social order is also an issue feminism places before us. Many women have felt that society imposes obligations on them that they ought not to have to shoulder. What gives society the right to do this? What gives it the right to interfere with individual freedom? In feminist literature, the issue sometimes appears in discussions of social contract doctrine, which holds that society and the state are grounded in the voluntary agreement of their members. This doctrine closely conforms with feminist concerns. Not that many would claim that societies and states ordinarily, if ever, originate in an explicit contractual agreement. The core of the doctrine is in what it says, not about the origin, but about the moral authority of social institutions. It says, in effect, that the obligations society "imposes" must be freely accepted. Social roles must be filled voluntarily or not at all. Many women have felt that their roles as wives, mothers, and homemakers are not only onerous but practically enslaving, even though originating in a freely undertaken contract of marriage. The burdens ahead are not clearly foreseen by naive young brides; and even if they are, society provides them with few alternatives. The social contract doctrine calls into question situations of this kind. Social and political obligations must be rooted in the will of the individual. This sounds reasonable—indeed, vital—to most people today.

But can society be based solely on the unconstrained choice of every individual? Can so mammoth a task as the bearing and raising of a new generation be accomplished if every individual is completely free to stand aside and take no part? Does the standard of voluntary agreement require that any individual, at any time, be free to abandon any relationship, with the simple declaration: "I did not know what I was getting into"? With questions like these we face again, as have political thinkers in all ages, a moral dilemma inherent in our collective existence.

6. Feminism also leads us to reflect on oppression in general. One cannot think about the status of women without thinking about the status of other groups that are, or feel, oppressed, such as racial minorities and the poor. If the position of women were altered in accordance with feminist ideals, would the end of all forms of exploitation and wretchedness naturally follow? This is to ask, first of all, what the status of women today rests on—on capitalism, which according to some analysts is the major cause also of poverty and economic inequality? Or does the status of women reflect an ancient patriarchal tradition (a tradition, that is, dictating male primacy) independent of capitalism or even underlying capitalism? Or does it reflect a pride and selfishness that will surface in any system, even in one with absolute equality between men and women? We are asking not just about the status of women, however, but about the sources of injustice. Are all forms of injustice founded on a single, underlying condition, so that correcting one of them is correcting them all? Must they all be attacked simultaneously? Or are they like weeds, diverse and independent, and continually springing up, so that the battle against them is necessarily disorganized and endless?

Questions such as these naturally spawn a great variety of answers. There are many feminist positions, and added to them are the positions of those who reject all feminist positions. The alternatives opened up by the question before us—whether men and women should always and in all ways be treated equally—are bewildering in their number and diversity. How can one avoid drowning intellectually in a sea of questions and answers?

To facilitate reflection—to save us from drowning—I shall mark out four broad alternatives: three types of feminism and one type of antifeminism. Simply for the sake of convenience, I shall give these names. One should remember, however, that these names are the author's; representatives of the corresponding positions do not all use them and some might reject them.

Feminist Separatism. For people who hold this position, the aim is not equality for women but rather a separate, or even superior, place for women. In that sense, their answer to the question of whether men and women should be treated equally is negative. While repudiating any form of subordination, they aspire to a distinct women's world, or even to a world ruled by women. Their attitude may be founded on the conviction that women are not merely equal to men, inherently, but are superior to them. For most people, such views are jarring; they seem extreme and unreasonable. But of course they are no more extreme, nor more manifestly unreasonable, than the assumptions of male superiority that have been commonplace for centuries. Representatives of feminist separatism have discussed the possibilities of technological developments allowing fetuses to be conceived and developed outside the womb. The perpetuation of the human race would then no longer impose on women the burdens of pregnancy and childbirth.

Exemplifying feminist separatism is a novel written over fifty years ago by an American feminist, Charlotte Gilman. Entitled *Herland* and valued still by feminist writers, it depicts a society made up entirely of women; the inhabitants had developed a capacity for self-initiated pregnancies—always producing female infants—thus maintaining the population. The society is a female utopia. All relationships are entirely harmonious and cooperative; beauty is everywhere, both in the countryside and in the towns; problems are handled with unfailing practicality and success; the inhabitants are handsome and lithe, and they are serious, inquiring, and cultivated as well. They have achieved a complete and satisfying existence entirely without men. At the end of the novel three men who had found their way into this paradise are accepted by three of the women as mates. Throughout the book, however, the men are again and again comically thrown off balance by the superior competence and discernment of the women. And it is made clear that the women who accepted them as mates were in no way dependent on them for their well-being.

Radical Feminism. In contrast, radical feminists are very much concerned with equality. Their answer to the question before us—

whether men and women should always and in all ways be treated equally—is yes. But they attach a major condition: that society be radically changed. They seek access, not to the present world of men, but to a transformed world—one more worthy of being shared than the one men have created. Patriarchal society is degraded by conditions like competition and violence, and imperialism and war. And not only do radical feminists call for social transformation; they are apt to believe that women can make a decisive contribution to the needed transformation through a spirit more personal and compassionate than men ordinarily evince. As one might infer, radical feminists are far less respectful of convention than of nature—that is, human nature—where they see potentialities that, with the liberation of women, could come to reality in a world profoundly in need of renewal.

The radical response to some of the issues discussed earlier is interesting. Concerning the dichotomy of public and private spheres, radical feminists do not necessarily call for its abolition. Some of them call rather for its reinterpretation. The private sphere would become a place into which one may rightfully withdraw but where one cannot be forcibly confined. The public sphere, on the other hand, would be opened up to emotions and concerns hitherto treated as private; it would become more personal and dialogical— less legalistic. As for the roots of injustice in general, it is common for radical feminists to see the liberation of women as the key to general human liberation. The patriarchal subjection of women is organically connected with, or even the basis of, all major forms of injustice, such as racial discrimination and class oppression. Thus a world renewed by the liberation of women would be new not only for women but for everyone.

Liberal Feminism. In their comments on the present status of women and the patriarchal attitudes of political thinkers of the past, liberal feminists sound much like radical feminists. How they differ from them might be summarily indicated by saying that they do not find the general structure of liberal democracies, that is, of most contemporary Western societies, completely unacceptable. While affirming the natural equality of the sexes, they are apt to be less sure than radical feminists that children can be well reared outside the home and away from the mother; and they are more open to the possibility that biology may impose unique obligations on women. Hence they are friendlier to the family than are radical feminists. Also, they are less hostile to the public world as presently constituted and consequently more apt to be satisfied if women gain more or less equal access to that world, and if men share more fully in the tasks of the home. Above all, as the term *liberal feminism* suggests, they wish for liberty—the liberty institutionalized in most Western societies and enjoyed more or less fully by men (at least by white, middle-class men) but partially withheld, feminists believe, from women. Indeed, real liberty would suffice. Society does not need to be transformed but only to be made fully accessible to women and fairly administered.

Patriarchal Conservatism. This is the camp of those who answer no to the question of whether men and women should always and in all ways be treated equally. They are not necessarily men; many women share this view. And if they are men, they are not necessarily what feminists call "male chauvinists." But they do accept prevailing arrangements, arrangements undeniably granting a certain primacy to men. To anyone conscious of the intelligence, learning, and passion characterizing much feminist literature, to accept the society so scorned in such literature may seem peculiarly backward and blind. But probably far more people occupy this position than any of the others we have discussed, and it would be hard to show that they all are lacking in intelligence and humane feelings.

The more moderate of the patriarchal conservatives would probably rest their case on the complementary character of men and of women. They would insist that men and women are different and that their differences are enduring and natural, not just products of convention. Whether they are absolutely equal would not greatly concern them. What would concern them far more would be the way typical male and female characteristics fit together in the working of society. They would hold, for example, that men tend to be aggressive and thus are suited for posts of large-scale management and leadership; that women are attentive and compassionate and thus good at creating harmony and warmth among small numbers, as in families; that there is a certain correspondence, in short, between the male temperament and the public world and between the female temperament and the private world.

To be mindful of this correspondence is vital alike to the conduct of public affairs and to the care of the family. To ignore it is to neglect the very structure of civilization.

The more moderate of patriarchal conservatives might also offer certain practical observations. For example, social order depends on degrees of authority and degrees of subordination. To insist mindlessly on absolute equality is to tamper with the basic conditions of a workable society. Men may sometimes, even often, lack the inherent qualities justifying their present primacy. But primacy has to be held by someone; to insist on its being held by someone demonstrably superior to everyone beneath reflects perfectionism of a kind that fits very badly into the actual world. Another of these practical observations might be that the present order is not oppressive for most women. Once the tasks of child-rearing are completed, women have extensive liberty and leisure, and through voluntary organizations, such as churches and public-interest pressure groups, have a multitude of opportunities for entering into the affairs of the larger world.

In sketching these positions, I have tried to show that none is absurd, none indefensible. On the other hand, it must be noted that none is free of serious weaknesses. A serious weakness in feminist separatism, for example, is that it fractures community. It rejects a major premise of this book, the ideal of unrestricted dialogue, with men and women equally taking part. As for radical feminism, its gravest weakness may lie simply in its revolutionary cast; it calls for immediate and sweeping social changes. But history comes close to proving (although events beginning in 1989 in Eastern Europe may require that this conclusion be reconsidered) that human beings cannot quickly and completely transform society. In trying to do so, they release uncontrollable human forces and create unmanageable situations.

Is liberal feminism, then, the answer? Not beyond all question, certainly. The weightiest argument against it, perhaps, is not that it is flawed as an answer but rather that, *from a feminist perspective*, it is no answer at all. It fails effectively to address feminist concerns. In accepting the present order of society, along with male definitions of liberty, and of public and private life, it leaves women with unjust handicaps and leaves society degraded by competition and violence. So, at least, radical feminists would be apt to argue. As for patriarchal conservatism, finally, despite an appearance of sobriety and good sense—an appearance far from wholly deceptive—it can be charged with skirting the issue of equality and thus leaving unchallenged institutions and practices violating the supreme standard of justice.

Readers who feel bewildered—not only by issues concerning the subordination of women but by issues concerning inequality and equality generally—should not be discouraged, for these are truly bewildering issues. This is one reason they have never been settled. If reflecting on them were a game, we might prefer not to play. But convictions concerning equality and inequality determine how society should be organized. And these convictions are explosive, having caused countless revolutions from the time of the Greek city-states to the present. Hence, again and again we are compelled to reflect on the troubling realities of inequality and on the enthralling visions of equality. We have little choice but to take on the bewilderment we naturally feel as we approach those things that "thought cannot think."

SUGGESTED READINGS

Plato. *The Republic*
Aristotle. *Politics*, Books I and III–VI
Locke, John. *The Second Treatise of Government*
Rousseau, Jean Jacques. *Discourse on the Origin of Inequality*
Kant, Immanuel. *Critique of Practical Reason*
Paine, Thomas. *The Rights of Man*
Tocqueville, Alexis de. *Democracy in America*, 2 vols.
Kierkegaard, Søren. *The Present Age*
Mill, John Stuart. *The Subjection of Women*
Marx, Karl. *Capital*, Vol. I
Nietzsche, Friedrich. *Thus Spake Zarathustra*
Ortega y Gasset, José. *The Revolt of the Masses*
Camus, Albert. *The Plague*

Orwell, George. *The Road to Wigan Pier*

Okin, Susan Moller. *Women in Western Political Thought*

Elshtain, Jean Bethke. *Public Man, Private Woman: Women in Social and Political Thought*

Benhabib, Seyla, and Cornell, Drucilla (eds.). *Feminism as Critique: On the Politics of Gender*

Coole, Diana H. *Women in Political Theory: From Ancient Misogyny to Contemporary Feminism*

POWER AND ITS POSSESSORS

The discussions of unity and disunity and of equality and inequality put us in an advantageous position from which to begin exploring the main subject of political science: power. Because people are disunited, power seems necessary for ensuring order; because they are unequal, power seems justified as a way of placing everyone under the rule of the best human qualities. Many of the controversies of politics, moreover, have to do with the impact of power on unity and disunity and on equality and inequality. Power may be used to separate human beings and to bring them together, as is exemplified in policies of racial segregation and integration in America; it may support inequality, as when special tax benefits are accorded to the wealthy; and it may support equality, as is done in many countries through systems of national health care. Perhaps it would be impossible to use power so that it would neither divide nor unite, neither discriminate nor equalize. It is because of these interconnections that the preceding two chapters have prepared us to reflect on power.

Some of the most basic and difficult questions about power arise from its moral dubiousness. Perhaps power is evil in essence. Certainly the use of power normally involves much evil; it tends to make those who possess it evil ("power tends to corrupt" in Lord Acton's well-known phrase) and it presupposes evil, as is evident in the conflicts that render order dependent on power. That human relations are pervaded by power is an unmistakable sign of the radical imperfection of human beings.

Perhaps even these few assertions, however, have carried us too far by expressing certainty about matters that in fact are far from certain. Is it true that human beings are radically imperfect? Is power really indispensable? There are renowned writers, such as the Russian novelist Leo Tolstoy, who have answered both questions negatively and have called for the drastic curtailment or even the total elimination of power. On the other hand, there are political thinkers of great reputation who have seen social order, and therefore civilization itself, as dependent almost entirely on power.

Here we have obviously encountered an issue that must be discussed before going any further. If politics is the use of power, one of the first questions we must ask is whether power really is necessary in human life and, if it is, how large a role it must have.

13   *Can Social Order Be Maintained Without Power?*

Countless political thinkers have argued that it can be *in part*. There are sources of order other than power. Human nature, the natural harmony of interests, and custom all have been seen—even celebrated—as grounds of human harmony and as enabling societies to dispense, in some measure at least, with power. Let us briefly examine each of these.

1. Human nature is a source of order if men and women are basically good. The argument that they are forms a thread running through the history of political theory and, as we have seen, is particularly visible and important in modern thinkers such as Rousseau and Marx. Another thinker whose work is shaped by an affirmation of human goodness is John Locke. In constructing the modern theory of liberal government, Locke's major premise, it might be said, is that human beings are at bottom reasonable. This meant two things—first, that most people have the sense to see that others have certain rights, such as the right to life, simply because they are human beings. It meant further that most people are disposed to respect these rights. In other words, reason is both a cognitive and a moral faculty—informing us concerning reality and guiding our conduct. Hence, human reasonableness for Locke meant both the capacity and the inclination to live by reason.

Natural law, which provided a kind of moral structure for the universe, had an important place in this outlook. Reason was the

faculty by which we discern and conform with natural law. The upshot is that social order is in large measure spontaneous. Power cannot be dispensed with entirely, but it can be relegated to the fringes
of life, having an occasional and peripheral but not central role in
the maintenance of social order.

2. The concept of the natural harmony of interests accom-
plishes the feat of arguing that social order is largely spontaneous
even though human beings may not be very good. The clearest il-
lustration of this principle is probably the theory of the so-called
classical economists, who flourished in the nineteenth century and
provided what is still the basic rationale for free enterprise. The classical economists did not regard human beings as good. On the contrary, they regarded them as materialistic and self-seeking. But they
did not conclude from this that social order must be created and
sustained with power. They believed that if governments would
merely ensure the main conditions of individual economic activity,
such as security of property and stability of currency, but otherwise
would not curb the freedom of individuals to seek their own economic advantage, according to their own selfish promptings and
calculations, large areas of social order—above all, areas made up of
or determined by economic relationships—would come into being
and endure naturally. An economic order not only conducive to efficiency, but just in itself, would take shape with little involvement
on the part of the government. And since life as a whole is shaped
decisively by economic interests and relationships, this is to say that
a good social order would spontaneously take shape.

The reasons the classical economists had for thinking this are
well known and not implausible. Within a free market, the products
most needed by society will be manufactured and put on sale without forcing anyone to do these things; the profit motive will provide
incentive enough. Moreover, the market will see not only to efficiency but also to equity; manufacturers will be fairly rewarded,
and buyers fairly charged, for otherwise no business will be trans-
acted between them. On the other hand, those unable or unwilling
to help in meeting the needs of society will garner no profits and
will thus be penalized without the slightest intervention by the police. Thus good order will arise from the operation of natural economic laws, with governmental power serving only to establish a
framework within which human interests can have free rein. For
the classical economists, order was contrived by what one of them

called the "invisible hand" of the free market rather than by the visible hand of the government.

3. Finally, a great many political writers see social order as arising spontaneously from habit, custom, and tradition. They do not take for granted either the goodness of humans or the harmony of nature. Rather they count on the human tendency to do what has from time immemorial been done, to think the thoughts of their ancestors, and to hold in awe things—like constitutions—that are ancient. Given a chance to develop peacefully, a society will gradually build up an intricate structure of traditional practices and beliefs. Such a structure will contain more wisdom than any social order or system of belief built at a particular moment in time because it will be the work of many generations and will have been long tested in practice. Power of course may have a role in safeguarding a traditional order, but it need not be a dominating role. To say that human beings are creatures of habit and custom is to say that they are orderly by nature.

The ideological tendency inherent in so high an evaluation of long-lasting and slowly-evolving social structures can be easily seen. If the principle of human goodness is radical, suggesting severe judgments of the established order and implying the feasibility of swift and sweeping changes, reliance on custom and tradition is conservative. Dismantling an old and well-established social order in behalf of an abstract design for a better order would be as heedless as tearing down one of the great medieval cathedrals to make room for a supermarket. Here we touch again on the views of Edmund Burke (discussed in Question 3), for whom the major sources of order are habit, prejudice, and awe.

In summary, there are three major sources of spontaneous order, as contrasted with humanly contrived and power-centered order. These are the innate goodness of human beings, natural forces tending to harmonize conflicting human interests, and the tendency of people to order their lives in accordance with past practices. On this basis, how must we answer the question as to whether social order can be maintained without power? Three possible answers present themselves.

The first of these is strongly affirmative and amounts to what is usually called "anarchism." Contrary to popular impressions, an anarchist is not someone in love with chaos and disposed to set off bombs in public places. Rather, an anarchist is apt to be an extraordinarily benign and hopeful person. In essence, anarchism is the belief that we can get along very well without power. Indeed, that is the only way we can live in accordance with our full potentialities, for power is not only unnecessary; it is always oppressive and destructive. In short, anarchism seeks the abolition of government. Such a purpose can only rest on the belief that one of the sources of spontaneous order, or perhaps some combination of them, suffices for ensuring order. Typically, however, it is human goodness that anarchists count on, for the other sources of order contain an element of coercion. To act under the sway of natural forces (such as the so-called "laws of supply and demand"), or of habit and custom, is not to be fully free. Only if human beings are so unselfish that, even when living purely as they please, they will live harmoniously with one another can the immemorial conflict of order and freedom be resolved without compromise on either side.

. Is such a philosophy credible? Not very, for it rests on what will strike most people as an unrealistic view of human nature. Accordingly, there have been relatively few anarchists in the history of political thought. Nevertheless, the idea should not be casually dismissed. For one thing, it is susceptible of modifications which enhance its credibility. It can be construed to mean, not the total absence of centralized administration and coherent groups, but rather radical decentralization and the abolition of all coercive agencies, such as police and armies. Then it becomes the vision of a social order entirely free of violence and infused through and through with the spirit of cooperation even though not subsisting altogether without deliberate contrivance and administration. For another thing, and regardless of how impractical it may be, anarchism represents an inevitable human longing, the longing for perfect understanding and peace among humans. Anyone who seriously entertains the hope that life on earth will sometime be what our conscience tells us it ought to be is an anarchist of a sort, for such a hope necessarily seeks the eradication of power.

A far more common answer to the question we are discussing is mildly negative. Social order cannot be maintained without any use whatever of power, yet it is not dependent entirely on power. This is the view held by the framers of the American Constitution and, probably, by most Americans still. We can call it "liberal," if we understand this word broadly enough to cover practically everyone, except anarchists, who believes in liberty—as do most of those we call "conservatives." According to this view a great deal of order arises spontaneously, but such order is incomplete and imperfect and therefore needs to be overseen and upheld with power. The three sources of spontaneous order are not sufficient in themselves. Human beings are reasonable and decent on the whole but still bear watching; and a few are quite unreasonable and indecent. Natural market forces can produce a great deal of economic justice and efficiency yet in some cases fail; there is needed a visible, as well as invisible, hand. Finally, although custom and tradition play an incalculably important role in sustaining civilization, they are far from infallible; they must sometimes be deliberately—perhaps through the application of centralized power—modified or even scrapped. The upshot is that power is merely supplementary, but it is still indispensable.

Such a view will seem to most people commonplace and unexciting—anything but a daring flight of thought. It has great importance, however, for it underlies the concept of ordered liberty which most Americans support and which America in some measure realizes. If there were no spontaneous order, then every relationship would have to be contrived and upheld by the government. Totalitarianism would be inevitable and liberty impossible. People can be in some measure free because they tend naturally to create not only chaos but order as well. In other words, government can be limited because a profusion of harmonious relationships arise spontaneously, without governmental contrivance. The disorderly tendencies of people rule out anarchism; their orderly tendencies rule out totalitarianism.

The principle that social order can be maintained in part, although not entirely, without power leads naturally to an emphasis on the importance of group life. Spontaneous order is apt to take the form not only of uniformities and harmonies prevailing throughout a nation but also of groups smaller and more specialized than the nation—clubs, corporations, universities, pressure groups, party caucuses, churches, and, more important probably than any other, families. The overall coherence of society is heavily dependent on the structural detail such groups provide. Moreover, the strength and independence of individuals depend on their not having to stand up to the central government unsupported and alone. Most scholars, consequently, view a stable, constitutional government as resting on a foundation of numerous and vital private associations. In his classic study of American democracy, Alexis de Tocqueville argued that the uncommon aptitude Americans showed in forming private associations played an indispensable role in the stability of ordered liberty.

We must note, finally, a strongly negative answer to the question: Can social order be maintained without power? No one, of course, can deny that there are sources of order other than power; at least occasionally people behave decently, reach good results through competition, and pay heed to custom. Some have felt, however, that these sources are entirely unreliable and that the disorderly tendencies in life far outweigh the orderly tendencies. Power, therefore, is the only effective source of order. Such a view can be derived from the Christian emphasis on sin, although Christians for the most part have favored limited government. It was the view of Hobbes, and was a logical outcome of the principle that human beings are essentially estranged. Its most notorious representative, however, is Niccoló Machiavelli (1469–1527), the Florentine statesman, exile, and writer who formulated many of the basic rules of power politics.

Contrary to his lurid reputation, Machiavelli probably had a somewhat less pessimistic view of the human race than did either Augustine or Hobbes. He wrote often of virtue and corruption in politics, showing that he did not consider humans to be wholly and incurably evil. Machiavelli saw virtue as consisting in qualities, such as loyalty and honesty, that predispose people to uphold order voluntarily; only when such qualities are lost is absolute rule inevitable. Nevertheless, Machiavelli regarded all uncoerced and uncontrived order as highly unstable, and this was the heart of "Machiavellianism." Human beings tend always to be fickle and selfish, and are ingenious and tireless sources of chaos. Hence, order depends—now and again, if not continuously—on the resoluteness and skill of political leaders. Machiavelli's two main works, *The Prince* and *The Discourses*, are reflections on the techniques and devices of political and military art. Machiavelli's central teaching is inherent in his pessimistic appraisal of human nature: order, hence civilization, rests not on human goodness but on the political sagacity of rulers.

Unhappily, the Machiavellian answer to our question is more plausible today than the answer at the other extreme—anarchism.

Every continent and civilization in our time is cursed by wars among nations, classes, races, and religions. Millions of young men were killed in the war between Iraq and Iran; tens of thousands have been slain in Latin America by death squads acting in behalf of the upper classes; Jews and Arabs have been locked in a violent confrontation for several decades; and in India, since independence from Great Britain was gained, Hindus have slaughtered Muslims by the millions. The idea that humans are deeply and irremediably chaotic is quite credible. Nevertheless, just as anarchism should not be casually dismissed, neither should Machiavellianism be casually accepted. This is because it leads readily to political despair, meaning by this the sense that constitutional government is impractical and liberty unattainable. Admittedly, one does not find such despair in Machiavelli himself. Still, if a human being is an irremediably disorderly creature, then for as long as the human race endures, societies are bound to be immersed in power and in all of the evils that unavoidably go along with power.

The question before us is obviously a rather practical one. For example, is it feasible now that the Cold War has ended for America to reduce drastically the scale of its military spending? Many say that it is, since the threat of a war between the superpowers no longer exists. Others say that it isn't, partly because, with the outbreak of ethnic and religious strife in areas where the Soviet Union once maintained peace, American armed forces may be needed in several places at once; and partly because, in view of the chaos in Russia, which has followed on the disintegration of the Soviet government, we have no assurance that Russia will not within a few years again be a hostile, imperial power. Your attitude toward this issue will be decided largely by how dependent on power you believe human order to be. Another example of the practical import of the conclusions you come to concerning the role of power is based on the spread of violence in America, where there are guns enough to arm every man, woman, and child; where casual killings occur every day in every major city; and where being President, or even being a celebrity of some sort, is to live in more or less constant peril of violent death. Does keeping order in American cities necessitate freeing police forces from procedural rules that may, while safeguarding individuals, inhibit effective suppression of crime? Again, your answer will depend largely on the amount of emphasis you place on power.

Readers are apt to have noticed that we frequently touched, in the preceding discussion, on facets of the first question in this book—are human beings estranged in essence? Not that it is one and the same thing for human beings to be disorderly and to be estranged. Disorder signalizes just one type of estrangement—that which issues in overt actions. Nor, conversely, can it be concluded that just because humans are spontaneously orderly, they are not estranged. As we have already seen, for example, some writers find humans profoundly estranged under a placid surface of custom and tradition; Marx thought they were estranged within capitalist order. But the two issues clearly are closely connected. If you believe human beings are essentially estranged you will easily be led to the view that they are irremediably disorderly. On the other hand, if you believe that they are essentially at one you will probably conclude that there is, or can be, a good deal of spontaneous order among them. Hence it may be helpful, at this point, to recall your reflections in connection with the first question.

Let us assume now that the anarchistic option, however appealing, has been rejected. Social order cannot be maintained without power. Immediately another important question arises. Who should have power: military leaders? men and women from the business world? intellectual aristocrats of some sort, such as scientists or philosophers? agents of the bourgeoisie, that is, of those who are propertied and successful? champions of the people? workers? Many of the tensions of politics center on this issue. Civil wars and revolutions are occasioned by opposing answers to it. And philosophers, since the beginnings of political thought, have tried to discover the final and unchanging principles in accordance with which power should be distributed and thus to answer the question that follows.

14 *Who Should Rule?*

"Anyone" and "no one" are among the answers that have been given to this question, as implausible as both may seem.

The answer "anyone" is implicit in the philosophy of Hobbes. One reason Hobbes was willing that anyone should rule lay in his cynical egalitarianism. Hobbes had no faith in "great men" or in elites of any kind; no one was exempted from his pessimistic appraisal of human nature. Therefore, he did not feel that it much mattered who ruled. Looking at things so pessimistically, however, could he not just as well have argued that no one should rule? No, for he thought this would result in intolerable chaos. His position makes sense if human beings, as Hobbes believed, are essentially estranged and thoroughly disorderly.

Still, we may ask whether intolerable chaos might not also result from giving supreme power to a specimen of Hobbesian humanity—a person invariably and uncompromisingly egotistical, who is merely a complex material object governed like the rest of reality by the laws of cause and effect. Hobbes thought not. His reasoning went roughly as follows. What every individual in his egotism desires above everything else is self-preservation; self-preservation can be gained only where there is peace; and peace is the product of a strong, well-ordered state. Such a state is a primary goal of the subjects of a ruler. What does the ruler desire? Like everyone else, self-preservation. In the ruler's case, however, the primary condition for fulfilling this desire is power. How is power to be obtained? Through organizing a strong, well-ordered state—the same end sought by the subjects. There is thus a fundamental identity of interest between government and people.

On these grounds Hobbes thought that anyone in command of a state would be about as effective as anyone else and would try to further, albeit for personal advantage, the interest of the governed.

Mistrust of power, of course, is common. But only a few thinkers, and those relatively obscure, have taken the extreme view that no one should be entrusted with power. These thinkers are anarchists, whom we discussed in connection with the preceding question. They are pessimistic in their conviction that power will inevitably be misused, but optimistic in believing that power can be dispensed with and that order and peace can be securely established without any coercion at all. To them, every form of power is both intolerable and useless. How can intelligent people affirm so seemingly self-contradictory a theory?

They affirm it by maintaining, as we have noted, that the misdeeds of those who govern do not reflect the essential nature of human beings. People in essence are cooperative and unselfish. This will be revealed when governments have been destroyed or perhaps when civilization has further evolved. On such suppositions anarchists have based, in compensation for the terrors many of them have experienced in their own lives, a daring hope: oppression, and indeed government itself, will die away and humanity will become a perfect community. This hope may strike one as strange and implausible. But it has generated a doctrine whose moral purity and philosophical audacity command respect.

When we consider the answers lying in between these two extremes we cross a path we followed in the preceding chapter—we encounter issues connected with inequality and equality. The question of who should rule has been thrashed out by two broad political and philosophical parties. These are the supporters of the few and the supporters of the many. A reasonable decision in favor of one side or the other can be made only after reflecting on whether human beings are essentially equal or not.

Are there certain virtues, attainable by a minority but not by the majority, that render those possessing them deserving of power? It has frequently been claimed that there are. Philosophical wisdom was such a virtue according to Plato; the divine authority supposedly inherent in ordination has occasionally been so regarded by Christians; and unique political capacities have often been attributed to some minority distinguished by family background, education, military achievement, or business success. Human beings show a surprisingly strong inclination to exalt some minority or other. Medieval priests and kings may have fallen, but the twentieth century has raised up its own priestly and royal authorities, as is evident in the trust that has been placed in Communist and Nazi elites as well as in scientists, technicians, and managers.

The idea of popular rule has received less support in the history of political thought than we might expect. It is true that twenty-five hundred years ago in Greece many people believed in participatory democracy, for a number of the city-states were direct (rather than representative) democracies. But the great Greek thinkers either scorned democracy or had serious reservations about it and the conquests of Alexander the Great, several centuries before the time of Christ, largely extinguished democracy, which has revived only in recent times. In the interim there were democratic movements, and people here and there believed in democracy. But political thinkers, while in theory often granting a significant measure of authority to the people, assumed that in practice this authority would be severely limited. Rarely did they advocate popular rule.

Whether the dearth of democratic thought was owing to a class bias among those who had the leisure to think and write, to a wisdom that discerned the insufficiencies of democracy, to the difficulties of organizing popular rule prior to the development of technological media of communication, or to some other cause is uncertain. In any case, not until the seventeenth and eighteenth centuries was the idea of democracy uncompromisingly affirmed. Rousseau was the first great thinker in whose writings this occurred.

For Rousseau, we are deprived of our humanity by having to live under a government in which we have no part. This diminution of humanity would take place even if the government were benevolent and wise. However, if a great many people were excluded from participation, the government would almost certainly be selfish and oppressive. Only government by the people can be truly and steadily devoted to the common good. Insofar as the people are neither corrupted by modern urban civilization nor frustrated by defective political arrangements, Rousseau thought they possessed what amounts to moral and political sanctity.

Is it really any more sensible, however, to rest confidence in great numbers than in some select minority? Do the doubts that most political philosophers have had about popular rule constitute a consensus of the wise, which we should hesitate to contradict? The modern experience with democracy and socialism, through which the people have gained more, if not total, power has prompted many misgivings. Numerous observers have judged the cultural tastes of the people to be crude and their political opinions to be based on ignorance and prejudice.

Some reply that in reality the people have gained little power and that their failings reflect the irresponsible influence still wielded by minorities, such as the commercial interests dominating television and the press. Democracy has never had a chance to display its virtues.

Obviously it is hard to decide between the few and the many. This is why numerous thinkers, from the earliest periods of political thought, have refused to take either side and have argued that aristocracy and democracy should be combined in some fashion. Aristotle thought that this could be accomplished by granting power to a large middle class. Rule by this class, he held, was likely to be more moderate and sensible than rule by either the few or the many.

Where a strong middle class does not exist, Aristotle's advice is inapplicable, for such a class cannot be created easily or quickly and perhaps cannot be created at all. Also, some people feel that while neither the upper nor the lower class should govern alone, each should share in power. Accordingly, political thinkers have given much attention to organizational devices whereby the few and the many might govern together. Some suggest, for example, that the executive power should be reserved for persons of special distinction while the legislature should express the will of the people.

A list of the great thinkers who have urged a combination of aristocracy and democracy would be an impressive collection of names. This fact and the arguments already discussed suggest that the idea has wisdom. There is one objection to it, however, that for some will be conclusive: it contains little promise of the radical social and political renewal that many call for. If all classes share in governing, nothing is likely to be done that seriously jeopardizes the interests of any class. Hence, the ideal of government that is neither by the few nor the many, but is mixed, is apt to appeal mainly to those who are satisfied with things as they are.

It is the unsatisfied who often pose most dramatically the question of who should rule. They are the ones most likely to claim that some particular group is not merely the best alternative as a repository of power, but that the favored group can redeem humanity from the vicissitudes and agonies of history. Plato made this claim for philosophers, Marx for the proletariat, and Lenin for the Communist party. When faced with such claims, we have to ask how much can reasonably be expected of rulers. Should we be satisfied with prudence on the part of our leaders and with a conduct of affairs that avoids disaster? Or should we look for redeeming wisdom, for a Moses to lead us out of our captivity within commonplace life and mediocre visions?

A final question concerning power deserves our attention. The modern answer to the question of who should rule is, on the whole, that the many should rule. The prestige of certain aristocratic institutions, like the Supreme Court in the United States, indicates that the answer is not unqualified, but most defenders of minority powers and privileges see such institutions as merely prudent restraints on what is predominantly and properly government by the people. Few openly attack the basic principle of popular rule. It is appropriate, therefore, to consider how popular government can best be carried on.

15 If the People Rule, Should They Do So Themselves or Through Representatives?

Idealists are apt to believe that direct (or "participatory") democracy is far superior to representative democracy. They feel, as did Rousseau, that "sovereignty . . . cannot be represented," and they agree with his famous animadversion on the English political system: "The people of England regards itself as free: but it is grossly mistaken: it is free only during the election of members of parliament. As soon as they are elected, slavery overtakes it, and it is nothing."[1]

Perhaps this view is correct. In view of the fervor and frequency with which the case for participatory democracy is made, however, we should remember that the arguments for representative democracy are not insubstantial. Consider the following.

1. The representative system makes it possible, while allowing the people as a whole to have the final word, to empower those who stand out for their intelligence, experience, and interest in political matters. Direct democracy tends to submerge such minorities in the masses.

2. Representatives can devote all of their time to government, whereas the people as a whole cannot. The consequence, since government must be carried on continuously, is that representative democracy can provide steadier popular control of day-to-day government than direct democracy can. Even in a very small state, the entire populace could not be expected to assemble oftener than once in every few weeks. Thus, most of the time government would have to be carried on by unsupervised minorities.

[1]Jean Jacques Rousseau, *The Social Contract and Discourses,* trans. with an introduction by G. D. H. Cole (New York: Dutton, 1950), p. 139.

3. A representative body provides better opportunities for leisured, unemotional deliberation than does a great popular assembly. Representatives are in daily, face-to-face contact, so their mutual antipathies may be tempered by personal understanding; also, because representatives are few in number and meet frequently, their relationships can readily be structured by formalities that protect the spirit and the processes of deliberation. Members of large multitudes, on the other hand, cannot for the most part be personally acquainted; the mere existence of a crowd discourages deliberation and incites inflammatory speech; and great numbers are more likely than the few making up a representative body to be carried away by some momentary emotion.

4. Direct democracy is workable only in polities that are very small in population and area; otherwise, frequent assemblies of the people are impossible. Representative democracy opens the way to large-scale, even global, political integration. Not only are there military, economic, and cultural advantages to linking together large numbers of people, but there is political safety in numbers. As James Madison (though not a proponent of universal suffrage) argued in the celebrated "Federalist No. 10," a polity may embrace so great a variety of interests that for a single faction, such as a racial or economic minority, to gain ascendancy and act in opposition to the public interest would be virtually impossible.

These four points constitute a sober and sensible case for representative democracy. Indeed, it is doubtful that proponents of direct democracy can present an equally sober and sensible one. This is not to say, however, that their position is weaker; rather, it is a position of another kind. Proponents of representative democracy usually stand on the ground of common sense; this means, among other things, that they expect people in the future to be what they have ordinarily been in the past, beings who en masse rarely manifest either acute intelligence or a firm sense of responsibility. On the other hand, proponents of direct democracy commonly rely more on hope than on experience, on what people might become than on what they have usually been. At least two compelling visions inspire the ideal of direct democracy and it is unlikely that either will be much weakened by the objections of common sense.

First, there is a vision of human beings as governing their own lives not merely in the negative and partial sense of having a sphere in which to behave according to personal preferences, but in the positive and complete sense of deliberating upon and deciding the whole order of life. The individual alone cannot be sovereign in this way, but a populace can. Direct democracy allows the individual to share in sovereignty, and where a large measure of agreement binds together the governing populace, the individual may feel that the decisions of the people are in effect personal decisions. In contrast, representative democracy means passive citizenship. As Rousseau asserted, you are free when you vote, but at other times you are a subject rather than a sovereign.

Beyond this, there is a vision of community that cannot be accommodated within the concept of representative democracy. Representation modifies but does not overcome the deep division between those who have power and those who do not, between government and governed. Few other circumstances so alienate human beings from one another. An enduring appeal of direct democracy is that it promises to bridge this chasm; no longer will humankind be divided between rulers and ruled. All will be ruled together and all together will rule. A direct democracy could be, fully and literally, a community.

Thus, matching the practicality of one side is the imagination of the other. How can you choose? Pondering the following questions might help you in defining your position.

1. How much of your time is politics worth? Rousseau asserted that "the better the constitution of a State is, the more do public affairs encroach on private in the minds of citizens."[2] But is it necessarily good for public affairs to encroach on private affairs? Rousseau thought it was, as must any whole-hearted supporter of direct democracy. But the private affairs crowded out by public activities might be the reading of literary masterpieces, the creation of works of art, the enjoyment of the company of friends and loved ones, the cultivation of personal skill in a sport or a craft, or the pursuit of scholarly or scientific research. Are these all less important than public affairs? Not everyone, certainly, will think that they are. Direct democracy places heavy demands on the time and attention of everyone, and it is doubtful that you can logically favor

[2] *Social Contract,* p. 93.

this system unless you believe that we fully realize our humanity only in politics and public life.

2. Is it possible for industrial societies to function without bureaucracy, that is, without a highly organized corps of professional administrators? If so (as Marx, for example, apparently believed), direct democracy may one day work. If not, the ideal of direct democracy is probably an illusion, for a bureaucracy is a kind of latter-day aristocracy, a more or less settled and privileged ruling group. Where bureaucracy exists, only limited, indirect democracy is possible, and even that is possible only if the bureaucracy is held strictly responsible to the people. Arguably, such responsibility is more likely to be achieved through representatives who possess a measure of expertise and meet continuously, than by a vast, miscellaneous assemblage of citizens who can meet only occasionally.

3. On what human qualities does the solution of political problems depend? If above all on expertise, that of engineers and social scientists, for example, direct democracy is a dubious ideal. Citizens cannot all be experts in all areas. As everyone knows, we live in an era of science and technology, and of complex and large-scale social phenomena, so it may seem that experts must rule. Are there any common human qualities, qualities attainable by ordinary men and women, to which expertise should be subordinate? It might be claimed that there are: character and common sense. But do common people really possess these qualities? And are they in fact relevant to the problems facing the modern state?

The whole issue reflects our efforts to reconcile power and personal dignity. The general idea of democracy is that to do this, sovereignty or ultimate power must be in the hands of the people. But how is this possible? Government by the people, literally, would not be government. The concepts of representative and direct democracy are two different ways of grappling with the issue. Representative democracy is the "realistic" solution in that it acquiesces in the inevitability of government, that is, of concentrated power, and requires merely that those who exercise this power be subject to periodic approval by the people. Direct democracy is the "idealistic" solution. It moves a long way toward anarchism; it reduces government to a subordinate administrative apparatus and calls on the people themselves to pass laws. Representative democracy does not overcome the alienation of government and governed, but in its realism does not try to. Direct democracy imaginatively attacks this alienation; the question is whether in the complex, industrial world of the twentieth century it is a real alternative.

These various disputes about the proper location of power are not, as everyone knows, ordinarily carried on in a spirit of detachment. On the contrary, they are acrimonious and impassioned. One of the main reasons for this is that power is something many people avidly desire. For such people, power is equivalent to life, and the prospect of powerlessness is dismaying. But is power really good for its possessors? Does it make for happiness, or is it, in fact, a burden? Does it enhance the humanity of the powerful—for example, by enabling them better to serve others—or does it make them arrogant and callous?

16 *Is It Good to Have Power?*

Two ancient and diametrically opposed answers dramatize the issue. For Aristotle, as we have seen, politics constituted a particularly favorable sphere for the realization of one's full humanity. When Aristotle said that "man is a political being," he meant in part that through political activity we can actualize our major potentialities. We are essentially united, in the sense that our essence, as expressed in virtues like courage, pride, and truthfulness, can be realized only by means of human relationships. The sum of all relationships is the state (or, more precisely, the *polis*) in that the state embraces and harmonizes all lesser groups. To become completely related to our fellow human beings requires conscious participation in the affairs of state, that is, in politics. In fine, Aristotle saw the possession of power, in company with other citizens, as providing an incomparable amplitude of life.

Aristotle was thinking both of virtue and of happiness. In modern times many people have regarded these as antithetical. For Aristotle, they were indivisible: political activity was at once duty and fulfillment.

Aristotle's views, however, apply only to political activity carried on in a good state. Aristotle saw no virtue or happiness in being, or supporting, a tyrant. True political activity is possible only where there is self-government and the rule of law.

A completely different position from Aristotle's was taken by another great thinker of antiquity, Epicurus (342?–270 B.C.). Having seen the downfall of the city-state, Epicurus sought serenity in a life of gentle pleasure and minimal pain. His viewpoint was summed up in the injunction "Live unknown." Epicurus was trying to deal with a general disorientation of life (not unlike the alienation of the present time), resulting from the passing of the city-state as a viable form of human life. In a world suddenly vast and strange, Epicurus wished to discover how a person might attain self-sufficiency and tranquillity. He was led, in his search, to repudiate the notion that "man is a political being." Politics means the very opposite of the good life; it means continuous vexation and daily dependence on others. Only in private life—a kind of tomb in the eyes of Aristotle—can a person find happiness and independence.

Today, an Epicurean observer of American life would say that those who seek political office, ascending perhaps from local and state posts to the summits of power in Washington, are foolish, for they will find only annoyance and anguish. He would equally condemn radical militants and activists, for they violate the rule of detachment as drastically as do members of the governing groups. An Epicurean would be unlikely to sympathize even with exhortations to vote. You might better concentrate on maintaining balance and peace in your own personal life, regardless of prevailing political conditions.

Aristotle and Epicurus stand at either end of a wide range of possible answers to the question of whether it is good to have power. Most Americans today would probably be unwilling to endorse either position. Many would probably say that wielding power may not improve a person's life in the sense of bringing fulfillment and happiness but nevertheless is a duty and so must at least improve a person morally. A position close to this was developed by the Stoics a century or more after the time of Epicurus and contributed to the political resoluteness needed to administer and defend the Roman Empire.

The Stoic conception of the universe as a divine order dictated the conscientious performance of the duties of one's station; each person should play a part, whatever the part might be. Political office should not be sought but should nevertheless be accepted by anyone led thereto in the normal course of affairs. A slave should accept a slave's lot, realizing that one's humanity cannot be destroyed by enslavement but only by failure to fulfill one's duties with a rational and imperturbable consciousness of taking part in the divine order of the cosmos. And once faced with political tasks, a person should perform them without being swayed by the uncertainties and discouragements that assail a conscientious person in a position of power; whatever the consequences, all is as it should be.

Whether or not this outlook is correct, we must admit that so austere an emphasis on duty might well prove useful in times of political trouble. Rome found it so, and perhaps times are coming when America will as well.

These three attitudes, the Aristotelian, the Epicurean, and the Stoic, all are relatively hopeful and constructive. The Epicurean and Stoic attitudes reflect disillusionment but tell us how to live well in spite of the evils surrounding us. There is a more cynical view, however, and in times as disturbed as ours, it is likely to have numerous adherents. According to this view, power may not be morally or socially beneficial but is eminently worth having, either for the opportunities it provides for a ruthless person to satisfy personal interests or merely for the pleasure and exhilaration of wielding it. We do not expect to find this attitude argued by philosophers but rather reflected in the lives of those too fully occupied with gaining and using power to have time for thinking and writing. To find it in the writings of a great thinker we must look beneath the surface.

As already noted, Machiavelli was not indifferent either to the ends sought by rulers or to the inherent morality of the means they employed. Success was not everything for Machiavelli. He was, however, deeply fascinated with power, so much so that he often evinced satisfaction with an adroit political maneuver and showed relatively little concern with either its ultimate consequences or its inherent morality. Moreover, the charm of power seems to have been enhanced, in Machiavelli's eyes, when it assumed violent and terrifying forms. While he did not explicitly defend the idea that power is an end in itself, much less the idea that it is merely a means for satisfying the private interests of the one who wields it, his writings do sometimes express the feeling that power is in some measure justified simply by the glory and excitement of political virtuosity.

Whether power is good for its possessors is a particularly pertinent question today. The politics of the twentieth century has been filled with confusion and violence; the problems facing modern governments are overwhelming in number and complexity; corruption has been rampant. It is far from clear that power is a source of happiness and fulfillment to those who wield it in any era. In the present era the possession of power seems an especially dubious privilege, particularly for those concerned with personal serenity and moral integrity. Thus, politics today often repels the most sensitive and honorable people and attracts those who seek above all wealth, fame, and power. Such a situation constitutes a crisis in the political order. If the best people spurn political power and the worst seize it eagerly, the conclusion that our troubles are bound to grow worse can hardly be avoided. How far these remarks apply to particular present-day societies can be debated, but it seems indisputable that they apply in some measure to many of them. Hence the significance of the question before us. Politics might become a realm of noble human activity could the principle that possessing power is good in the fullest sense of the word be established and become widely accepted. If this principle cannot be established, however, then pessimism—concerning not only the immediate future but human history as a whole—seems inescapable.

At any rate, let us assume that we have become convinced both of the practical necessity of power and of the moral legitimacy of wielding it. What about those subject to power? Why should they submit?

17 *Why Obey?*

To possess power is, at least superficially, honorable and glorious. To be without power and subject to the power of others, however, is at least superficially degrading. Why should a person accept such a position? This is one of the central questions in political thought; if it cannot be answered, then the entire political order, with all of its offices, laws, and dignities, is indefensible.

Another way of posing the question is to ask what makes power legitimate or what turns it from naked force into authority. Throughout history human beings have been offended by stark power, by a demand for obedience unsupported by any reference to moral right. But not very much has been required to overcome this feeling of offense; disobedience is dangerous, and a fragile claim to legitimacy may suffice to reconcile most people to subordination. Nevertheless, it is not just a handful of radicals or peculiarly conscientious people, such as Quakers, who ask why obedience is owed to a government. The self-respect of practically all human beings depends on assurance that the government they obey has a moral right to be obeyed.

Probably the oldest and most durable answer to this question is one that today seems absurd: the divine right of kings. Until just a few centuries ago most governments claimed their power was given them by God. This claim was made well before the rise of Christian societies. "From the beginning of history," writes the historian Christopher Dawson, "the king has been distinguished from the tyrant, the magistrate or the official by the possession of a *charisma* or divine mandate which sets him apart from other men."[3] One inference drawn from this principle was, of course, the requirement of absolute obedience. Political resistance was rebellion against the divine.

The concept of the divine right of kings, however, may seem an effort not to answer the question but to stifle it. Granted, power entails an immense moral strain for those subject to it, and it is not surprising that in religious ages people relieved this strain by conceiving of power as divinely sanctioned. The idea of divine right, nevertheless, is thoroughly irrational, not primarily because it is based on a religious premise, but because the premise—that God is—does not justify the conclusion. The idea that God has sanctified every government is no more necessitated by religious faith than is the idea that God has sanctified every revolution. One element in the durability of the idea that kings rule by divine right may well be the desire of governing classes to suppress an explosive question. Certainly the idea was not reached by open-minded inquiry and could not long withstand such inquiry.

A complete change of mind has apparently occurred in recent centuries. Worldliness and religious skepticism have rendered the principle of divine right wholly implausible, and the ideal of personal freedom has shifted the burden of proof, in questions of obedience, to the side of the government. At the same time, rising self-confidence and political awareness among the masses have given

---

[3]Christopher Dawson, *Religion and Culture* (New York: Meridian Books, 1948), p. 109. The italics are Dawson's.

disobedience history-making potentialities. Thus the question *Why obey?* has been asked with mounting and ominous insistence.

The simplest defense of obedience, aside from the theory of divine right, may be that contained in the idea of consent. As Locke put it, "Men being . . . by Nature, all free, equal and independent, no one can be put out of this Estate, and subjected to the Political Power of another, without his own *Consent.*"[4] A person is not obliged to obey unless he has voluntarily agreed to do so. At one point, at least, Locke seems to imply that not only does the founding of a government require consent but that every governmental act significantly affecting a person's life or rights requires consent, for he writes that "the *Supream Power cannot take* from any Man any part of his *Property* without his own consent."[5] If this injunction were followed literally, payment of taxes would be voluntary. Indeed, if we are under no obligation to obey unless we consent to do so in each particular case, then strictly speaking we are under no obligation to obey at all.

The theory that political obligation is based on consent subordinates government to freedom. Even assuming that Locke did not mean to go so far as to require consent for every particular governmental act, his general point is that nothing can be rightfully demanded of us that does not accord with each one's uncoerced and conscious will. Not surprisingly, some political thinkers sought to formulate a doctrine of obedience with less anarchistic overtones. One result is the theory of the "general will," which was definitively formulated by Rousseau, although it had been implicit in other political philosophies, such as those of Plato and Aristotle.

According to this theory, the obligation to obey does not depend on a prior act of consent (although it happens that Rosseau did incorporate the idea of consent into his political theory). A government deserves obedience if its commands conform to what Rosseau called the general will. What is the general will? Or, to put the question in a more convenient form, what qualities make a will general? Not simply its being the will of everyone, for this would

---

[4]John Locke, *Two Treatises of Government,* ed. Peter Laslett (Cambridge: Cambridge University Press, 1960), p. 348. The italics are Locke's.

[5]*Two Treatises,* p. 378. The italics are Locke's (as is the spelling of "supreme").

make the theory of the general will only another form of the theory of consent.

Rousseau explicitly distinguished between "the will of all" and the general will, and asserted that they often differ greatly. The will of all, he wrote, is "no more than a sum of particular wills."[6] The distinctive quality of the general will, according to Rousseau, is that it "considers only the common interest."[7] For a will to be general, then, it must be directed toward the good of everyone. It is not necessary to ask now whether there can be such a good, a value shared equally by every member of society. This depends on whether, in answer to Question 1, human beings are essentially united. The point is that the theory of the general will tells us that a government can legitimately claim obedience only when its commands represent the true, ultimate interest of all the people.

Rousseau acknowledged that the people are subject to error, so that the will of all is not necessarily the general will, which has led to the idea that a single ruling person, even an absolute dictator, might represent the general will. Accordingly, some writers have claimed to see in regimes such as Lenin's and Hitler's a Rousseauean spirit. This, however, is based on a misreading of Rousseau. In spite of all the complexities of *The Social Contract*, Rousseau's own words seem quite conclusive. "The general will," he wrote, "to be really such, must be general in its object as well as its essence . . . it must both come from all and apply to all."[8] Thus, while the will of the people may be mistaken, a will directed toward the common good is not the general will unless it also is the will of the people.

Rousseau was not so unrealistic as to demand unanimity in every decision, however. He did not mean it literally when he said that the general will must "come from all." He was willing to accept a majority, with its size depending on circumstances, as a surrogate for "all." Government need not depend in every act on unanimous consent. This seems reasonable enough. However, the whole idea of the general will introduces a possibility that is startling but quite important. This is, that in obeying the general will, even under duress, you are free. Obedience and freedom, usually assumed to be opposites, in these circumstances are identical. How can this be? The an-

[6] *Social Contract*, p. 26.
[7] *Social Contract*, p. 26.
[8] *Social Contract*, p. 29.

swer is logical. You are free, presumably, when you do what you really want to do; in turn, what you really want to do is realize your own ultimate good. If you live in a just society, however, your own good is identical with the common good; and the common good is the object of the general will. Hence you follow your own real will—you do what you *really* want to do—when you obey the general will. The conclusion is inescapable: in obeying the general will you are free. This would be true even if you felt threatened or crushed by that will.

This inference is stated so starkly in order to make the basic theory clear, not to induce the reader to reject it. If the theory be rejected, it should be only after careful reflection, for Rousseau's view is not absurd. It is a restatement of the ancient conviction that we are essentially united and hence are human—and in that sense free—not in following some wayward individual impulse but in playing the part of active and loyal citizens. And this is true even if we are imprisoned, so long as we are justly imprisoned; and it is true even if some great sacrifice, such as life, lost perhaps in battle, is required of us, so long as the requirement accords with the will and the good of the whole people.

The main problem presented by the question of obedience is the reconciliation of obedience with liberty. "To renounce liberty," as Rousseau asserted, "is to renounce being a man."[9] But the essence of government is to demand obedience and thus, apparently, a renunciation of liberty. How then can even the best government mean anything but the destruction of the humanity of those living under it? Anarchists claim that it cannot. The theories of consent and the general will, on the other hand, both attempt to justify government by showing how a person can obey and still be free. The principal difference between the two theories is that one conceives of freedom only in terms of conscious will and tries to legitimize obedience by tracing it back to an act of consent; the other conceives of freedom in terms of a will that may not be fully conscious, since in willing my own welfare I may not know what political measures will promote it. The theory of the general will maintains that even though a law does not rest on explicit consent, it may yet command what contributes to my real good and thus may enhance my freedom.

[9] *Social Contract*, p. 9.

Both theories involve serious difficulties. The theory of consent is simple and comprehensible on the surface, but it is hard to see how it could be put into practice. It cannot mean that the legitimacy of every governmental command depends on a separate act of consent; this would be incompatible with stable, effective government. Thus, it must mean that the legitimacy of each governmental command follows from some prior act of consent. The trouble is that a command rarely has this kind of consent behind it; people do not normally give their clear and specific consent to the government over them. In reading Locke, one can sense the embarrassment this difficulty causes him. In a passage on taxation, he asserts that when property is taken from a citizen, it must be "with his own Consent, *i.e.*, the Consent of the Majority."[10] Thus, individual consent is equated with majority consent. But there is no manifest justification for doing this, and it merely sharpens the question of obedience: why obey the majority? In another passage, Locke asserts that a person gives tacit consent to a government merely by traveling freely on its roads or simply by being within its territory.[11] Judged by this standard, however, the most despised tyrannies have rested on the consent of the governed.

A further question is this: is a person bound by consent that was given in ignorance or confusion? Was a young German who swore allegiance to Hitler when he first came to power morally obliged to obey every command of the Nazi government? These are a few of the questions provoked by the theory of consent.

The theory of the general will, on the other hand, is scarcely free of difficulties. It implies that a person might, as stated in a notorious phrase of Rousseau's, be "forced to be free." You might be free in doing, under the supervision of the police, something that you do not at all want to do. You might even be free in prison. Hegel argued, in the spirit of Rousseau, that criminals really will their own punishment, which suggests that a government wisely and justly carrying out its penal responsibilities liberates people by locking them up. This idea is not at all nonsensical, any more than it is nonsensical to speak of a criminal as being enslaved by an evil will. But the idea gives one pause. Is there perhaps some dangerous sophistry concealed in the equation of force and freedom?

[10] *Two Treatises*, p. 380.
[11] *Two Treatises*, p. 366.

Another difficulty involved in the theory of the general will is somewhat like the difficulty just pointed out in the theory of consent; it cannot be readily applied. True, government in accordance with the general will is not as far beyond the realm of possibility as government literally by consent. Nevertheless, the theory of the general will, as Rousseau conceived it, requires active and continuous popular participation in a process of legislation that produces just laws and a just order of society. None of the Western democracies comes close to meeting this standard.

This fact makes it apparent that the major theories of obedience do not set our minds at rest and enable us to obey the governments over us with good conscience. On the contrary, they cast the legitimacy of these governments into doubt. In telling us when to obey, the theories of consent and the general will also tell us when not to obey; and the standards they set are very demanding. Hence they are doctrines not only of obedience, but also of disobedience and revolution. They have proved this in practice; Locke's philosophy played an important role in the American Revolution and Rousseau's in the French Revolution. Today for these philosophies to be applied rigorously and seriously would be destabilizing. Why, then, aren't the Western nations, condemned by the major theories of legitimacy, seething with revolutionary fervor?

The primary reasons, of course, are that revolution is an extremely dangerous and difficult act and that most people in the Western nations are (whether they should be or not) reasonably contented. Popular contentment is due above all to material abundance; flatly contradicting the predictions of Marx, the progress of industrialism has undermined revolutionary will. In nations like the United States and Great Britain, exceedingly few desire revolution; and with the governments commanding highly sophisticated administrative and police organizations, revolutionary efforts have scarcely the slightest chance of success. It is not just popular contentment or stark impracticality, however, that stands in the way of revolution. For the time being, at least, revolution has been discredited. This has happened because the most dramatic revolutions witnessed in the twentieth century all have ended tragically. All have brought into power tyrannical governments. There has arisen in response a widespread feeling that revolution transcends human capacities, that it expresses the kind of arrogance the Greeks called *hubris* and considered a forerunner of disaster. This feeling may be ill-founded, but there is little doubt that it exists, and it reinforces the stability brought by industrial prosperity.

The prevailing indifference and skepticism concerning revolution, however defensible or indefensible in general, leave the whole issue of obedience unresolved and place us in a dubious relationship with governmental power. Most people in the Western nations are normally acquiescent, but their acquiescence is habitual rather than thoughtful and reflects little respect for their governments. If they think about the matter, they are more or less conscious that the governments over them do not measure up to the highest standards of legitimacy, but for all of the reasons cited earlier they do not contemplate revolution or, indeed, any form of principled, as distinguished from personally expedient, disobedience. But this is a morally unsatisfactory situation. Obeying always and as a matter of course means nothing less than abandoning selfhood; the center of choice and responsibility is shifted from the self to those who command. Moreover, one is implicated morally in the injustices done by government and society, for obedience is support; only through obedience do governments and societies stand. Such considerations are probably not as far from the minds of ordinary citizens as one might suppose. A vague sense that the moral stakes are high is what makes most people desire some assurance that the government they obey is legitimate.

Is there any way we might recover and affirm a sense of responsibility in matters of obedience and disobedience? It is doubtful that this should be done by trying to reanimate the revolutionary spirit of 1776 (America) and 1789 (France); the contemporary sense that a revolution is usually a tragedy has much to commend it. And to advocate casual and persistent disobedience, even without revolutionary intentions, would be irresponsible. Civilization depends on obedience being normal and disobedience exceptional; otherwise, the fundamental order undergirding a cultivated life would break down. Nevertheless, obeying is a serious responsibility, and it bears on every human being, even on those—the majority— who never think of it. A revolutionary spirit carries a consciousness of that responsibility, and the passing of the revolutionary spirit, however realistic, is not without a moral price. The question, *Why obey?* occurs only to human beings, not to beasts. Hence, never to ask the question is literally bestial.

These reflections drive us irresistibly to the idea of civil disobedience. Does that idea tell us how we might recover and affirm a full sense of political responsibility? Civil disobedience can be contrasted both with casual and with criminal disobedience. Unlike casual disobedience, it is selective and purposeful. One disobeys a law that is considered unjust or symbolic of an unjust condition; and one disobeys in the hope of furthering a political purpose, such as changing the law. Unlike criminal disobedience, civil disobedience aims at a public, not merely personal, value, and it affirms the principle of law by acquiescing in the penalties attached to disobedience. Practicing civil disobedience requires not only courage but political sophistication—a knowledge of techniques and strategies. A solitary individual is not likely to possess the requisite knowledge, and a significant measure of civil disobedience is therefore not likely to emerge merely from scattered personal decisions. A movement, or some kind of collective effort, is needed. Should a civil disobedience movement be mounted? Should thoughtful people begin mastering and spreading the knowledge on which civil disobedience depends? Would this help to revitalize the question *Why obey?* and thus render the state of obedience—which is no doubt normally incumbent on us—more thoughtful, responsible, and fully human than it is at present?

SUGGESTED READINGS

Plato. *Apology*
———. *Crito*
———. *The Republic*
Aristotle. *Politics*, Books I–IV
Marcus Aurelius. *Meditations*
Saint Augustine. *The Political Writings of St. Augustine*, ed. by Henry Paolucci, Chapters 1–3
Machiavelli, Niccolò. *The Prince*
Hobbes, Thomas. *Leviathan*, First and Second Parts
Rousseau, Jean Jacques. *The Social Contract*
Paine, Thomas. *The Rights of Man*
Mill, John Stuart. *Representative Government*
Marx, Karl. *The Civil War in France*
Green, Thomas Hill. *Lectures on the Principles of Political Obligation*

Tolstoy, Leo. *Resurrection*
Niebuhr, Reinhold. *Moral Man and Immoral Society*
————. *The Children of Light and the Children of Darkness*
Tillich, Paul. *Love, Power, and Justice*
Arendt, Hannah. *The Origins of Totalitarianism*
————. *The Human Condition*
Márquez, Gabriel Garcia. *The Autumn of the Patriarch*
Kundera, Milan. *The Unbearable Lightness of Being*

Chapter 5

LIMITS ON POWER

Because all power is morally dubious—hard to justify and likely to corrupt—the confinement of power to its proper bounds is a central problem of civilization. Power constantly tends to become arbitrary and limitless, and tyranny is one of the ancient afflictions of our collective existence. But never in history has power been so boundless and destructive as in the totalitarian dictatorships of the twentieth century. These regimes have made it plain that, contrary to Hobbes, not only the lack but the lawlessness of a central power renders life "solitary, poor, nasty, brutish, and short." To ask about the proper limits on power and how these limits can be enforced is to inquire how life can be decent and civilized.

Limits on power are basically of two kinds: moral and constitutional. Moral limits are those deriving from moral law, or from what is believed to be moral law; their efficacy depends solely on moral convictions. For a government to refrain from using murder as an instrument of foreign policy, even when murder is within the scope of its legal powers, would exemplify respect for a moral limit. Constitutional limits may derive ultimately from moral law, but what makes them constitutional is their embodiment in a basic written law—a law that takes precedence over all others and is upheld by society and enforced in the courts. This law may be represented by one supreme document, as in America, or it may be merely the content of a body of customs, statutes, court decisions, and historical documents, as in Great Britain. A constitutional government is one that is limited by such a law.

We shall discuss both moral and constitutional limits, beginning with moral limits because they must in some sense underlie constitutional limits. First we shall consider what may be the oldest, most fundamental question concerning the relationship of morals and politics.

18 Should Governments Be Under the Same Moral Limits as Individuals?

One great political thinker, Machiavelli, has become notorious for arguing that they should not, because they cannot. We have already noted Machiavelli's belief that there can be no order among human beings and nothing accomplished in human affairs without power. A companion belief in Machiavelli's mind was that effective use of power is incompatible with strict observance of the moral law. No ideals can be realized without doing evil. To perceive the somewhat tragic coloring of Machiavelli's argument, it is necessary to understand that Machiavelli never expressed indifference to the moral law and never glorified evil. The greatness of Machiavelli's thought depends on the tension inherent in the idea that there is a moral law but that rulers on occasion must break that law.

No such necessity, however, can be claimed by private individuals. Rulers must sometimes be immoral in order to establish and preserve the state; for the sake of the same end, subjects must always be moral. Social order would collapse if private individuals considered themselves free to break the moral law when their interests require it. The political universe thus is morally unique.

By setting forth this point of view, Machiavelli gained one of the most unsavory reputations in the history of thought. Shakespeare referred to him as "the murderous Machiavel," and among the synonyms of "Machiavellian" in Roget's *Thesaurus* are "false," "crafty," and "dishonest." What is most striking about the opposing arguments, however, is how faint and infrequent they are. So far as I am aware, the chief works of political thought contain no comprehensive and systematic argument, answering to Machiavelli's, for the same uncompromising morality among rulers that is expected of private individuals. One great thinker who disagreed with Machiavelli was Immanuel Kant (1724–1804), but in none of his major works does he systematically take issue with the Machiavellian argument. Many thinkers have believed that the health of the political order depends on the moral rectitude of its members. But Machiavelli too believed this; his writings abound in expressions of admiration for the honor and probity of the ancient Romans.

Where Machiavelli differs from the others is in saying explicitly what they seldom deny: while political order depends on respect for moral standards, it depends also on the capacity of rulers occasionally to violate those standards. In view of the silence of the great political thinkers concerning so unsettling an idea, one wonders whether it is Machiavelli's chief distinction to have divulged a distressing truth (one writer speaks of his "appalling sincerity")—a truth others have been reluctant to acknowledge.

Opposition to Machiavelli, then, comes less from political philosophy than from common moral convictions. But can people with these convictions hold their ground in the face of political reality? Let us consider lying as an example. Anyone who is repelled by the evasive and deceptive speech common in the political world might consider these two questions: (1) Could a government operate successfully without often concealing its plans and withholding much of the information at its disposal and to this extent practicing deception? (2) Should a government refuse to lie outright if it might thus gain some great good like ending a war or helping an underprivileged group? It is possible to answer both questions affirmatively, but that is not the side of plausibility and common sense. Rather, these questions suggest the Machiavellian conclusion that we cannot demand from rulers the same candor and truthfulness we expect of personal associates.

But having moved this far toward Machiavelli, we should ask whether *every* moral limit is conditional on political circumstances. If rulers may lie to reach political goals, may they kill? Machiavelli said yes, defending not only political deceit but also political murder. But if we go this far, what is left of ideals and conscience? Is it in the nature of things that profoundly evil means can be used to attain good ends? The Communist regimes of Russia and China have been willing to engage in large-scale killing for the sake of perfect and lasting community, but neither has attained, or even approached, its goal.

Underlying this question is an issue concerning the nature of moral law. To define this issue we may usefully employ a distinction made earlier—that between moral absolutism and moral relativism. The former, let us recall, is the theory that there is a moral law, usually said to derive from nature or from God and independent of the interests and opinions both of individuals and of societies. The latter, moral relativism, is the theory that morality is determined by and is in that sense relative to some variable circumstance, such as the desires of the individual or the needs of society. Your choice between these alternatives predisposes you to one side or the other of the question as to whether governments should be under the same moral restraints as private individuals. Absolutism indicates the same moral law for everyone, in public and private life alike, whereas relativism opens the way to distinctions between governmental and private morality.

Before exploring this theme, however, it would be well to recall a cautionary note sounded earlier in this book; that is, that issues in the field of political theory can seldom be conclusively settled merely by making a direct inference from some philosophical principle. Thus, in the present instance, it might be argued that governments must sometimes break a moral law (incumbent invariably on individuals) that is in some sense nevertheless absolute. For example, we are apt to think of "Thou shalt not kill" as an absolute law; we are also apt to assume that under certain conditions, as in war, governments may justifiably kill. You can object that absolute means unconditional and thus that the word should not be attached to a law that must under certain conditions be broken. But surely acts such as killing and lying are evil regardless of the circumstances in which they are committed, and in that sense the laws against them are absolute. And it is even thinkable that one who kills or lies is in some sense guilty even though circumstances made those acts unavoidable.

On the other side, whether relativism opens the way for an affirmative answer to the question of the right of rulers to ignore moral limits depends on exactly what the moral law is relative to. If it is relative to each individual's desires and circumstances, then those who possess power are not subject to the same moral restraints as those who do not; but if morality is relative to the nation or the culture, then both rulers and ruled may logically be subject to identical laws.

These remarks are intended as warnings against oversimplification, however, not as indications of the way people usually think or of the main logical forces inherent in moral absolutism and relativism. There is no doubt that moral absolutism tends to bar any distinction between the morality of politics and the morality of private life. It affirms a single all-embracing moral order, thus placing governments under the same moral restraints that are incumbent on private individuals, so that any violation of these restraints requires a special justification. And even such a justification may not relieve from all guilt those who violate the moral law. Dietrich Bonhoeffer, who took part in the resistance against Nazism in Germany, felt himself guilty for conspiring to kill Hitler even though he was doing only what he felt he had to do. From this standpoint, politics may be viewed as a sphere of moral tension and even of moral tragedy. It still must be viewed, however, as having a uniform and authoritative moral structure.

Moral relativism wonderfully simplifies matters. It allows the argument that political leaders and private citizens inhabit two different moral universes or even that political leaders are not within any moral universe at all. For example, if morality were held to concern only relationships among citizens of the same nation, then international relations would not be subject to any moral rules; political leaders would be free, in their diplomatic and military activities, to act without compunction as circumstances dictate, responsible only to the moral bonds uniting them to their own subjects. Moral relativism might also take the form of the argument that possession of power entails liberation from all moral rules whatever. In this situation, political leaders would not need to feel morally inhibited in any sphere of activity. For reasons of state they might kill and mislead even their fellow-citizens.

In a sense, moral relativism clears the air. It does not subject political leaders to the terrible strain of acknowledging the authority of certain moral rules and then being forced to break them. They can act, with clear consciences, under their own separate rules. The shadows of moral strain and failure that are cast over political life by moral absolutism are dispelled. In general, the atmosphere of moral absolutism can be heavy, even ominous. Moral rules are taken with utmost seriousness, and infractions of them are not apt to be regarded as mere mistakes, easily corrected and appropriately passed over and forgotten. The very term "absolute" is indicative of something that is unyielding, something unconcerned with varying human temperaments and situations. Defying, or transgressing against, the absolute may result in a fate of such ultimate and unlimited gravity that to name it fittingly the word "damnation" is needed. Moral relativism dissipates the absolutist atmosphere of gloom. It goes readily with the sense that human beings, while fallible, are not really wicked, and that they never suffer anything so ultimate and transcendental as damnation. Moral relativism does not bind someone trying to work out a practical problem—a diplomat, say, or a political leader—in the steel shackles of moral absolutes.

This may at first strike the reader as wholesome. As can easily be seen, however, there are serious risks in granting rulers such freedom. If "power tends to corrupt" under the best of circumstances, then surely this tendency is enhanced where power means liberation from all moral limits, or at least from all unconditional moral limits. Further, if government is exempt from the moral standards that apply to ordinary citizens, then it apparently is exempt from their moral judgment. And if government is exempt from their moral judgment it must be, for the most part, exempt from their political judgment as well. And if that is so, it is unchecked and irresponsible.

Can you perhaps circumvent a host of moral dangers and philosophical difficulties by simply insisting on the same moral standards for everyone and refusing to grant any exceptions? Perhaps you can. But this possibility may invite an idealistic distortion of reality. The political scene in the twentieth century has displayed so many paradoxes and terrors that we are bound to doubt that political realities can be dealt with as unequivocally as the moral law, in its majesty and simplicity, seems to demand.

Today, the question of whether governments should be under the same moral limits as individuals is put forcefully to Americans by their role as citizens of a superpower in a world of war and brutal factional and international rivalry. There is, for example, the issue of assassination. Amid the conflicts and tensions of power politics, a nation often has an interest in the death of a foreign figure—a leader, perhaps, or a secret agent. The ax-murder of Trotsky, who had been exiled by the Soviet government and was living in Mexico, by a Stalinist agent is only the most lurid example from recent times of official assassination. It is public knowledge that the United States has attempted, and carried out, acts of assassination in recent decades. How should Americans feel about this fact? Relativists will perhaps be undisturbed, for in their minds there may be no moral laws governing the relations of one nation with another. Machiavellians may be disturbed but will nevertheless consent in principle (in principle only, since any particular act of assassination would have to be politically necessary in order to be justified). But anyone who believes in absolute moral laws will be tempted to say that a nation should in no circumstances whatever engage in murder. Would an absolute ban of that kind make sense? Would it make sense in all circumstances whatever, for example, even if the very safety of the nation were in peril? If a nation is willing to kill enemy soldiers in battle, as every nation must be, is it logical for it to recoil from killing, however it can, foreign civilians who seriously threaten its interests?

An issue weighing more heavily on many minds than the morality of assassination is the morality of nuclear war. The end of the Cold War has changed our images of how a nuclear war might come about and be waged; no longer do we envision it mainly as a conflict of superpowers. Unhappily, however, the end of the Cold War has not lessened the likelihood of eventual nuclear conflict. Indeed, it has enhanced it by furthering the process of nuclear proliferation. We are therefore in no position to cease thinking about the question of when—if ever—the use of nuclear weapons can be justified.

Americans have a personal interest in this issue, since they are the only people who have ever used nuclear weapons in combat. The bombs dropped on Hiroshima and Nagasaki took over two hundred thousand lives, most of them civilian lives. Is America's use of the bombs morally defensible? The argument over Hiroshima and

Nagasaki begins with the question of necessity. Couldn't the bombs have been dropped on an uninhabited area? If it was not necessary that cities be the targets, few would defend the President's act. But suppose that devastation in uninhabited areas would not have swayed the Japanese leaders, and that hundreds of thousands of lives—both American and Japanese—would have been lost in the invasion of the Japanese home islands. One might argue on those grounds that it was necessary to bomb Hiroshima and Nagasaki. Might one argue, in response, that on moral grounds that "necessity" should have been rejected?—that the bombing was mass murder and unjustifiable on any grounds? If so, then shouldn't the United States have refrained from countless other acts of violence committed during the war with ordinary weapons: the bombing of Tokyo and Berlin, for example? Would you say yes even if such restraint would have prevented the United States from winning the war? On the other hand, if you sanction the bombing of Hiroshima and Nagasaki, aren't you accepting the principle that governments may rightfully employ terror against civilians? It isn't easy either to affirm or deny the invariable subordination of governments to moral law.

Stated broadly, the question is whether waging nuclear war can under any circumstances be a moral act. During the Middle Ages, political thinkers developed the concept of "just war." It was argued that war was just when it met certain conditions, such as having a reasonable purpose and having prospects of attaining that purpose without inordinate destruction. The principal thrust of the concept was that war can be moral. It is often asked today whether the concept of just war hasn't been nullified by nuclear weapons. How can a nuclear war be moral? It seems that a nuclear war would have to be purposeless, since at the end nothing would remain—no civilization, perhaps no human beings at all. What ends could justify such means? What moral calculus could warrant universal annihilation? The legitimacy of nuclear war must appear doubtful even in the eyes of Machiavellians and moral relativists.

If the legitimacy of nuclear war is doubtful, however, then so is the very possession of nuclear weapons, for such possession is pointless unless accompanied by an implicit threat to use them in certain circumstances. This issue has been extensively debated, in connection mainly with the so-called policy of deterrence which the United States followed throughout the Cold War. That policy consisted primarily in the building up of a vast arsenal of nuclear weapons and in threatening, albeit more tacitly than openly, to use them if attacked by like weapons. Can such a policy possibly be moral? Would such a policy be moral if practiced by presidents who pretended to be ready to strike yet were secretly resolved never to do so—not even in response to a nuclear attack on the United States? Or is so paradoxical, secretive, and restrained an attitude impossible for human beings to maintain for very long? On the other hand, what alternative is there to a policy of deterrence? Can a responsible person soberly urge the United States to disarm itself in a world where the number of nations with nuclear weapons is steadily mounting?

Such questions do not lead quickly to clear answers. They do, however, make clear the urgency of moral reflection. In the unparalleled crisis of civilization to which nuclear arms have brought us, one is not seriously tempted to abandon all moral considerations. That would be like abandoning the helm and all navigational aids during a storm at sea. To understand the relationship of governments to moral law may literally be a matter of life and death.

Pondering the moral limits on power leads to the matter of constitutional limits. These are different, as we have seen, in that the former rest on moral consciousness, the latter on law. Both, however, give rise to similar doubts when imposed on the possessors of power—doubts about the wisdom of subjecting governments to invariable limits without regard to variable circumstances. Hence the question that follows.

19 *Should Governments in All Circumstances Be Under Constitutional Limits?*

The issue has been forcefully posed by the twentieth-century conflict between democratic and totalitarian nations. During World War II and the early stages of the Cold War, it was tempting to see the democracies as altogether good and the dictatorships as altogether bad. But there came a realization that good and evil are not so neatly distributed. Although the dictatorships still look very bad, we cannot quite say that the democracies look very good. Not only is there much evil in those countries where government is under constitutional limits; the evil appears in some cases to be protected by the limits. For example, in the United States, the richest country in history, many people are hungry and homeless. Why this is so, of course, is not absolutely clear. It can be asked, nevertheless, whether it would be so if numerous substantive and procedural restraints laid down in the Constitution did not render it virtually impossible for the government to bring about any appreciable redistribution of wealth and income.

No political idea in the West has greater authority than constitutionalism. For more than two thousand years there has been a remarkably wide and stable consensus that government ought to be carried on within publicly known and enforceable limits. Perhaps the most influential modern expression of this consensus is found in the writings of John Locke. But Locke is only one of several great modern thinkers who have been firmly committed constitutionalists. Locke's views, moreover, were drawn from a solidly established medieval tradition, itself the outgrowth of an ancient Greek and Roman constitutionalist tradition. Few other ideas can claim so impressive a background. Time after time, from the beginning of political thought, lawless government has been condemned as monstrous and unnatural.

The opposition to this tradition, however, is substantial—in the quality of those representing it, at least, if not in their numbers. No great thinkers have actually advocated totalitarianism, that is, governmental control of every detail of life, but several have been enemies of constitutionalism. Four stand out in the history of thought, and each represents a different motive.

1. Plato opposed constitutionalism because of his faith in the wisdom of a few. Later in life, when he faced the improbability that the wise could ever gain power, he endorsed constitutionalism. But earlier, when he seemingly believed that philosophers might become rulers, he opposed the subjection of government to preestablished limitations. He did this on the logical grounds that perfect

wisdom is quite competent to decide for itself how far its power should reach. Plato likened the philosopher-ruler to a doctor, who is not hampered by prior rules but in each particular case can prescribe precisely what the health of the patient requires.

Today we do not have Plato's faith in philosophers. But we do accept the Platonic ideal in a somewhat different form; we assume, or many of us do, that our social problems can be solved by experts. It is scientific and technological intelligence, rather than philosophical, that commands our trust. Thus we may logically ask whether America, with a government confined by limitations established in the eighteenth century, can attack such problems as poverty and urban disorder with the full resources of twentieth-century social and physical science. The American Constitution makes it next to impossible for a scientific plan to be uncompromisingly applied to any major social problem. This is partly owing to the procedural forms for decision making that are inherent in constitutionalism and that the American Constitution imposes. These forms ensure that every measure finally decided upon embodies a great number of compromises; these compromises may render the measure acceptable to the various interests affected by it, but they inevitably rob it of scientific integrity. Moreover, beyond procedural limitations are substantive limitations. Under a constitutional government, people cannot be forced to move, alter their living habits, take certain jobs, or do any number of things that science might deem necessary for solving social problems.

It is not too much to say that constitutionalism and scientific government are incompatible. Which is of greater importance? This is the question Plato puts before us.

2. Hobbes opposed constitutionalism because of his pessimistic appraisal of human nature. Many passages in Hobbes's writings show that he did not desire or even envision the possibility of anything like modern totalitarianism. Nevertheless, he regarded human beings as far too restless and selfish, too inherently chaotic, to afford governments that were barred absolutely from certain areas of life. Hobbes's views on religious toleration exemplify this attitude. While far from being a dogmatist wishing to impose a single set of beliefs on everyone, he thought that government must have the power to regulate religious creeds and forms of worship. An in-

violable rule of toleration would invite a reopening of "the war of all against all."

In quiet American suburbs today Hobbes may seem a mere doctrinaire pessimist. But look beyond the suburbs: are not the cities, with their poverty and racial tensions, Hobbesian worlds? Is not the whole globe Hobbesian, divided as it is among suspicious, heavily armed nations?

The impact of such conditions on constitutional government is apparent in society today. Some people, looking to safety of life and property, demand that police be allowed to deal with criminal suspects with whatever harshness and guile are necessary for uncovering and suppressing crime; certainly they should not be bound by every rule a careful judge might find implicit in the Constitution. A very Hobbesian demand! Hobbesian sentiments are also behind the willingness of many people—those, for example, who oppose all congressional restrictions on a president's power to wage war—to set aside constitutional limits in foreign affairs. The principles applied to domestic crime and to international conflict are the same: order is prior to all other values, and in some circumstances order depends on authoritarian rule.

3. If Plato opposed constitutionalism out of faith in the few, Rousseau did so out of faith in the many. Granted, such a statement must be severely qualified. Rousseau never explicitly attacked constitutional government. Moreover, he was passionately committed to one aspect of constitutionalism—the principle of government by law. He held that no command of the sovereign populace was valid unless it took the form of law. (The idea of government by law is constitutional because it implies a certain limitation on government—it must always adhere to the form of law. It is only one aspect of constitutionalism, however, because, while adhering to the form of law, a government might regulate religion, speech, and every other individual activity.) Nevertheless, the example of Rousseau demonstrates that government by the people can take on a totalitarian flavor. Just as Plato assumed that no human agency had the wisdom or right to restrain the philosopher-rulers, so Rousseau held that no human agency could properly impose limitations on the people except the people themselves. Rousseau seems to envision a commonwealth in which the lives of individuals are

absorbed into the common life and regulated in every detail by the popular will. Rousseau calls for a "civil religion," for example, "a civil profession of faith of which the Sovereign should fix the articles, not exactly as religious dogmas, but as social sentiments without which a man cannot be a good citizen or a faithful subject."[1] Rousseau demands that anyone refusing to subscribe to the articles of this faith be banished and that anyone who does subscribe to them and then "behaves as if he does not believe them" should be put to death.

Democratic totalitarianism is remote from the spirit and the structure of the American Constitution, but during the sixties the actions of militant students often had a totalitarian flavor. In campus uprisings the normal proceedings of universities were disrupted, opponents were shouted down, and "nonnegotiable demands" were the order of the day. Student gatherings were often characterized by an impassioned unanimity that may have been in some sense democratic but, in its intolerance of disagreement and its lack of restraint, was far from constitutional.

Social critics have often asserted that the established pattern of restraints, both within universities and in society at large, is designed to preserve the status quo, along with inequalities and injustices that ought to be destroyed. Perhaps this is so. However, the assertion raises rather serious questions. Is constitutionalism harmful, rather than valuable, when unaccompanied by justice? Is constitutionalism a lesser value than justice?

4. In asking these questions, we have come upon a fourth possible reason for opposing constitutionalism: it stands in the way of justice. A great many powerful people in our time have thought this. Perhaps the most influential and gifted of them was Vladimir Ilyich Lenin (1870–1924), the principal creator (with Trotsky) of the 1917 Bolshevik Revolution and of the Soviet state. Lenin had studied thoroughly, and accepted almost unreservedly, the doctrines of Marx. Hence his basic principles were democratic; the very purpose of overthrowing capitalism was to give liberty and power

---

[1]Jean Jacques Rousseau, *The Social Contract and Discourses,* trans. with an introduction by G. D. H. Cole (New York: Dutton, 1950), p. 139.

to the people. But Lenin had inherited Marx's cynical view of Western constitutionalism (it only masked the limitless power of the ruling class), and, in addition, he discovered something Marx had not seen: working people did not spontaneously become revolutionary as capitalism advanced, but rather, they developed an inclination to compromise with the upper classes and to accept the continuance of capitalism so long as they benefited from occasional improvements in wages and working conditions. In Lenin's words, they developed "trade-union consciousness" rather than revolutionary determination. The conclusion that Lenin drew was simple and daring, and it was fateful for modern civilization. The working class could not be allowed to develop spontaneously. It had to be aroused and disciplined by an absolutely dedicated and united elite of revolutionaries. This elite, "the vanguard of the proletariat," would lead the working class first in overthrowing capitalism and then in forcibly suppressing the last remnants of capitalism, thus laying the foundations for universal liberty and authentic democracy. This was the philosophy of the Communist Party, which Lenin founded and led.

Lenin's outlook is reminiscent in some ways of both Plato's and Rousseau's. Lenin's elite, like Plato's, is scientific. True, Lenin's conception of science, derived from dialectical materialism, was very different from Plato's; but Communist revolutionaries, like philosopher-rulers, were assumed to understand perfectly the determining forces and the final ends of human existence. Although Lenin was an active revolutionary during all of his adult life, he always applied himself to theoretical questions with intense earnestness. Lenin's outlook is reminiscent of Rousseau's in that the ultimate aim was democracy. Indeed, Lenin's vision of democracy was more sweeping than Rousseau's; government itself would finally disappear and the people would rule without the relatively slight restraints inherent in the very existence of government. This expectation, however, signals one way in which Lenin differed from both Plato and Rousseau—that he did not believe in government at all; he was an anarchist (despite the ironic fact that he was also the founder of the modern totalitarian state).

Lenin dramatically represents, and did much to create, or at least to spread, a view widely accepted in the twentieth century—a view that prevails far beyond the boundaries of Marxism. This is the view that constitutionalism (and democracy as well) depends on a certain degree of industrial development and distributive justice; it is futile to ask for constitutional safeguards in countries that are nonindustrial, poor, and governed by oppressive landowning oligarchies. The conclusion usually drawn is that agrarian nations must pass through a transitional period—a period in which the ruling oligarchy is overthrown and eradicated, a degree of industrialization is effected, and wealth is redistributed. While these things are occurring, it is not only appropriate, but necessary, to dispense with constitutionalism. Countless scholars and students—many of them not Marxists or Leninists—share these assumptions.

Given the strength and prevalence of Leninist assumptions, it may be that Lenin offers many readers the most convenient center for their reflections on the question of how important constitutionalism really is. Are we, perhaps unconsciously, being condescending in assuming that poor and illiterate peasants neither understand nor care about constitutionalism? After all, constitutionalism is, in some measure at least, liberty—a matter of universal interest. Further, are we being naive in supposing that a generation or so of revolutionary tyranny will pave the way for constitutionalism? It is hard to see that anything of the sort happened in the Soviet Union. Dostoevsky foresaw a hundred years ago that in times to come "sages" would proclaim that there is no crime and no sin, but only hunger; that is, antisocial behavior would be attributed to economic circumstances. Therefore, Dostoevsky said, reformers would write on their banners: "Feed men, and then ask of them virtue!"[2] Lenin fulfilled Dostoevsky's prophecy, as do the multitudes who consciously and unconsciously follow him. Dostoevsky believed that postponing "virtue"—respect for moral standards, decency in human relations, and above all liberty—would be catastrophic; it would threaten the permanent loss not only of liberty, but of the very qualities that make us human.

[2]Fyodor Dostoevsky, *The Brothers Karamazov,* trans. Constance Garnett (New York: Modern Library, n.d.), p. 262.

Considering the importance of the question before us, let us look at it briefly from a different vantage point. There is a broad consensus among political thinkers that power can be kept within constitutional limits only by being divided. Hence, supporters of constitutionalism are almost invariably supporters of divided power; on the other hand, those who favor power wholly responsive to the will of those wielding it, unrestrained by constitutional limits, practically always favor concentrated power. Thus we may rephrase the original question so that it reads: should there be more than one main center of power in society? From this angle, we may see things that were not apparent in the preceding discussion.

The idea that power should be divided among two or more independent centers rests on a tradition no less ancient than that of the idea of constitutional government. When Plato faced the improbability that philosophers would ever gain power, he concluded that concentrating power in any single group would be unwise; instead, power should be divided between those with characteristics indicative of wisdom (such as age) and those chosen by lot, thus representing the populace as a whole. This idea, touched upon briefly in our consideration of the question *Who should rule?* is one version of the principle of divided power. It was probably old, as common sense if not as political philosophy, even when Plato was writing, and it has endured both in common sense and in political philosophy to the present day. It has assumed a great many different forms, including the form prescribed in the American Constitution. Throughout its long history and in all of its varieties, it has been rooted in one primary conviction: totally concentrated power menaces civilized existence.

Even Christian orthodoxy, which might be expected to dictate priestly sovereignty, contains its own unique version of the principle of divided power. This is the "doctrine of the two swords," set forth by Pope Gelasius I near the end of the fifth century and followed in some form by almost every succeeding Christian thinker. According to this doctrine, not all power should rest in the same hands, not even in the hands of the Pope. Human beings should not be under the exclusive control of a single sword. True, most Christian thinkers, not only during the Middle Ages but well into modern times, held that there should be only a single church. However, most did not argue that this one church either should govern or should totally control those who do govern. The task of ensuring temporal order, as distinguished from that of guiding people toward salvation, should be under a separate authority.

Protestant and atheistic critics are quick to point out that Christian thinkers of earlier times were rarely tolerant; accordingly, the doctrine of the two swords was often construed in a way that set the Church over the state so decisively that it denied the spirit of the doctrine although not its letter. All of this must be admitted. Nevertheless, the tenacity of the doctrine of the two swords remains impressive. It shows that even devout Christians, certain as most of them were in earlier times that God had authorized a particular human organization to interpret and guard his word, shared the traditional Western mistrust of concentrated power.

American institutions, it can be seen, derive from ideas many times older than America itself. The separation of powers among the three branches of government is a variation on a theme that can be traced back at least as far as Plato and the Greeks. The separation of church and state is a version of the medieval principle that even authority derived from God does not justify undivided power.

Thus one can hardly help feeling that there should be more than one main center of power in a society. Perhaps, however, there are other things of greater importance, such as achieving scientific government, order and peace, complete democracy, or justice. It is striking that every thinker just cited as an opponent of constitutionalism was an opponent also of divided power. For Plato, philosopher-rulers would not check one another, even when sharing power, for all possessed perfect understanding and therefore could not disagree; and for people of lesser understanding to check them would be intolerable. For Hobbes, any division of power was an invitation to chaos. Rousseau regarded the dispersal of power among separate centers as undesirable since it meant limiting the sovereignty of the people. Lenin opposed all checks on Communist rulers.

As pointed out in discussing the constitutional limits on power, these thinkers are not out of date. They represent attitudes still powerful in the twentieth century. Plato calls for the comprehensive and organized use of knowledge in solving social problems,

Hobbes for the utmost efficiency in keeping order, Rousseau for the unchecked ascendancy of the people, and Lenin for absolute justice. All these demands are insistently voiced in our time, and all, at least implicitly, are demands for concentrated power. Are there good grounds for resisting them?

The issue before us is where and how to mark out the boundaries of power. We have reflected on the moral and constitutional boundaries. These are like disputed borders between nations, the scenes of many battles. There is a third boundary, perhaps even more fiercely contested—the economic. The issue here is whether the economic system ought to be free of governmental intervention. Does it work according to laws of its own ("the laws of supply and demand") that will only be thrown askew by governmental tampering? Does it tend naturally toward a more just and efficient order than governmental planning can achieve? The issue is whether government should keep its hands off the main centers of economic power.

20 Should Governments Ordinarily Leave the Ownership and Control of Industry in Private Hands?

This question is broader than it looks. The word *industry* is used as shorthand for all major means of production—land, mines, electrical power, communications, and so forth, as well as factories. Nor is the question concerned with production only, apart from distribution; whoever controls production controls distribution as well. In sum, this question asks about our responsibility for the earth—for the whole physical setting of human life and for all the materials we use for the maintenance and improvement of life.

An old idea, accepted by both Locke and Marx, the fathers respectively of "free enterprise" and of socialism, is that the earth is the common possession of humankind. By a primal right, established by God or inhering in the nature of things, it belongs to all. But how can humankind actually take the earth into its possession and use it—by allowing individuals freely to appropriate parts of it, or by placing it in the custody of governments?

The answer endorsed in one way or another by all defenders of capitalism was given by Locke when he asserted that "the Condition of Humane life, which requires Labour and Materials to work on, necessarily introduces *private Possessions.*"[3] While the earth *belongs* to the entire human race, it can be *used* only by individuals; and for individuals effectively to use things, they must own them. Hence the government's responsibility for the earth is fulfilled in protecting the rights of private property. Thus ran Locke's argument.

Is it true, however, that efficient use of the earth requires individual appropriation? Doesn't the history of industrialism indicate, on the contrary, that exploitation of the earth depends on immense economic organizations and that the individual alone can do almost nothing? Locke asserts that a person has a right to keep "the Acorns he picks up under an Oak, or the Apples he gathered from the Trees in the Wood."[4] What relevance have such examples to the industrial systems of the twentieth century? Today in America hardly a single item in daily use is the product of individual labor. Our cars, clothing, food, and household utensils are produced by large, complex business organizations, and these organizations in turn are integrated into vast national and international economic systems.

Furthermore, doesn't the history of capitalism indicate that free appropriation by some brings deprivation to others? It has been urged, of course, that those who are able to appropriate a great deal vindicate by this very ability their right to all they appropriate, while those who have little thus prove how little they deserve. We may well be suspicious, however, of a logic that begins with the principle of our common ownership of the earth and ends with the principle that a few can rightfully take most of it for themselves. Not surprisingly, this logic has failed to achieve universal acceptance.

It has also been urged, of course, that individual appropriation is not only just, whatever the inequalities that result, but also beneficial for everyone. The few who gain wealth for themselves, it is said, at the same time create wealth for others. America, with its

[3]John Locke, *Two Treatises of Government*, ed. Peter Laslett (Cambridge: Cambridge University Press, 1960), p. 310. The italics are Locke's.
[4]*Two Treatises*, p. 306.

vast concentrations of private wealth along with the historically unparalleled prosperity enjoyed by the majority, is evidence in favor of
this argument. But not conclusive evidence. Given America's natural advantages, an economic system other than capitalism might
have produced goods just as abundantly while distributing them
more equitably. Further, as has often been noted in recent years,
while great numbers in America are prosperous, a sizable minority
is not. In view of the ugliness and squalor of the inner cities, America's poor today must be as wretched as the poor in most other societies in history.

The major idea underlying the case for individual appropriation—the idea on which thinking might be advantageously focused—is that of the natural harmony of the free market. This idea
was briefly explained in connection with Question 18. The gist of it
is that where people are free to produce, sell, and buy as their own
economic interests dictate, the economic system will perform efficiently and justly. The things people want will be produced, because
that is in the interest of the producers; they will be sold at prices acceptable to both sellers and buyers, for otherwise the two parties
will not deal with one another. The myriad daily decisions involved
in the working of a vast economic system will be made, not by a distant government board trying in vain to comprehend the infinite
complexity of a nation's economic life, but by multitudes of private
individuals, each one impelled by self-interest to be realistic and rational. This, of course, is what Americans know as "free enterprise."
It is one of the most attractive ideas ever formulated, for it promises
material abundance, fairly distributed, without any sacrifice of individual liberty. But does it, realistically, make sense?

Surprisingly (in view of the somewhat utopian flavor of the
idea), it does; at least most people nowadays believe that it does.
Not that so many political leaders and writers and scholars would
trust an entirely unfettered market. But there is widespread recognition, even in Communist nations, that many economic problems
are better resolved through free competition than through bureaucratic control. The chief issue now is not whether to rely on the free
market at all, but how far to rely on it—almost entirely (the view of
those often called "conservatives") or only guardedly (the typical
position of "liberals")?

This issue no longer stirs the ideological passions it once did; many people, both on the right and the left, agree that the extent of governmental intervention is a matter to be decided experimentally. It should be noted, however, that the issue will never be allowed to rest entirely on practical grounds. The greatest weakness of "free enterprise" is probably that it violates the Western moral tradition. It sanctions selfishness and materialism. It tells us to concentrate on personal advantage and to interpret personal advantage in terms of money. It tells us to forget about the welfare of others and the public interest; let others take care of themselves and let the market take care of the public interest. It has nothing to say about values, such as wisdom or beauty, that cannot be readily translated into market prices. There are always people, many of them taking pride in their "hardheadedness," who can follow such a doctrine with untroubled consciences. But there are always others, viewed as "soft" and "sentimental" by the realists of the free market, whose allegiance to such values as equality, the common good, and cooperation, will lead them in another direction.

It is understandable, then, that a number of thinkers have sought alternatives to individual appropriation. These alternatives all amount to socialism of one kind or another.

Socialism in the broadest sense stands for the idea that humankind must assert its primal right to the earth by actually taking the earth into its possession and using it cooperatively. Socialists have not agreed whether this should be done through governmental action or in some other way. But they are united in their unwillingness to tolerate private appropriation of the earth.

Socialism has drawn much of its moral force from the democratic tradition, according to which government should be carried on only with the consent, if not the active involvement, of the governed. Power belongs to the people. But property, of course, is power; thus, large concentrations of private property are by democratic standards suspect. Most socialists think democracy and capitalism are flatly contradictory. Socialists often see themselves as extending to the economic sphere the democratic principles already widely accepted within the political sphere.

A contrary opinion, of course, is often heard in America, where democracy in politics and capitalism in economics are widely regarded as natural allies. Democracy is thought to be threatened more by concentrations of governmental power—which socialism is apt to effect—than by concentrations of private property.

One of the most serious questions about socialism is whether *common* appropriation can, in practice, mean anything but *governmental* appropriation. Most socialists would refuse to assent to any such equation. Socialist literature is filled with ideas for voluntary cooperation. Many socialists are scarcely more trustful of government than are typical capitalists, and Communists of course go so far as to anticipate "the withering away of the state."

In practice, however, common appropriation has nearly always meant governmental appropriation; and communism, as everyone knows, has led to something very different from the withering away of the state. Do we see here signs of an insuperable difficulty in socialism? Perhaps if all of us together are to appropriate the earth, this must be done through the one agency that represents all of us together, namely, the government. An economic enterprise might be taken over by a cooperative group smaller than the whole society; a factory, for example, might be run by its workers. But this is not common ownership, and a worker-run factory might behave no more responsibly in relation to society as a whole than a capitalist-run factory. Government may be a socialist's only recourse.

The trouble is that governmental ownership and common ownership are not at all the same. It never occurs to Americans, for example, to think of the postal service, with all its buildings and equipment, as common property; it belongs to the government and that is a different matter altogether. This is not to suggest that governmental ownership is necessarily a bad thing. It may in some circumstances contribute both to efficiency and to public responsibility. But such advantages cannot be taken for granted; even if they are realized, governmental direction of the economy, with the powerful officialdom and pervasive red tape that inevitably evolve, is far from the ideal of common appropriation that is the inspiration of socialism.

There is one way, indeed, in which governmental control of the economy may be even further from common ownership than is private ownership. Governmental control unites the political and economic centers of power. Thus, these do not check one another, as they occasionally do in a capitalist system. This might not matter if the government were fully responsible to the people. But governmental responsibility is imperfectly realized even in the most democratic countries, and as government becomes larger and more complex, popular understanding and control may grow weaker; bureaucrats may overshadow the people and their representatives. In this way socialism could mean, contrary to its intent, that power is more concentrated and uncontrolled than it would be under a system of private ownership.

If the signal weakness in the case for individual appropriation is the amorality of the market, that in the case for common appropriation is bureaucracy and all it has come to stand for: impersonality, inefficiency, uncontrollability. Not, of course, that such adjectives describe bureaucracy altogether. The administrative branches of the federal and state governments in America help citizens in innumerable ways, and they help many who are greatly in need—the retarded, handicapped, and unemployed; the poor, sick, and old. They employ countless able and conscientious people. And they are checked in diverse ways to assure their responsibility to the public—by legislatures, elected executives, courts, interest groups, and citizen's lobbies. Still, governmental bureaucracy (and in some measure the smaller bureaucracies in business and elsewhere) is an ominous presence in twentieth-century industrial nations. A bureaucracy is a kind of human machine, so far as such a thing is possible, and is designed to carry out efficiently (and regardless of the political opinions of the bureaucrats themselves) the directives of top officials. Hence set functions and prearranged relationships (as in the design of a machine) belong to the essence of bureaucracy. It seems to follow that impersonality, as well as the kind of inefficiency associated with red tape, are bound to characterize a bureaucratic organization. And while a bureaucracy can be reasonably responsive to elected officials and to public feelings, it is hard to see how a nation under a large bureaucracy could realize the degree of popular political involvement called for by the ideal of democracy.

One of the most disquieting characteristics of bureaucracy is its tendency continually to grow. Ideally, of course, a bureaucracy would be merely as large as is needed, growing at some times and shrinking at others. But once a bureaucratic agency is established, those who staff it and those whom it serves have a vested interest in its continuance and are usually able to exert strong political pressure in furtherance of that interest. The result is that bureaucracy rarely shrinks, although it often grows.

Hence, just as proponents of individual appropriation and market economics may properly be challenged with the query, What about cooperation and public service? so proponents of common appropriation may fairly be asked about bureaucracy. It is said that a competitive market interferes with cooperation among citizens and common devotion to the public good. Doesn't a bureaucracy do the same thing? It is charged against the market that it brings about gross and unjust inequalities. But won't a bureaucracy inevitably be a privileged group, enjoying a level of remuneration and degree of security far higher than do ordinary citizens? A free market supposedly leads to concentrations of economic power that are incompatible with democracy. Doesn't a bureaucracy involve concentrations of managerial power that are also undemocratic? Such questions might be multiplied indefinitely.

In this kind of impasse, common sense immediately suggests that the truth is somewhere between the two extremes. And indeed such a suggestion is not without weight. In the history of political thought it is probably Thomas Aquinas (1225–1274), the author of what has since become the official philosophy of Roman Catholicism, who has most clearly delineated a theory that sanctions neither unrestrained individual appropriation nor total governmental control. Aquinas argued that property should be held by individuals but regulated by law and custom to ensure its being used in the common interest. He maintained, as an American in business might, that one will look more carefully after what is one's own than what is held in common, and that the economy will, therefore, be better managed under a system of private property than under any other. At the same time, Aquinas condemned the use of property primarily for personal profit; it should be used for the common good, and society has a right to see that it is. On this side of his thought, Aquinas seems less like an American in business than like the kind of socialist the businessperson would excoriate as a dangerous radical.

Is the issue thus resolved? Not necessarily. In political practice, it is often sagacious to profess a middle position; in political theory, however, such a tactic is often only a way of avoiding issues. Thus one must ask whether the Thomist position resolves the dilemma of private versus governmental ownership or merely obscures it.

Does the right of individual ownership, according to the middle position, mean that an individual can appropriate and use some significant part of the earth according to purely personal desires and contrary to the will of society? If so, then what is ostensibly an intermediate position turns out to be, in essence, an individualism like that made explicit by Locke. If it does not mean this, however, and the individual's use of personal property can be supervised and controlled by society, then one might question how significant the right of individual ownership actually is. In substance, the theory would seem to be one of common ownership. If, finally, sometimes the individual and sometimes society is responsible for the earth, where should the line between the two be drawn, and how should disputes between them be decided? Unless those questions are answered, what is offered is less a theory of property than an argument to the effect that property questions cannot be decided in a general theory. That may, of course, be the truth.

The question of whether individuals should be free to appropriate the earth has always been important but never as momentous as it is today, because technology has placed the earth much more fully at our disposal than it has ever been before. The right of individual appropriation is a far more sweeping power than it was in the days of Locke. Private persons have used the earth in ways that have affected whole nations. In the twentieth century, for example, the lives of the American people have probably been shaped as much by General Motors as by the Supreme Court. Is is right, then, that General Motors is private property? On the other hand, if you mistrust government, then the immense power of private property may be just what makes you oppose any scheme of public ownership or control, for that would greatly increase the power of government.

Is there any way, then, of fulfilling the spirit of the biblical assertion that "the heaven, even the heavens, are the Lord's: but the earth hath he given to the children of men?"[5] Is there any way hu-

---

[5]Psalm 115:16.

manity can possess the earth without being possessed in turn by the powerful?

Power is so dangerous that the quest for limits has been a quest for firm and unchanging limits—for eternal moral laws, understood by all; for constitutional rules impervious to the shifting sentiments of rulers and peoples; for a clear and lasting knowledge of where governments must stop when tempted to intervene in the economic system. The quest for limits has been for *preestablished* limits, for boundary lines not subject to continual reconsideration and change. And that is where much of the trouble lies.

The idea of government under preestablished limits and the idea of government without such limits are equally unsatisfactory. The former implies that good rulers will be hindered; the latter, that bad rulers will not. The former means compromise and delay in carrying out the best of plans; the latter, expeditious accomplishment of the worst. It is not surprising that people have long sought to avoid both horns of the dilemma by finding ways to keep governments from doing evil but not from doing good. Several possible solutions might come to mind—for example, arranging matters so that the interests of rulers and ruled are identical. One solution, however, stands out from the others for its simplicity and appeal. Governments might be restrained from doing what they ought not to do, but not from doing what they ought to do, by placing them in the hands of persons with perfect understanding and wisdom. Is there any validity in such a notion?

21 Can Political Power and Perfect Knowledge Ever Be Joined?

Flawless, all-encompassing knowledge has been the object of perennial hope. Plato powerfully expressed this hope in his ideal of the philosopher, a man or woman who had ascended from the cave of ignorance into the light of "the Good." Many Christians have believed that perfect understanding has been given to us through Christ, although we could never have found our way to such understanding through reason and cannot fully grasp it during our earthly lives. In modern times, faith in Christ has seemingly declined, but faith in reason, comparable in intensity to Plato's, although based on a different concept of reason, has reawakened with the progress of science.

Can government ever be made the servant of such knowledge? The idea that it can has naturally accompanied the hope that perfect knowledge might be attained. As we have seen, Plato thought that philosophers should be rulers. Medieval Christians, in spite of the doctrine of the two swords, were continually tempted to grant the Pope a power as limitless and unified as they believed Christian revelation to be. The modern political mind has long been fascinated by the idea of technocracy, government carried on by masters of technology and science.

The idea of joining power and perfect knowledge may have serious flaws, but at the very least it is noble and attractive. It represents the ineradicable feeling noted in connection with constitutionalism; one of the greatest of all evils is to be helplessly subject to the blind and selfish will of another human being. The idea of constitutionalism is that rulers should be compelled to stay within certain legal boundaries. The idea of subordinating government to perfect knowledge is much more radical. It proposes to eliminate the very willfulness and ignorance that necessitate legal boundaries. It envisions doing away with arbitrary government by cutting its roots in human nature. What constitutionalism would merely check—capriciousness and stupidity—perfect knowledge would wholly abolish.

The notion that this is possible, however, rests on two assumptions: that perfect knowledge is available, at least to some; and that this knowledge has the power of determining the behavior of its possessors, of transmitting to them, as it were, its own perfection. Both assumptions have frequently been challenged.

As for the first, a widespread attitude of the last century or two has been what might be called "epistemological discouragement," that is, discouragement over the possibility of gaining sure and comprehensive knowledge (*epistēmē*, in Greek). In the past, especially in the Middle Ages, it was widely believed that such knowledge, comprehending humanity's origin, nature, and end, had been given to us by God; reason might help us lay hold of it, but ultimately it rested on a divine guarantee. Now, however, that faith is alive only in the minds of a few. Church leaders may cite figures showing widespread religious belief, but one suspects that they are more likely to study human nature by reading social science than by pondering the New Testament.

It is often assumed that faith has been defeated by science. That is an oversimplification. It is an ominous fact that we have lost faith not only in Christian revelation but in science as well. Of course, everyone would agree that scientists have made striking discoveries. The question is whether there is any absolute truth contained in these discoveries. Do they concern reality itself or only our perceptions of reality?

David Hume (1711–1776), a skeptical philosopher, a lucid writer, and a major figure of the Enlightenment, argued that neither observation nor reasoning can validate the universal and invariable physical laws that scientists claim to establish. At the center of Hume's argument was the contention that there is no necessary connection between cause and effect—not, at least, so far as we can *know*. We see that an experience of one sort, say, the rising of the sun, is usually or always followed by an experience of another sort, in this case the spread of daylight. But we do not see any necessity binding together these two experiences. If tomorrow the rising of the sun were accompanied by the spread of several feet of water over all the earth while darkness continued, that would provide a *different* experience than we had ever had before, but not one in conflict with any law established by preceding experiences. Nor would it be in conflict with reason. We are able by reason to infer that Socrates is mortal if Socrates is human and if humans, by definition, are mortal. We are not, however, able to infer that light will spread over all the earth when the sun rises; all we *know* is that we have seen it happen that way in the past. (Likewise, we cannot know that all humans are mortal, only that all humans have been observed to die; the conclusion that Socrates is mortal depends on the *assumption* that all humans are mortal). Hume did not deny that our "laws" are convenient generalizations and very useful for everyday living. But the universality and necessity that make them laws in the strict sense of the term cannot be verified and are not, therefore, matters of scientific knowledge. By virtue of this argument, and similar arguments concerning other elements of "knowledge," Hume was one of the major sources of our "epistemological discouragement."

The most profound and influential attempt to answer Hume and to show that true and certain knowledge is possible was made by Immanuel Kant(1724–1804), who is widely regarded as among the greatest philosophers of all time. Kant's *Critique of Pure Reason,* a classic in philosophical literature, has as its immediate intent a defense of science. A crucial point in Kant's response to Hume was that the concept of causal necessity is a precondition of coherent experience. With that and other concepts, we link together our sensations and form the things around us and the world in which we live. Without it, we would fall into a chaos of sounds and colors, without form or stability. This implies, however, that scientific laws derive their universal and invariable character from the structure of the human mind rather than from the structure of reality itself. Reality is unknowable; indeed, it is unwarranted to think that reality itself even has a structure. Thus Kant's defense of science is highly equivocal. It offers assurance that scientific laws can have absolute validity. But this validity consists only in telling us how reality must appear to us if our faculties are properly used; in telling us only how reality must appear to us, and not what it is in itself, scientific laws are purely relative.

Thus Kant, too, became a source of epistemological discouragement, contrary to his own intentions. A dramatic sign of Kant's influence today and of the weakness of our faith in science is existentialism. Many different philosophies and attitudes have been referred to as existentialist. But if a single theme is common to them all, it is probably the idea, deriving ultimately from Kant, that a human being is not an object of knowledge—at least not that and nothing more. A human being is a subject—one who may *have* knowledge but who is not included within that knowledge. A person may gain understanding of humanity by looking inward, but not by objective analysis.

If this is so, the changeless, all-inclusive knowledge envisioned by Plato and by many admirers of modern science cannot be obtained. The ideal government, dedicated to the service of such knowledge, is no better than a dream.

Many do not agree with these critics of reason; not everyone is totally discouraged about the possibilities of knowledge. Few would deny, however, that the critics have done much to set the mood of our time—a mood in striking contrast with both the confident faith of the Middle Ages and the bold nationalism of antiquity. Today it is hard not to wonder whether we can know anything at all except, perhaps, that we inhabit an impenetrable darkness.

The possibility of perfect knowledge, however, is not all we have to consider. In asking whether governments can ever become servants of perfect knowledge we must also ask whether, if such knowledge were gained, people would be disposed to respect it. They might not; they might know all things, yet behave impulsively and foolishly. The human race might finally fill out and perfect the physical and social sciences, yet still be stupidly and brutally governed. It is not obvious that perfect knowledge means perfect virtue.

Some thinkers have held that while the equation of perfect knowledge with perfect virtue may not be obvious, it is nevertheless valid. Socrates apparently believed that full moral knowledge—that is, knowledge of human nature and needs, and knowledge of what is really good—leads inevitably to moral excellence. A person who knows, fully and certainly, what is good is bound to choose it; an evil person must be an ignorant one. It follows that knowledge—full and profound knowledge—cannot be misused.

Socrates' identification of knowledge and virtue has been a powerful influence in history. It underlay Plato's concept of the philosopher-ruler and antiquity's long-sustained commitment to the cultivation of reason. It has no doubt also contributed substantially, albeit indirectly, to the unhesitating enthusiam with which most of us, in modern times, have supported the advance of science. We have assumed rather casually that the progress of science is bound to mean the improvement of life.

In recent decades this assumption has appeared increasingly dubious. We have gained vast quantities of knowledge through the physical and social sciences, but we seem as likely to use this knowledge for evil ends, like nuclear warfare and brainwashing, as for good ends, like peace and the elimination of poverty. We now feel menaced, rather than saved, by our knowledge.

Why is this so? Is it because our knowledge is still imperfect and incomplete? Or was Socrates wrong and is it possible to understand all things and still be selfish and cruel?

During the past century or two, the most resolute defenders of the ideal of joining power and perfect knowledge have probably been social scientists. This is not to say that every social scientist is a utopian, without reservations about the possible perfection or social utility of the knowledge being sought by sociologists, psychologists, and political scientists. Such reservations, nonetheless, have not been prominent in the writings of social scientists. On the contrary, the effort to establish social sciences comparable to the physical sciences in precision and certainty has been pressed so aggressively that those favoring intuitive or philosophical approaches have had to fight for survival.

Few would deny that social scientists speak with a certain moral force. They seek an end to the guesses, approximations, biased opinions, and unsupported sentiments that compose much of the content of present-day political discourse. They also want to provide governments with the capacity for effective action. These aims go back to the time of Plato and have an indisputable moral dignity. Few would deny, moreover, that they are in some measure realizable. That we can gain precise, objective knowledge of aspects of society and that this knowledge has practical uses has already been demonstrated. The question is, How far does such knowledge extend? Can all major social problems be solved scientifically? This question comprises two subordinate questions.

1. Can all social realities be understood scientifically? Those who claim they can must assume that all realities, including human beings, are in the nature of "things," that is, subject to the laws of cause and effect and accessible in their entirety to observation by anyone with normal faculties and the necessary training in scientific procedures. If this is so, then precise statements about human behavior can be formulated and tested, and a science of human behavior is a reasonable goal. But doubters are apt to have a different impression of the nature of reality. They may, for example, be unwilling to set aside as illusory our strong conviction that when faced with alternatives we are able to choose; they may believe that freedom is a reality. If they are right, then our glaring inability always to foresee what human beings are going to do is owing to something essential and enduring in human beings—their freedom—and not to a temporary defect in our knowledge. In addition, some human qualities may not be observable in the same way something under a microscope is observable. A physical scientist does not need to (and cannot) identify with an object under a microscope, but a student of social phenomena may be unable to understand human emotions without experiencing them or at least vividly imagining them. Perhaps no one can understand terror, hatred, lust for power, and the other passions of the political universe without actually feeling and

being moved by them. In short, whereas effective observation of the physical universe seems to require detachment, effective observation of the social and political universe may require involvement—at least, the involvement of empathy. If there is substance in these conjectures, then novelists and philosophers will often understand society better than social scientists do.

2. Is the scientific understanding of society always beneficial? If governments know what is good for society and how to attain it, will they necessarily choose it? Social scientists are practically always silently or outspokenly Socratic; they assume that all the knowledge we can gain will be good for us. They do not often, like nuclear scientists, envision with apprehension or horror the ultimate consequences of their research. Their critics, however, have not been so confident. Many have granted that although a scientific knowledge of human beings may be possible, governments are not reasonable and responsible enough to be counted on to use this knowledge for the best purposes. For example, if everything a human being feels, thinks, and does is a product of objective social and psychological forces, and we can understand those forces scientifically, then we are potential masters of human consciousness and behavior. And who is "we"? Presumably, teams of social scientists and civil servants. Possessed of powers of manipulation such as human beings have never had before, might they not make slaves of us, *even if they made us happy?*

The Western tradition provides a weighty alternative to the Socratic viewpoint. While Socrates apparently believed that every effort should be centered on knowing good and evil, the Book of Genesis seems to say, in the form of a great myth, that such knowing is the very essence of iniquity. Adam and Eve were cast out of paradise for tasting, contrary to God's command, fruit from "the tree of the knowledge of good and evil."

The myth of the Fall is not something anyone can confidently interpret. It suggests, however, that the state in which we were intended to live was one of such complete unity with the good that we did not know anything *about* the good because we did not in any degree stand apart from it; and we did not *choose* the good because we were not conscious of any alternative to it. The destruction of this state was an act of deliberate self-estrangement. We deliberately set ourselves apart from reality. And we did so arrogantly;

the motive was pride, sheer self-assertion. Our objectifying and calculating minds, then, and our consciousness of good and evil, come from sin; but they are also punishment, and a curse, for they make us aliens in the universe. Such a view sounds extreme, but it is not entertained solely by religious believers. Many American students in recent decades, not to speak of poets and writers in earlier times, have sought a spontaneity of life and immediacy of experience precluded by the Socratic premises underlying Western institutions such as universities.

The dilemma of our civilization may be symbolized in terms of these two great sources of understanding: the Greek and the Hebraic. One exalts the human mind and leads logically to the idea of government simultaneously directed and restrained by a knowledge comprehending all needs and all means to their satisfaction. The other humbles us and tells us that as long as we seek to be "as gods, knowing good and evil," we will suffer the anguish of labor, estrangement, and mortality.

Here we can hardly help feeling that we are in the presence of the mystery of being—of the things that "thought cannot think." Perhaps this is why the biblical view is set forth not as a theory but as a mythical event in the lives of the first human beings. We are trying to think about something that is not accessible to observation and is not even an event except in a metaphorical sense. We are trying to think about the roots of the human situation. In doing this most of us find it impossible to choose one side or the other, as we might in dealing with a question of fact. We find ourselves drawn toward the paradox that both interpretations are somehow true.

We must remember, however, that the very function of a paradox is to keep thought alive. Anyone who simply says that both Socrates and the author of the Genesis myth are probably right, and then comfortably sets the whole question aside, has misused the concept of paradox. Any truth contained in a paradox is hidden; it cannot be reached by accepting the paradox in the same way we accept a statement of demonstrable fact. It is of the essence of a paradox that formal acknowledgment of the kind we accord a demonstrable fact is nonsensical. A paradox is true not in itself but in the understanding it impels us to seek.

We must therefore try to understand *how* the Socratic and biblical views might both be true. We might ask, for example, why Socrates was habitually ironical, as though what he said and what he meant were—paradoxically—quite different. Was he hinting that the theoretical inquiries he pressed so indefatigably could not possibly succeed, or rather that they could succeed only through failing—disclosing truths of a kind that no theoretical conclusions could embody? Pursuing this line of thought, we might ask whether the Genesis myth can be interpreted so that it yields a similar idea. Is it a condemnation only of the presumption of thinking that good and evil can be completely and securely known? Does it allow for the strange wisdom that Socrates seems to exemplify—a wisdom that is not found at the end of a search but in the search itself?

SUGGESTED READINGS

Plato. *The Republic*
Cicero, Marcus Tullius. *On the Commonwealth*
Saint Thomas Aquinas on Politics and Ethics, *ed. and trans. Paul E. Sigmund*
Machiavelli, Niccolò. *The Discourses*
Hobbes, Thomas. *Leviathan*, Second Part
Locke, John. *The Second Treatise of Government*
Rousseau, Jean Jacques. *The Social Contract*
Hamilton, Alexander; Jay, John; and Madison, James. *The Federalist*
Hegel, G. W. F. *Philosophy of Right*
Mill, John Stuart. *On Liberty*
Koestler, Arthur. *Darkness at Noon*
Orwell, George. *1984*
Strauss, Leo. *Natural Right and History*
Lippman, Walter. *The Public Philosophy*
Friedman, Milton. *Capitalism and Freedom*
Berlin, Isaiah. *Four Essays on Liberty*
Rawls, John. *A Theory of Justice*

Chapter **6**

THE ENDS OF POWER

Power must be used as well as restrained. In carrying on political thinking, therefore, we must consider the ends of power. This is no easy undertaking; it incorporates two large and refractory problems. First, what are the ends of human life? Clearly it is impossible to understand anything about the purpose of government without understanding something about the purpose of life itself. But this has been an enigma for every generation. Some of the thinkers of our own day—Jean-Paul Sartre, the French existentialist, is perhaps the greatest—have reached the seemingly despairing conclusion that human life has no purpose whatever. But once we have identified the ends of life, we must estimate what power can do to help us reach them. Power cannot do everything: it cannot, for example, make one person love another. Thus, thinking about the ends of power can go astray in two ways—by misconstruing the ends of life and by misunderstanding the capacities of power.

The difficulty of thinking about the ends of power, however, is matched by the importance of doing so, especially now, when we are deeply confused about the proper activities of people and governments. Our confusion no doubt has many sources; the ceaseless, unplanned rearranging of our lives by technology and the permeation of thought and feeling by the fads cultivated by commercial television may disorient us far more deeply than we realize. Whatever the causes of our confusion, the political consequences are likely to be significant. Lacking wise and settled purposes, we devote our resources and attention to secondary problems—exploring space, rather than eliminating poverty, is a possible example—and we will be fortunate if we do nothing worse than that. The time may come when we will be sorely tempted to escape the burden of discord and uncertainty by placing absolute power in the hands of a leader or party pursuing unity through propaganda and terror (a short definition of fascism). In one way or another, if we sink unprotestingly into doubt and indifference regarding the ends of power, those ends are likely to be set by the irresponsible and insensitive.

For these reasons, reflecting on the ends of power is not a leisurely diversion but an urgent and practical duty. But with so difficult a task, where should we begin?

A person's first response, when asked what government should do, is likely to be that whatever the value pursued, it should be one that all can share. The good at which power aims should be a common good. This may seem elementary. But is it? Is there any such thing as a value all can share? And do not those who have power always pursue their own good in preference to the good of others, even when their intentions are idealistic? Let us ask at the outset whether every government does not necessarily pursue the good of only the few—the few who control the government.

22 Does Every Government Serve Merely "the Interest of the Stronger"?

The phrase, "the interest of the stronger," and the argument that it describes the goal of every government are attributed in *The Republic* to a contemporary of Socrates, Thrasymachus. In effect, Thrasymachus held that human beings are estranged in essence; hence it is meaningless to speak of the common good or the general welfare. The ends of each person are purely personal, and they are likely to be in conflict with the ends of others. People with power, consequently, seek their own good alone and readily sacrifice the welfare of others to attain it. It follows that every social and political order, the most ancient and venerated and the most carefully designed (excepting only naked tyrannies), is fraudulent. Governments usually claim the sanction of both God and the people; but that is false, because what they actually do, and are intended to do, according to

Thrasymachus, is to further "the interest of the stronger," of those who have power.

No great thinker has wholly agreed with Thrasymachus. Some, though, have been so deeply suspicious of established governments that they have assumed that most do, in fact, serve only "the interest of the stronger," although they may believe that under some exceptional condition, like philosophers becoming rulers, the case would be otherwise. Karl Marx, for example, had this attitude.

Marx, of course, believed that the working class was destined to seize all power for itself. With this event, government would come to serve the interest of all so completely and so obviously as no longer even to be coercive; the state would "wither away." Until that time, however, governments would inevitably betray the interests of most of the people. As already noted, Marx saw the liberal democracies of his time as little better than disguised dictatorships carried on in the interest of the upper classes. Such devices as written constitutions, representative assemblies, and popular elections, which supposedly compel governments to serve the welfare of their subjects, were instruments of fraud, elaborate devices for veiling the tyranny of landowners, industrialists, and financiers.

Marx's view stemmed partly from his conviction that decisive power in any society lay in the hands of those owning the means of production. Less decisive were the various governmental instruments of power, such as legislatures and police. In certain circumstances governments might gain independence from class control, but they usually were agents of the dominant economic groups. Thus, governments were normally in no position to serve the common good. But a more crucial point for Marx was that there could be no common good in a society divided among warring classes; the interest of one class was necessarily the oppression or destruction of another class. Even a philosopher-ruler, in a Marxist universe, could not devise a formula to unite the bourgeoisie and the proletariat.

These considerations placed Marx provisionally on the side of Thrasymachus. Marx qualified Thrasymachus's position by adding "until the Communist revolution"; otherwise, he agreed that the "justice" maintained by governments is nothing but the "interest of the stronger."

It would hardly be too much to say that refuting Thrasymachus has been the principal aim of political thought. Plato devoted the whole of *The Republic* to this task. Of course, not all thinkers have had Thrasymachus consciously in mind, but most have tried to show that government can further some state of affairs that is not merely in the interest of the stronger but in the interest of all. Even so cynical a thinker as Hobbes argued emphatically that peace is needed by everyone. Rousseau and Marx, who thought that governments rarely if ever sought a common good, concentrated on showing how the reign of selfishness might be overcome. When liberalism, in response to Marxist criticism, tried to show that liberal and democratic regimes could act in the interest of workers as well as of owners, they were simply renewing the ancient effort to refute Thrasymachus.

Can he be refuted? Your answer will depend on whether you believe that people are in essence estranged or united. Even in a just society some members must get less—leisure, job satisfaction, wealth, and so forth—than they desire and than others get. This is strikingly true of soldiers who lose their lives in battle, of workers who perform indispensable but stultifying jobs, and of criminals who are punished. The problem is to show that these people are not being sacrificed to the interest of the strong, but are somehow contributing to a common good. This can be done, thus refuting Thrasymachus, only if all are essentially united and society so organized that those who, voluntarily or under compulsion, sacrifice conscious desires for the good of others actually make those sacrifices for a common good, thus for their own highest good, and are not merely means to the ends of others.

This idea may seem farfetched, but in actuality it is not distant from common sense. We do not generally think of a soldier who has died in war (unless, perhaps, unjustly drafted or in an unjust war) as having been victimized by the strong. Nor do we ordinarily think that of a criminal in prison. We feel the fate of each to be in some way justified. How? Presumably by serving some end, such as the survival of the nation or the maintenance of justice, which is assumed to be more important to each person even than life. People do not always feel this way, but they usually do; otherwise the governments over them would depend purely on force to survive.

But rather than facing such complicated questions, can we not simply say that each person has interests that, while purely selfish, here and there coincide with the interests of others, thus making society possible? In this way we avoid speaking of such mysterious things as a "highest good" that is also a "common good" even if completely unknown to the individual. But unfortunately we cannot resort to so attractively simple an expedient. The reason is that the *conscious* interests of millions of people rarely, if ever, do coincide. Not even such elemental values as order and peace are desired by absolutely everyone; revolutions and wars always produce examples of people who profit from chaos. Social order therefore depends on a degree of coercion. This usually takes the form of peaceful pressure, although no society can avoid the occasional use of open force. This coercion is simply an assertion of the "interest of the stronger" unless it is exercised in behalf of a common good. And if the good is truly common, it must be the good of those coerced, but it must also be unperceived by them or else they would not have to be coerced. In short, since people cannot be united in their *conscious* interests, they must be united in their *real*, but often unrecognized, interests. Otherwise, every government serves merely "the interest of the stronger."

The issue of moral absolutism versus moral relativism is closely linked with this question. If there are absolute moral laws or absolute values, they must in some way define a common good, otherwise they would not be both good and absolute. Thus a moral absolutist might regard justice as a good to which every purely individual interest is properly subordinate; the imprisonment suffered by a criminal would then be demanded by the criminal's own essential nature.

On the other hand, if all moral rules and values are relative to circumstances or persons—if they merely represent someone's idea of what is good and not good in itself—then it is questionable whether the idea of a truly common good makes sense. A moral relativist may be logically bound to side with Thrasymachus; certainly, Plato's attack on Thrasymachus was an attack on moral relativism in general. But the paths of thought are intricate enough to make the assertion of an invariable rule in this matter inadvisable. Many relativists have been as hostile toward the outlook of Thrasymachus as Plato was.

In speculating on this question, we are traversing some of the most rugged and uninviting terrain in the whole realm of political thought. But there is no way of avoiding it. A political system is essentially a set of arrangements by which some people dominate others. How can this be made morally tolerable? Civilization is carried on under a great moral shadow—a shadow cast by the political order. Unless we can show that Thrasymachus was wrong and that government can serve the interest of all, we shall have to regard civilized life as founded on the exploitation of the weak.

One way of pursuing the question is to ask: if there is a common good, what is it? If such a good be defined, then Thrasymachus is refuted. By trying to define the common good, however, we do not leave the rugged and uninviting terrain we have been crossing. This is not only because of philosophical difficulties attending the question but also because of what might be called personal difficulties. In asking about the good, you are asking what, above all else, you care about. To ask that is to put heavy demands on your willingness and ability to look into your own mind and spirit.

It may help to put one widely accepted answer at the center of our discussion. This answer comes clearly to our ears above the din of modern history. It is liberty, the idea of organizing society so that individuals can live as they choose. The cry of liberty is heard in the French and American revolutions; liberty is the central value in the liberalism which has dominated European and American political life for two centuries or more. This is not a unanimous answer, as shown by communism, where equality and community are given priority over liberty. But communism is a conscious revolt against the liberal tradition that has hitherto been dominant in the West. The same is true of other antiliberal movements, such as fascism; their rebellious temper testifies to the ascendancy of the liberalism they reject. Let us then ask whether, buffeted as we are by the ideological hurricanes sweeping through our century, we can find refuge in the liberal tradition.

23 Is the Final Goal of Government Simply to Enable Individuals to Live as They Choose?

An affirmative answer has a powerful appeal today. This is because it enables us to bypass the moral diversity (not to say confusion) of our times in defining the purpose of government. People at present differ concerning the good—to some, for example, it is equal justice, to others it is the opportunity for those with ability to gain great material wealth; to some popular music and most television programs are good, whereas to others only such things as classical music and Shakespearean drama deserve the name of "good." To ask the government, or society in any form (say, the schools), to decide who is right may seem to be asking for the impossible. Even philosophers disagree on the nature of the good. Doesn't it make sense, then, to let individuals decide for themselves what is good and to organize their own personal lives accordingly? In other words, doesn't it make sense to say that the only *common* good is liberty?

A great many say that it does. Among these there are two quite distinct sorts. One sort is made up of moral relativists. These people, as we have seen, say that there is no absolute good, that is, no good which is good in all circumstances and for everyone. The good is entirely a matter of personal preference, and preferences, as we all know, vary. There are no grounds on which one person can say that what another person considers good is not really good. From this point of view it would be absurd to give any lawmaker, or judge, or chief executive, or even teacher, authority to prescribe for others their purpose in life. All we can do is give all people the liberty to live their lives in accordance with their own individual purposes.

Such a view has manifest plausibility in our time. It requires no leap of faith and commits one to no grandiose (but questionable) ideals. It suits an age that has seen strong convictions take the form of terrorism and splendid ideals go up in the smoke of disillusionment. The notion that governments should concentrate simply on enabling individuals to live as they choose is credible to a disenchanted, sometimes cynical, generation—to people sure of little except the self and its momentary satisfactions. Such people (that is, most of us today) are drawn to a minimal politics, a politics making no large assumptions about our human essence or our highest ideals and thus placing few demands on us. Such could even be called a politics of self-concern. It is bound to be, at least implicitly, contractual; one obeys the law not because it serves justice or some great common purpose but because it provides a framework in which one's own desires can be pursued. Citizenship is premised on self-interest.

Perhaps the most obvious difficulty involved in this view is that if every absolute good is denied then liberty too ceases to be an absolute good. It can be recommended only on the grounds that for most people it helps them get what they want. But someone with the soul of a gambler, or with vast self-confidence, may feel better able to thrive in a society where no one has much liberty but a few have great powers, privileges, and riches. A moral relativist has no way of arguing with such a person. This is far from being a mere theoretical consideration. A populace filled with moral doubt does not offer a solid foundation for liberty. It seems likely that moral confusion and uncertainty underlay the coming of Nazism to Germany; otherwise Germans would not have supported a regime which from the beginning perpetrated moral atrocities. Granted, people for whom the good is nothing more than personal preference may in certain moods support liberty. But if they are frightened (as Germans in the pre-Nazi era were by economic instability), or hate certain minorities (as Germans in that era typically hated Jews), or are resentful at loss of national power and prestige (exemplified by German attitudes toward the Versailles Treaty), and if a demagogue plays skillfully on these emotions (as did Hitler), they may repudiate liberty.

In other words, moral relativism is only accidentally, not essentially, liberal. It is therefore important to note that among those who see liberty as the central aim of the state there are also moral absolutists. These are of two basic kinds.

For moral absolutists of one kind, liberty is not merely something one happens to like. Rather, as the liberty of all of my fellow-citizens and not simply my own, it is the substance of an unconditional moral obligation. If I will liberty for myself, in elemental fairness I must will liberty for everyone. Mood is irrelevant. In supporting liberty I am conforming with a moral law which does not ask people whether they are frightened or resentful or in the grip of some other illiberal emotion. Rather it tells them, categorically—that is, without regard to feelings or circumstances—what they must do. Nor does personal advantage have a governing role in such moral calculations. I support liberty not because liberty serves my own interests but because by willing liberty for everyone I affirm my universal humanity. (This point of view is ordinarily called "deontological," a word designating the idea that moral behavior consists in doing what is right regardless of consequences.)

For moral absolutists of another kind, consequences are of decisive importance, for moral behavior consists in living in a way that enables one to realize the good. While it is granted that the nature of the good is debatable, the very notion that an absolute good exists is not denied. What is denied is only that there can be any governmental definition of the good. For some, this is because the good by its very nature must be freely chosen; the idea of forcing people to choose the good is absurd. For others, the crucial consideration is that in modern times the social and cultural conditions for pursuing the good in common do not exist. Something that might be called "moral pluralism"—a state of disagreement concerning the good—is seen as a condition of modern culture which, at least for the present, is unsurpassable. Moral pluralism is our fate and we must live with it, and this means allowing people to define the good for themselves. For whatever reasons, then, any official definition of the good would be highly inappropriate. But a personal definition is quite another matter. For private individuals to seek the good accords with our dignity as moral and thinking beings. The very purpose of liberty is to allow individuals to do this. The moral neutrality of the state, it might be said, is a strategy, not an ideology. It is not claimed that anything anyone happens to like is necessarily good, nor that liberty has the function merely of allowing people to pursue private pleasures and preferences—although it does do that. More important is that it allows people to search for the good and, if they find it or think they have found it, to devote their lives to it—so long as they do not trespass in any way on the liberty of others. (This point of view is often called "teleological," in contrast to the "deontological" attitude. Whereas the latter asserts that there are unconditional moral laws, valid regardless of consequences, the former, the "teleological" outlook, rests on the notion that rules of conduct are valid by virtue of their contribution to the attainment of the essential purpose, or *telos*, of human life.)

At some risk of oversimplification, those who support liberty on the grounds that there is no absolute good may be called "hedonists," since pleasure of one sort or another will usually be the aim that is sought. On the other hand, those who support liberty, whether on the deontological grounds that it is unconditionally right to do so or on the teleological grounds that it allows individuals to pursue the good in their own ways, may be called simply "moralists," for morality has a role in their attitude which it does not have among "hedonists." Moralists and hedonists alike we may refer to simply as "liberals." For both schools liberty is the common good. And for both of them it is a special sort of good. It is nonexclusive. It is, so to speak, a good which readily shares the universe with many other concepts of the good. Hence it seems particularly appropriate to an age of moral doubt and diversity.

In view of the variety of values embraced in modern culture, the attitude of liberals is highly reasonable. Indeed, one may wonder how anyone can disagree with them. Nonetheless, the opposition to them is formidable, and it does not come, in its most substantial form, from fanatics such as fascists. It comes from people dedicated to a less easygoing, undiscriminating concept of the good than liberty. For such people, public life is impoverished if the good is so far subordinated to rights of personal choice as liberals demand. They do not necessarily deny liberty altogether; it may have a role in relation to whatever they conceive the good to be. But they do not necessarily accept liberty, either, and they are ready to limit it, or even to set it aside altogether, when it conflicts with more ultimate values. Today people who take values so seriously are suspect in many quarters, for it is feared that they endanger liberty, and perhaps they do. One can question, however, whether civilization would exist if there had not been such people in the past, for it is not clear that mere liberty can inspire the greatest acts of human creativity. A deep commitment to values of one sort or another gave rise to the cultural brilliance of ancient Greece, the peace and order of the Roman Empire, and the depth and splendor (as typified in Gothic cathedrals) of the Middle Ages.

What sort of values might be regarded as more important than liberty? For us briefly to examine a few of these values will not only answer this question. It may also help readers to discover what they most deeply care about and where they stand in relation to the issue of whether the end of government is simply to enable individuals to live as they choose. Those who discover a good seemingly worthy of personal dedication will, at the very least, reject hedonistic liberalism. If the good discovered seems of commanding importance, they will reject moralistic liberalism too. On the other hand, those in whom contemplating several different concepts of the good gives rise mainly to personal doubt or to an impression of irresolvable social differences, will be impelled in the direction of liberalism. The following are a few of the chief values to which serious thinkers and leaders have given a significance transcending liberty.

1. *Justice.* The ideal of justice has an uncommon majesty. This is reflected in the fact that it constitutes the subject of the first and perhaps greatest classic of political philosophy, Plato's *Republic*. For

Plato, justice is the proper order not only of society but of the individual soul. It is consequently inseparable from humanity. An unjust human being is not, if we use words with care, truly a human being. In all ages there have been people who valued justice more than their lives. If majestic, however, justice is also impersonal and demanding. It does not go comfortably with liberty and may require the sacrifice of happiness. It tells us that liberty is less important than justice and that those who are not freely just must be coerced. It tells us too that happiness is trivial unless it is found in the true order of human relations and the human soul.

Clearly, there can be varying interpretations of justice. There is at least one great dividing line running through the camp of justice. On one side are those who interpret justice mainly as recognizing the special virtues and achievements of a few. *Excellence* is apt to be the watchword on this side of the line, and justice is conceived in terms of inequality. Plato affirmed this kind of justice, as have almost all conservatives. On the other side of the line are those less impressed with the differences among human beings than with the similarities. Justice therefore is equality; the watchword is apt to be *compassion*. Marx affirmed this kind of justice and socialists of various kinds have followed him in doing this. It needs to be emphasized, however, that on both sides of the line, justice is uncompromising. People concerned seriously with justice, whether they speak of it in terms of hierarchy or equality, breathe a completely different spiritual air than do people who regard the good as a matter of opinion or personal preference.

2. *Tradition.* I use this word to designate the complex of customs, institutions, myths, and time-honored beliefs that grow in a society over decades and centuries. Tradition has seemed to some people a society's most precious possession. It is the primary condition of our humanity. A human being stripped of everything derived from tradition is no longer human, except in potentialities, but is rather a peculiar kind of beast. Thus, for example, wisdom is not something possessed or even attainable by philosophers—contrary to Plato—but is rather the understanding of human ways and needs that is built up over a long period of historical evolution and is deposited bit by bit in the institutions, beliefs, and practices that make up a tradition. In a sense, a tradition is wiser than any person.

For all of its wisdom, however, a tradition is fragile. It can be destroyed not only deliberately, through political revolution, but also negligently—perhaps through reckless technological and social innovation. And once destroyed, it cannot quickly be rebuilt. It is of the very essence of tradition that it is not a deliberate human construct but a creation of time. Defenders of tradition are usually called conservatives. In their view, a government has no other end quite as important as safeguarding the inherited decencies and insights that make up a tradition.

This is why conservatives are not, properly speaking, liberals. Not that tradition is an exclusive value. A tradition ordinarily embodies standards of justice, liberty, and other political values and in this way, like liberty, is a concept of the good which brings into its universe other concepts of the good. Most conservatives are in favor of some measure of liberty. But the conservative understanding of liberty is far more qualified than the liberal's understanding of it. Liberty, and all other values an individual might choose, are defined by tradition; moreover, if carelessly defined they can threaten tradition. Edmund Burke remarks that before praising people on account of their liberty he will ask how they plan to use it. That perfectly expresses the conservative view of liberty—a view far more qualified and restrictive than most liberals can countenance.

3. *Community.* The sovereignty of personal choice is not nearly so old and durable an ideal as someone living in a liberal nation like America might imagine. From the age of Pericles to the present day many of the greatest minds and most serious reformers have believed that we are all, in our essential being, at one and that the ultimate aim of politics is to make our essential oneness a reality. Both Plato and Aristotle held to such a view, as did practically all medieval philosophers; and in the modern world the ideal of community has been represented by thinkers as profound and diverse as Rousseau, Hegel, and Marx.

It is noteworthy that interesting restatements of the communal ideal have come from feminists. The ideal of community, conceived and carried forward almost altogether by men, has been more or less rationalistic; the moral authority and integrating power of law, for example, has been stressed repeatedly. Various feminist thinkers, suspicious of male rationalism, have tried to envision community in a more concrete and inclusive fashion. They have brought within the circle of community personal concerns and dia-logical relationships which often in the past have been seen as alto-gether private. The point should not be exaggerated. There have been male philosophers, such as the great Jewish thinker Martin Buber, who have formulated unsurpassably warm and personal doctrines of community. Nonetheless, when one remembers Kant's insistence that if a society were disbanding and had one prisoner awaiting execution for a capital offense, it should without fail carry out the execution before disbanding; and when one remembers that Kant, with his doctrine of the human race as implicitly and ide-ally a "Kingdom of Ends," was perhaps the major source of the modern concept of community; then one may feel that traditional theories need an injection of less implacably legalistic attitudes.

In principle, it should be noted, the ideal of community is not necessarily antithetical to liberty. If liberty is living according to your essential self, and if your essential self is at one with all other selves (in other words, if human beings are essentially united, and not estranged), then liberty in the truest sense of the word is expe-rienced in community and only in community. But liberty here has been redefined. It is not liberty as understood by those who believe that the main function of government is to enable you to live as you choose. You may not choose to heed the demands of your essential self. Then, for the sake of community, you will have to be somehow reshaped—coerced, inspired, reeducated, or in some other way brought into line with your essential being.

Justice, tradition, and community are not the only versions of the good which offer alternatives to liberty. They do, however, offer a basis for reflection. The question is simply whether any of them—or any other concept of the good—warrants giving up the simple and appealing aim of living as you choose. How can one go about tackling this question?

Perhaps it will help to note that much depends on how you an-swered the first question in this book—whether human beings are estranged in essence. Any thinking done in connection with that question can here be turned to account. If your answer was yes (human beings *are* estranged in essence), then you have pretty much ruled out justice, tradition, and community as final ends. More than that, you have largely ruled out the notion that any absolute good exists, for an absolute good is good for all of us together; it must in some sense unite us in essence. In other words, if you believe that human beings are estranged in essence, then liberty is your logical political ideal. Liberty makes it possible for us to live together in spite of our natural estrangement. On the other hand, if your answer to the first question was no (human beings are *not* estranged in essence, but rather are united) then ideals such as justice, tradition, and community are within easy reach, for if we are united in essence, we must share a common and absolute good. Correspondingly, your attitude toward liberty may be somewhat qualified. If we are united in essence, a society in which separate individuals pursue their own separate values and satisfactions can hardly be the ideal.

It also may be possible to turn to account any thinking done in connection with the other primary question in the book (Question 7): are human beings unequal in essence? If you think that they are, you are strongly positioned for affirming the kind of justice that recognizes special virtues and achievements. Also, you might easily accept tradition as a political goal, since a tradition ordinarily embodies and recognizes marked inequalities. But you cannot—at least not without acrobatic intellectual maneuvers—deny any absolute good whatever; nor can you affirm liberty unqualifiedly. The idea of essential inequality implies a natural human aristocracy. That, in turn, presupposes absolute values of some sort and rules out the ideal of a society in which individuals live according to their own separate values. On the other hand, if you believe that human beings are *equal* in essence, a variety of routes become available. If their equality lies merely in the absence of any absolute standards according to which they can be distinguished, the realm of hedonistic liberalism lies open before you. If their equality is thought to lie in the possession by each one of absolute value, however, you might opt for egalitarian justice or for community as the common good.

It can help, in thinking about issues as abstract as these, to resort to concrete examples. And in thinking about the goals of government, some of the most relevant examples are issues concerning governmental coercion. Where are you willing for the state to interfere with force? Pondering this question might help you decide what goals you deeply believe government should pursue. The following three topics may serve to bring the question before us.

1. *Suicide.* Suicide is self-murder. Practically everyone supports the right of the state to prevent, and punish severely where it cannot prevent, the murder of others. Why? Because murder denies the right of people to live as they choose? Or, rather, because murder violates some great and absolute good, such as life? If the former, it is logical to affirm a right of suicide; it is living as you choose. If the latter, then it is hard to see how suicide differs basically from any other act of murder. It is noteworthy that people often defend the right of suicide in conversation but rarely do so in concrete instances. When the police use nets and lassoes to prevent someone poised on a high place from jumping, there is never a storm of public protest. Why not? Are we irrational to interfere when someone embarks on so deeply personal an act as suicide? Or does an actual attempt at suicide bring momentarily to light a deep, perhaps unrecognized, sense of values more important even than liberty?

2. *Abortion.* This is commonly defended on the grounds that whether a woman has a child is her own affair entirely and that government cannot rightfully interfere. A permissive view of abortion fits comfortably with liberalism, particularly with hedonistic liberalism. Feminists have emphatically, and it seems unanimously, or nearly so, claimed the right of each woman to make her own decisions in the matter. Their central contention perfectly illustrates the ideal of living as you choose; if a woman can be forced to bear a child, they maintain, her body and her own separate life in effect can be taken away from her. Those who oppose them on this issue argue that so unqualified an affirmation of liberty as this would justify not only abortion but infanticide as well, and that when it comes to the life of a human being, or potential human being, our right to live as we choose must be limited in behalf of our common humanity. This stormy issue, then, arises ultimately from the question of whether we are essentially estranged. If we are, then to force someone to bear and care for a child is an intolerable interference in personal life. If we are united in essence, however, then the termination of a pregnancy perhaps concerns us all.

3. *Pornography.* Freedom from every kind of censorship is a dominant ideal among liberals. The supporting argument usually is based on the presumed right of people to live as they choose; the kind of magazines they read or movies they watch is no one's business but their own. This is not a bad argument. If we are essentially

estranged, and my life is entirely mine and no one else's, then any governmental interference in private life is intrusive and presumptuous. Many who might otherwise accept such arguments, however, have had second thoughts. This is partly because children have increasingly become objects of pornographic attention. It is also because feminists have become sensitive to the way pornography degrades women. As a result pornography faces more formidable opposition than it has for some time. The question here is what values this opposition presupposes and reveals. Can the disgust most people feel when they contemplate the exposure of children to the lusts stirred by pornographic magazines be explained as due mainly to the sense that they are not old enough to choose such roles on their own? Or does it represent revulsion before the violation of some crucial and common value, such as care for the innocent and helpless? And does the concern felt by women about the degradation they suffer through pornography reflect an instinct of self-protection, or is it an awakening to a great and common evil—an ostensibly private amusement that in fact debases not women alone but *human beings?*

Questions concerning the ends of power are excruciatingly difficult. It may therefore be worthwhile stepping back and looking at them from a different angle. One way of doing this would be to pick one or two values, often regarded as absolute and as more important than liberty, and to ask whether government has any business supporting them. Hence the following question.

24 *Does Government Have Any Responsibility for Truth and Morality?*

No one, of course, would deny that people in public office ought to be reasonably truthful and moral. But the question does not concern anything so uncontroversial as the need for trustworthy government officials. What it asks is whether those officials are responsible for upholding truth and cultivating morality in the societies they govern. Have they any proper role in defining what people should believe or how in their personal lives they should behave? Is government concerned merely with maintaining order and protecting personal freedom, or is it concerned with the true and the good? In a word, does government have any *spiritual* responsibilities?

Today one is likely to be surprised that such a question is even asked. Secularism has become axiomatic in Western politics, and secularism means among other things that the relationship of citizens to ultimate matters—such as the true and the good—is not the business of government. If any organization is to be involved in a person's spiritual affairs, that organization is normally the church; and church and state must be strictly separate. And whether the church, or any other organization, or anyone else at all, is in fact to be involved in an individual's spiritual life must be left for the individual alone to decide. The individualism once taken for granted in economic matters is now taken for granted in spiritual matters.

This is perhaps a good thing. It is worth noting, however, that some of the greatest thinkers have not been of the same mind as contemporary Americans; they have not shared either our spiritual individualism or our political secularism.

Moreover, aside from what has been thought in the past, isn't it doubtful that so fundamental a question has been absolutely and permanently settled? Perhaps not, if truth and morality fall altogether within the purview of churches. But do they? Are not human beings, whatever their attitudes toward religion, intrinsically spiritual—concerned with the true and the good? And if so, are they not concerned with these values in all of their relationships, beyond as well as within the churches? And can society and the state be sound if they are unconnected with truth and morality? Clearly we need to think further on this matter.

Let us begin with the first value, truth. Does government have any responsibility for truth, or, to bring the question nearer to the point, for the beliefs of those it governs? The idea that government should be wholly detached in matters of belief, and individual men and women left completely on their own, developed fairly recently, only two or three hundred years ago. Locke defended such a doctrine near the end of the seventeenth century. He was not the first to do so, but he spoke for an idea that was still controversial and generally unacceptable.

Moreover, the reasons earlier thinkers advanced for asserting governmental responsibility for beliefs were not absurd. They may have been inadequate, but they were not incomprehensible or manifestly unreasonable. To begin with, these thinkers thought that we can know with assurance what the truth is. The question "Who is to say?" would have been attributed by most of the great Greek and medieval thinkers to bad character or lack of intelligence—to something obscuring the importance and availability of objective truth about humanity and the universe.

Why not let one discover the truth for oneself? Most of these thinkers would have made the sensible (although possibly erroneous) response that discovery of the truth is difficult even for the greatest minds and altogether beyond the capacity of average minds. Consequently, if government and society do not help the individual decide what to believe, most people will suffer paralyzing uncertainty and, finally, despair. The result for society, since social order depends on common—and true—beliefs, will be weakness and disorder.

Most thinkers of the past would not have inferred from these considerations that government should have an exclusive and unchecked right to proclaim the truth. Nor would they have inferred that government should try to uphold the truth with violence and terror. Aristotle, for example, held that scientists and philosophers had primary responsibility for finding the truth and making it known, and the typical medieval thinker believed that supervision of belief was the duty primarily of the spiritual power, the Church, rather than the temporal. Even Plato and Augustine, thinkers of a more radical and impassioned temper than many others, were far from desiring that truth be promoted by force. Education was the way taught by Plato; and Augustine sanctioned the use of violence against heretics only after long hesitation and with utmost reluctance.

But none of these thinkers, and few others until recent times, ever entertained the modern idea that government is spiritually neutral. To know the truth was for them one of humanity's principal aims, and government was far too great an influence on human life to be barred from participating and helping in the common pursuit of this aim.

It is noteworthy that Locke based his individualism, in economic and spiritual matters alike, on the same broad principles, and that the typical American liberal has rejected these principles in regard to the one area but clings to them in regard to the other. Locke assumed a certain essential estrangement among human beings.

This meant, in economics, that the use one makes of personal property is not the business of anyone else; it meant, spiritually, that the beliefs of one person are of no proper concern to anyone else. Locke also assumed that, despite estrangement (which does not necessarily eventuate in conflict), there is a natural harmony among individuals. Thus, he thought, if each person acquires and uses property according to the dictates of selfish interest, order and prosperity will naturally ensue; likewise, in the spiritual realm, if each one is left free to seek out and affirm one's own personal truth, universal truth will emerge spontaneously. Finally, Locke conceived of freedom primarily as the absence of governmental restraint. One is economically free, therefore, if not interfered with in acquiring and using property, even though, as a matter of fact, one may have little property and even be starving. Correspondingly, Locke apparently saw people as spiritually free so long as their beliefs were self-chosen, even if those beliefs were false and in some way spiritually destructive.

The typical liberal of the present day has left Locke's economic theory far behind. In considering economic questions, a contemporary liberal is likely to assume (1) that human beings are not essentially estranged, but that each has some responsibility for the welfare of all others; (2) that there is no natural harmony, that unrestrained accumulation of profits by individuals leads to drastic inequalities and to cycles of inflation and depression, and that a just and stable economic order consequently depends on governmental action; and (3) that freedom to starve is not real freedom.

With respect to personal belief, however, the same liberal is likely to remain an unreconstructed follower of Locke. Does some underlying logic hold together this seemingly divided consciousness? It does not seem so.

If you still think government should stay out of personal beliefs, test that idea. Imagine that a belief you despise—for example, that white people constitute a superior race or that America should be organized and governed by the military—has won the allegiance of a large and powerful group in the country. Would you object if the government took steps to ensure that this belief was not taught in the public schools or proclaimed in the nation's press?

Let us turn to another dimension of our spiritual life, morality. During antiquity, people were less concerned than we are today with material welfare and less concerned than people of the Middle

Ages were with faith. They gave much attention, however, to morality—not as a puritanical discipline denying worldly pleasures for the sake of life beyond death, but as a discipline for living fully within this world. Correspondingly, they viewed government as occupying a position of moral leadership. Thus were the spiritual and the political fused. Is this appropriate? Does government have any responsibility for the moral character of individuals?

For most people today the answer would be an emphatic no. To begin with, it is commonly held, moral theories are very open to doubt. Anyone who presumes to say what is good and what is evil is indulging a mere personal opinion, something that cannot be proved and thus should not be forced on others. The notion that governments should define the good and impose it on people is particularly outrageous, for governments are not wiser than private individuals; on the contrary, they are often uniquely benighted. If morality is the capacity for living well, then one person has as good a claim to being moral as another. Each of us has personal and unique ideas of what it means to live well and should be allowed to practice these ideas without interference. Besides, even if it were right for government to try to make people moral, how could it? A moral action must be freely done, whereas government can only coerce. An act done under governmental command could not possibly be moral.

These statements represent familiar attitudes in twentieth-century America; if sometimes thoughtlessly delivered, they are not baseless or arbitrary. Beneath them lie some of the major principles of modern liberalism, such as individualism, moral relativism, and the idea that government belongs on the periphery of life and not at its center.

However, the notion that government does have some responsibility for the moral character of individuals is represented by thinkers of the stature of Aristotle and Thomas Aquinas and is not as unsound as many Americans would suppose. Aristotle's argument might be reduced to the following chain of principles: living well is not doing just as one pleases but depends on understanding and adhering to a pattern of life that is valid for all human beings; discovery of this pattern requires unusual insight as well as the gradual development of tradition; most people, therefore, need society to provide moral illumination and structure for their lives;

government is the principal agent of society and thus is properly involved in the fulfillment of society's moral responsibilities.

This argument would not justify a government's deciding all by itself what is moral and then forcing it on people. Political power should serve a moral consciousness that is the mind and tradition of a whole culture and not something created by a government. Moreover, the moral responsibilities of government should be carried out less through coercion than through example, through education, and through the respect, rather than fear, inspired by the laws.

These two views concerning the moral functions of government (we may call them the liberal and the moralistic) involve two very different conceptions of law and its place in life. In the liberal view, the principal purpose of law is protection; the law should ensure security for persons and property and provide the individual with a sphere in which one can live as one chooses. In the moralistic view, law should prescribe what is right, not merely what serves the convenience of individuals, for the primary purpose of law is to give moral form to life. The liberal must feel on the whole that the less law there is, the better. The moralist, without being totalitarian, feels that the individual should have the law at hand as a guide and monitor.

Most Americans easily see the weaknesses in the moralistic view. It accords government a dangerous eminence and evinces relatively little respect for the freedom and uniqueness of personal life. Because the weaknesses of the liberal view are not so obvious, it seems appropriate to point them out.

For one thing, liberals often rely on the notion that moral rules are purely subjective and personal; this is why they believe governments should not lend their weight to such rules. But are not some rules incumbent on everyone? Presumably those against murder and theft are. If we admit that much, we have given up the casual relativism so often expressed (but perhaps not so often really believed) by liberals and have acknowledged that every human life should be carried on within a common moral structure. But even if we stick to the claim that we care nothing about universal morality but only about harm to others, is the argument saved? Why should we care about harm to others if we are indifferent to morality? A person who is really indifferent to morality would care only about harm to the self and only for selfish reasons would accept social arrangements that protect everyone. This is one form of the social-contract doctrine. Perhaps no argument can forcibly dislodge a person who consistently adheres to this position. But such a person has to assume that one of the most persistent of human feelings—that of moral indignation—is no more than a prejudice.

Another weakness in the liberal view is that it places a burden of moral discernment on the average individual that may be too heavy to bear. During the last generation or two we have come to realize that the *material* well-being of an individual is decisively affected by conditions prevailing in the whole society and manageable, if at all, only by the whole society; thus in time of severe unemployment an ordinary laborer is likely to suffer severely regardless of personal initiative and ability. But is not the *moral* well-being of an individual also decisively affected by society? An individual's ideas of right and wrong are, by and large, learned from society. Surely it is inevitable, then, that individuals living in societies that are morally degraded or empty will suffer demoralization, that is, the confusion and apathy that a person must experience when unable to see that any one course of action or way of living is preferable to any other. Does not the individual need moral as well as material help?

Finally, we may ask the liberal whether it is possible, let alone desirable, to place government on the periphery of moral life. Through such influences as personal example, education, and law, government inevitably has a powerful effect on the moral attitudes and practices of its citizens. Would it not be best, then, for political leaders, rather than trying in vain to separate themselves from morality, to acknowledge the influence they inevitably have and exercise it as wisely as possible?

I suggested earlier the possibility of testing one's principles by imagining governmental efforts to suppress beliefs that seem false and dangerous. Here a similar experiment may be in order. Imagine that the government is trying to encourage moral attitudes that are apparently valid and desirable. Imagine, for example, that public education, and the urging and personal example of leaders, are being used to cultivate a sense of fairness toward all races. Would that be objectionable?

The old idea of a wall between church and state obviously does not come near to resolving the issue before us. The relationship of

the temporal and spiritual realms, assumed by many to be a problem we have left far behind, appears after all to be among the
perennial questions. To establish this, I have presented arguments
primarily on one side of the issue.

We should not forget the other side, however. Although we
have found the question of a government's spiritual functions more
alive than most people today suppose, it would be reckless—and re-
actionary—to think of government as the major spiritual power in
society. The arguments separating the spiritual and the temporal,
however commonplace endless repetition and frequent oversimplification may have made them, are weighty.

These arguments are based on the nature of political and spiritual leadership and the differences between them. Political leadership necessarily involves the use of power—molding minds and in-
fluencing behavior in order to reach preconceived goals. This fact
casts a deep shadow over all political life, for power relationships
are inherently base; some people are objectified and used by others.
And such relationships tend to become worse in actuality than they
necessarily are by nature, since power encourages arrogance among
its possessors and irresponsibility among the powerless. Politics is
the darkest area of our collective and historical existence, and that
is why ancient wisdom tells us to beware of mixing the political and
the spiritual. Political leaders are not ordinarily very spiritual people, and the moral precariousness of their position can only be enhanced by spiritual aims and the consequent lure of spiritual pretensions.

Spiritual leadership, on the other hand, is closely linked with
powerlessness. It is said of the Messiah depicted in the Book of Isaiah that "he will not cry or lift up his voice, or make it heard in the
street" and that "a bruised reed he will not break, and a dimly burning wick he will not quench." Rather than having power, spiritual
leaders may have to suffer from the power of others. The Messiah is
likened, in another passage in the Book of Isaiah, to "a lamb that is
led to the slaughter."[1] The fusion of spirituality with powerlessness
and with suffering is consecrated by the New Testament through
the image of the Crucifixion. And it is not in Christ alone that this
fusion is realized; it becomes an authoritative pattern for all Chris-

[1]Isaiah 42:2–3 and 53:7 (Revised Standard Version).

tians. Paul "boasts" in one of his letters that he has been lashed five times, beaten with rods three times, on one occasion stoned, and three times shipwrecked; that he has been "in danger from rivers, danger from robbers, danger from my own people, danger from Gentiles, danger in the city, danger in the wilderness, danger at sea, danger from false brethren"; and that he has experienced "toil and hardship, through many a sleepless night, in hunger and thirst, often without food, in cold and exposure." "Who," he asks, "is weak, and I am not weak?"[2] Jesus and Paul were anything but men of power. On the contrary, the story of the Crucifixion and Paul's account of his own tribulations carry the unmistakable intimation that spirituality and powerlessness are mysteriously conjoined. Spirituality is apt to be impaired, or even destroyed, one may surmise, if mixed with political power. We glimpse here the intuition underlying the doctrine of the two swords.

If the idea of the separation of state and church is worth recalling, so is the idea of tolerance. It bears on both beliefs and morals: individuals should be free to hold and voice their own conceptions of the truth and also to live according to their own visions of the good. The idea of tolerance is easily misused and distorted. Sometimes it represents nothing better than an absence of moral convictions or indifference to others. And it is often pressed too far; not everything can be tolerated. But it rests on a compelling fact—that there can be no genuine life and no true relationships if there is no tolerance. If people have to think and act in conformity with official, or even with merely social, requirements, then everything is falsified. Tolerance thus is one of the primary requisites of life. And tolerance merely for true opinions and right actions will not suffice; since it means no more than tolerance for opinions which the government considers true and for actions the government considers right, there is always and everywhere tolerance of that sort. There must be tolerance for beliefs we consider erroneous and actions we deem immoral. Tolerance must extend far enough to be dangerous. Otherwise it is a mere formality, a courtesy I extend to those who think and act on the whole as I do, and not a policy that accepts important disagreements and differences and does this in an effort to make room for abounding life and serious communication.

[2]II Corinthians 11:24–29 (Revised Standard Version).

The sinister possibilities inherent in joining political and spiritual leadership and denying tolerance are indicated by the totalitarian states of our time. Nazi Germany was at once a political and (in however debased a sense) spiritual organization, and Hitler took responsibility for both the worldly order and the beliefs and morals of the German people. The intolerance of the Soviet regime rested on the presupposition that the rulers were responsible for spreading truth and destroying error. It is noteworthy that these exalted conceptions of political responsibility have not simply fallen short of perfect realization; they have led to unprecedented horrors.

Having opened up this question, so seldom seriously discussed in our day, we are in a good position to consider a closely related question. One spiritual function that everyone grants the government (although some might say it is not a spiritual function) is defining and dealing with crime. Let us consider in a very general way how this function should be fulfilled; we may conveniently do this by reflecting on punishment.

25 *Is Avenging Crime a Proper Aim of Government?*

This is a question about retribution; it concerns the requirements, not of a thirst for vengeance, but of justice. In spite of similarities of sound and appearance, the word *avenge* has very different connotations from the words *vengeance* and *revenge*. A crime might be *avenged* dispassionately and even regretfully. A crime is *revenged*, however, only in a resentful and vindictive spirit. One is a matter of justice; the other, of *vengeance*. The distinction is important because it is difficult to make out a strong case for revenge or vengeance. There are obviously poisonous passions at work among the vengeful, and there are terrible dangers for society and individuals once the sequence of injury, retaliation, and counterretaliation has been set afoot. But justice is another matter entirely. It is not personal rancor that causes us to care about justice, but a sense of the primal order of being. For a crime to pass unavenged seems, to many at least, like a derangement of the cosmos. Some sort of balancing seems imperative.

But doubts still can arise. Is dispassionate justice the highest standard of human relations? What about mercy? Is there not something deeply offensive in the cold and implacable execution of a human being, even when the human being is a murderer and the execution is just?

To reflect on the question as to whether avenging crime is a proper end of government requires giving some thought at the outset to the nature of crime. In our time, crime is probably more often thought of as evidence of sickness than of sin. In fact, even to speak of sin in discussing social problems is sure to raise eyebrows. A student of social problems usually does not accept the kind of moral absolutism the word *sin* suggests and does not regard the law as based on morality so much as on mere social convenience.

The sickness evident in crime is often seen, moreover, as a sickness of society rather than of the criminal. Crime is traced back to social conditions, such as broken families and unemployment. When this is done, the criminal comes to be seen as a victim and society, in a sense, as the criminal.

There is some truth in this way of looking at crime. If the criminal were not in some measure a victim, how could one explain the higher crime rate in slums as compared with suburbs? Indeed, if there were not some statistical correlation between crime rates and either social or psychological conditions, crime would be a thoroughly senseless phenomenon, entirely outside the sphere of reason.

The question of whether crime can be regarded as *altogether* an illness rather than a moral transgression, however, cannot be decided by statistics. And this question is of utmost importance; your answer to it involves your whole conception of the individual and the relations of individuals and society.

The first issue to be decided is whether the individual is wholly comprehensible through causal explanations. Can persons be completely understood in terms of various laws—physical, psychological, and social—or do we stand in some sense above the various causal sequences? In other words, are we free? The view that a person is entirely explicable in terms of causes may be termed *naturalism*, for it sees human beings as belonging completely to the order of nature. Let us call the contrary view *voluntarism*, because it maintains the possibility of free or voluntary acts. Naturalism is the basis of the view that crime is sickness. Presumably sickness is not freely chosen, but caused.

Where does retribution—avenging crime—come into the matter? For naturalism, clearly, it does not at all. If humankind is viewed naturalistically and crime is regarded as illness rather than sin, retribution is senseless. A physician would not punish a patient for contracting pneumonia. From a naturalistic viewpoint, crime presents two problems: the reformation of the criminal and the prevention of future crime. The first is connected primarily with the welfare of the person who committed the crime, the second with the welfare of society. Both, however, are problems of control and management rather than morality. The criminal must be rehabilitated in order to be no longer a criminal, and society must be reorganized so that it is no longer a breeding ground of crime.

One question about the naturalistic approach is whether it is possible to control either the criminal or society in a way that will assure desirable results. Certainly not as yet. A more serious question is whether the naturalistic approach, in however benign a fashion, is degrading to human beings. Does it treat them as things that psychiatrists and social planners can mold as they please? Does the dignity of the individual disappear?

Voluntarism obviously offers a very different perspective. Assuming the reality of a moral law, the principle of retribution inevitably takes on a certain amount of authority. First, avenging a crime can be seen as a way of vindicating the moral law. A crime is implicitly an attack on that law (for the sake of simplifying and abbreviating the discussion, we pass by the complicating issues that arise when legality and morality do not correspond). Retributive punishment—"eye for eye, tooth for tooth, hand for hand, foot for foot, burning for burning, wound for wound"[3]—is a reassertion of the moral law. It is thus a restoration of true order.

Second, a voluntarist or moralist can think of a criminal as deserving punishment in the sense of having a right to be punished. This idea sounds very strange. Yet if human dignity is connected with our being, unlike animals, subject to a moral law, then one suffers an indignity when treated as being exempt from that law—which is apparently what happens if breaking the law does not call forth from others its reassertion. In other words, a person is treated with disrespect if allowed to break the law without being punished.

[3]Exodus 21:24–25.

Thus Hegel declared that an individual "does not receive . . . due honour . . . if he is treated either as a harmful animal who has to be made harmless, or with a view to deterring or reforming him."[4]

The principle of retribution, then, does not threaten the dignity of the individual, as the naturalistic approach to crime seemed to do. It is, nevertheless, surrounded by difficulties, some arising from the side of nature and some from the side of morality. The former result from the unquestionable fact that a person at least in part is a natural being and crime—at least in part—is an illness. Crime can in some measure be treated and cured. In some cases retribution and therapy can be combined, but not always. For example, retributive standards might call for a long prison sentence, which would perhaps complete the moral destruction of the criminal; therapeutic standards might call for a period of hospitalization that would leave a crime largely unpunished. The principle of retribution provides no way out of this dilemma.

A similar difficulty, also rooted ultimately in our natural being, arises from the standpoint of the interest of society. The dilemma is that the prevention of crime is imperative yet is not necessarily accomplished through retribution. For example, crimes might best be prevented by executing everyone who commits any crime whatever, but by the standard of retribution, this would be grossly unjust. The problem of prevention, like that of individual therapy, must be addressed, but the principle of retribution provides no way of doing so.

Yet another difficulty involved in the idea that avenging crime is a proper end of government is that it presupposes powers of judging human character and motives that we do not very clearly possess. Let us assume that we have determined with certainty (although this is not always easy) that a particular person has perpetrated a particular crime. Can we determine with certainty the moral gravity of the perpetrator's offense? To do that, wouldn't we have to know every detail of the criminal's life and be able to weigh with absolute accuracy every extenuating circumstance from the moment of birth to the moment of the crime? Wouldn't we have to

[4]Georg Wilhelm Friedrich Hegel, *Philosophy of Right,* trans. T. M. Knox (Oxford: Clarendon Press, 1952), p. 71.

be able to enter into the mind of the criminal and understand even better than the criminal the motives of the crime? Often people unthinkingly convert the horror they feel at a particular crime into horror at the criminal and then unhesitatingly prescribe savage punishments. It can be argued, however, that the gravity of a crime does not always accurately indicate the moral fault of the criminal, and that justly avenging a crime requires a knowledge of the latter as well as the former.

Our inability to judge the moral fault behind a crime—assuming we suffer from such an inability—is both natural and moral. It is natural because it stems in part from the mere fact of our finitude; our knowledge of the past and of other persons is always limited. It is moral in that our misjudgments are worse than they have to be. We are often prejudiced and we are persistently unwilling to admit how limited our knowledge really is. We love to judge because we love to assume the lofty position of one righteous and wise enough to pronounce upon the sins of others. That is, we love to forget our fallible humanity and act like God. Hence the command and warning of Jesus: "Judge not, that you be not judged."[5]

Finally, in assessing the principle of retribution, we need to consider the matter of forgiveness. Owing largely to the influence of Christianity (although Christianity is not the only religion calling for forgiveness), we feel that we stand on a higher moral plane when we are merciful than when we are punitive. To exercise mercy is presumably to withhold punishment. Some theologians have denied this, but it is hard to see it as just that a criminal might receive a fitting punishment and yet remain guilty, with forgiveness still necessary for "clearing the books." On the other hand, it is hard to see what forgiveness can mean if it is not an alternative to punishment. It is necessary, therefore, to ask whether some crimes should be forgiven rather than punished. If so, which one's? Should crimes sometimes be punished, but with less than the commensurate penalty and with forgiveness, as it were, "making up the difference"?

In the Christian view, forgiveness manifests the height of human moral consciousness. The principle of retribution, therefore, is seriously in question. Nevertheless, forgiveness is difficult to under-

[5]Matthew 7:1.

stand. It expresses a willingness to pass over legitimate grievances. That is not only beyond the capacity of most of us; it can be asked whether it is reasonable and prudent. Doesn't it mean that people can get away with anything? Isn't chaos and rampant unfairness the inevitable result? It must also be asked whether there are pre-conditions of forgiveness. Must the criminal repent? How can we judge the degree and sincerity of repentance? The biggest question about forgiveness, however, derives from the standard of justice. Isn't it unjust to refrain from punishing someone who has committed a wrong?

Such questions become even sharper in the realm of politics. Can forgiveness be a *political* virtue? Could a person gain and hold power, even in a constitutional and democratic state, without judging and retaliating against opponents? Could a government maintain order if it closed its prisons and practiced forgiveness? Could a nation assure its security if, in place of power politics, it followed a policy of universal mercy? It would be a mistake to regard such questions as purely rhetorical. The figure of Abraham Lincoln shows that. Lincoln was severely realistic and highly effective as a politician, yet he was much given to forgiveness. This was expressed in his attitudes toward both deserters from the Union Army and the rebellious Southern states. There is another matter in the world of political realities that may serve even better than the example of Lincoln, however, to show that the principle of forgiveness cannot be barred from the realm of political thinking. This is the issue of capital punishment.

The proposition that avenging crime is a proper end of government leads inevitably, if practiced, to executions. Anyone who has illegally killed someone else must, in turn, be killed. And perhaps there are worse crimes than murder, such as treason; if murder is a capital crime, then these presumably would also be capital crimes. The argument in favor of capital punishment is often based on the claim that it constitutes a deterrent. That, however, is an impossible argument (even if it *is* a deterrent), for we cannot sacrifice lives merely for law and order. The argument from deterrence would collapse in a moment were it not for the unspoken assumption that executions will be carried out only in conformity with the standard of retribution: only those will die who deserve to die. No one suggests capital punishment for stockmarket swindlers or corrupt politicians or tax evaders, although such people may do more harm to society at large than murderers do. The principle of capital punishment has weight for one simple reason alone: apparently it is just.

Opponents of capital punishment, like those on the other side, often stray onto misconceived grounds of contention. It is said, for example, that "two wrongs do not make a right." But that is not obviously true; it is contradicted by the concept of retribution, which represents one of the oldest and most tenacious of human instincts. More precisely, a "wrong" visited on the perpetrator of a wrong is not clearly a wrong; the standard of justice seems to say that it is right. Opponents of capital punishment often conjure the horror experienced by someone awaiting execution; it is far worse, it is said, than the horror experienced by a murderer's victim. But that is a highly conjectural argument, and no doubt the truth varies from instance to instance; little is accomplished by speculating on the feelings of criminals and their victims. And even if it could be established that being executed is more painful than being murdered, does that make capital punishment wrong? It is not clear that feelings alone decide the issue. Opponents of capital punishment have also gone seriously astray owing to their concern with race. They have demonstrated that in America the penalty of death often has not been imposed in a racially equitable fashion. That is a serious criticism of our penal practices. But it is not a serious criticism of capital punishment; the death penalty would have to be accepted if the racial inequities were eliminated.

I suggest that there are only two strong (although not necessarily conclusive) arguments against capital punishment, and these are the main arguments against the principle of retribution itself. The first is that we can never appraise the character and motives of a person surely and finally enough to warrant our deciding that the person deserves to die. Sentences other than death are alterable (a prisoner may be paroled or have a prior sentence reduced) and flexible (a prison term may be anything from a month to life); but death is irrevocable and has no degrees. Human beings do not have the wisdom, it can be argued, to deal in such penalties. The other strong argument against capital punishment rests on the principle of forgiveness. We should be merciful enough to let people live, it is claimed, even people who have committed grave crimes. We need not refrain altogether from punishing them (for example, with life terms in prison) but only from killing them. While guarding society and doing justice, we should leave room for mercy.

Broadly, the issue here is between law, in its impersonal and majestic generality, and, to speak boldly, love, in its personal perceptiveness and adaptability. The studies indicating that women have a distinctive moral sense, more intuitive and situational than that of men, suggest that the issue might be construed in terms of gender. Resolute enforcement of the law, and fair but unrelenting retribution for every crime, would be a male version of social harmony; a female version would allow for more personal spontaneity and would season justice with forgiveness. But this is obviously too simple. Numerous men have taken the side of love, and women at times (as in cases of rape) have upheld law and retribution. It may be that the issue is rooted in the existence of two different temperaments or minds, a legalistic and a personalistic. Or perhaps it stems from the fact that some have power and some do not, with the former (predominantly men) inclined to insist on implacable enforcement of the law and the latter (including both men and women) more sensitive to the nuances of situation and person, and more sympathetic toward the powerless. No doubt one should be cautious in employing dichotomies of this kind. Without question, however, there is a deep divide, both personal and philosophical, between those in whom the word "crime" immediately arouses thoughts of law and punishment and those who think first of understanding and mercy.

We have now reflected rather extensively on the uses of power—on its ultimate purposes as well as on its limits. We may appropriately bring these reflections to a close by asking how great a role, in general, government should have in human life.

26 *Should Governments Try to Create Societies That Fulfill All Needs and Desires?*

This question brings us to a position overlooking one of the great chasms in the Western political mind. On one side lies what can be called "the politics of redemption." Some of the greatest thinkers in history—Plato, Rousseau, Marx—represent this general outlook, which is that the goal of politics and of political thought is a life on earth that is altogether good. There are no great, unconquerable evils in human nature or in the essential structure of earthly life. Felicity is not a gift of God, nor is it reserved for a heavenly existence or a time after death. It can be attained through human wisdom and planning here on earth.

Exponents of this view are not generally bland optimists; they have often felt a deep antipathy toward the social and political world about them. But their mood has not been the resigned disenchantment of those who take it for granted that worldly happiness is unstable and unsatisfying. Rather, it has been tinged with the impatience and disgust of those who feel that we have betrayed our potentialities. Finding themselves in hell, they have called for the creation of heaven. The Communist vision of vital, universal community, arising from the conquest of all poverty, injustice, and enmity, exemplifies the politics of redemption.

On the other side of the chasm lies what I shall call "the politics of convenience." This is a politics based either on skepticism about the capacities of human beings and the possibilities of life on earth, as in much Christian thought, or on satisfaction with things as they are. Both attitudes prompt a politics of low expectations and low demands, since the world either cannot or need not be much improved. Government is not called upon to bring salvation but only to enhance the convenience of life.

Locke exemplifies the politics of convenience based on satisfaction with things as they are. He did not assert that life without government would be terrible or impossible. He would not have dreamt of saying what Rousseau said, that when "man" founds a government and enters into the civil state, "his faculties are so stimulated and developed, his ideas so extended, his feelings so ennobled, and his whole soul so uplifted, that, did not the abuses of this new condition often degrade him below that which he left, he would be bound to bless continually the happy moment which took him from it forever, and, instead of a stupid and unimaginative animal, made him an intelligent being and a man."[6] That is the voice of redemptive politics. For Locke, a government may save time and

[6]Jean Jacques Rousseau, *The Social Contract and Discourses*, trans. with an introduction by G. D. H. Cole (New York: Dutton, 1950), pp. 18–19.

annoyance by doing for its citizens what they otherwise would have to do for themselves. But that is all; it cannot turn hell into heaven.

A chasm, not a mere line, divides these two concepts of power, because each has allied concepts and attitudes; each, therefore, is the center point of a whole political philosophy. Those who speak for the politics of redemption are often preoccupied with the state of the human soul—for example, with one's relationship to the true and the good (Plato) or one's moral perfection (Rousseau); those who speak for the politics of convenience are usually concerned primarily with mere external arrangements and with their efficient and orderly control.

Again, on one side all attention is given to the public realm, since politics can bring about redemption only if private lives and purposes are completely subordinate to public life and public purposes. The politics of redemption contains an inherent tendency toward totalitarianism, if only as a temporary expedient. So exalted a goal as the redemption of a people or of the human race renders the concerns of private life trivial by comparison. Moreover, if each person is guaranteed a private sphere of existence, then each person can in some measure stand beyond the reach of a redemptive government—can, in short, remain defiantly unredeemed. On the other side, where government is intended to serve convenience, the security of the private realm is a prime consideration. Life at its best is apt to be thought of as private life, where individuals are able to pursue their own interests and enjoy their own pleasures, even though these may look paltry in comparison with redemptive visions. From this point of view, the public realm is not thought of as broad and ennobling; it is not a place where human beings realize the human essence. Rather, it is properly narrow and utilitarian and exists primarily to secure conditions in which private life can flourish.

Correspondingly, thinkers engrossed in the state of the soul and the possibility of its renewal through reformation of the public world generally view the earth as the possession of all human beings in common and wish either to regulate severely or to abolish private property; Plato, Rousseau, and Marx were all, in differing ways and degrees, enemies of private property. On the other hand, those thinkers who are concerned mainly with external arrangements and with protection of private life will usually, like Locke, be strong defenders of private property.

Finally, the politics of redemption is likely to be a politics of concentrated and unlimited power. Admittedly, this is not true of Marx, for whom the final redemptive act in history, the proletarian revolution, prepared for the disappearance of the state. But the man who first put Marxism into practice, Lenin, was an exponent of unlimited, highly centralized power, and both Plato and Rousseau were more or less opposed to dividing or limiting power. On the other side, the politics of convenience is typically embodied in ideas such as constitutionalism and the mixed state. It is easy to understand why. To divide power, and draw constitutional bounds around it, is obviously prudent (unless one shares Hobbes's view of human nature) when one's aim is merely to eliminate some of the inconveniences of daily existence and to ensure the safety of life and property. It is prudent, but it is no way to bring about "new heavens and a new earth"; if that is the aim, there must be a new political order as well.

Not that everyone must be on one side or the other. It would be hard, for example, to know where to place Hobbes; and some readers may, in developing their own political ideas, discover ways of combining redemption and convenience—or, perhaps, of choosing neither one. But I do suggest that we encounter here a profound and dangerous issue for modern society.

At this stage of history, having seen both the Soviet and Chinese revolutions eventuate in tyranny, the politics of redemption arouses misgivings among most of us. It seems to express self-deification on the part of its practitioners. Political leaders claim the power that the Old Testament attributes to God alone—that of erasing and avenging all injustice and of guiding humanity to its destined fulfillment. The politics of redemption seems also—since human beings do not in fact possess the power of redemption—certain to bring severe disappointments. Thus it prepares the way for disillusionment and political apathy. Perhaps the most troublesome thing about the politics of redemption, for many, is that its means seem likely to be as boundless as its ends. Political leaders who conceive of themselves as redeemers are not apt to be careful about moral and constitutional limits. Can the niceties prescribed by conscience and constitutions be allowed to inhibit the attainment of justice and community for all humankind? Magnificent ends may justify atrocious means, and a politics of redemption may turn out to be also a politics of treachery and terrorism. In contrast, the politics of convenience goes naturally with sobriety and moderation in the choice of means. The ends are not so glorious as to justify limitless violence. The politics of convenience is founded on a temperate estimate of human virtues and powers; its practitioners will naturally be disposed to mistrust intemperate means.

Albert Camus (1913–1960), a French essayist and novelist who was swayed by his humane and poetic disposition toward a redemptive politics yet was checked by a stubborn streak of sanity, devoted much attention to this issue. He brought many of his concerns to a focus on the issue of political murder. As a participant in the French Resistance during World War II, he was in contact with many Communists during the Stalinist era, and he felt acutely that he was living in murderous times. Politics, he said (obviously not thinking of all politics, but of the politics of extreme situations, which includes all redemptive politics), involves killing; therefore, to meet our political responsibilities, we must know when and by what right we can kill. He was concerned especially with limits. How can there be a political murder that does not immediately shatter all limits and open the way to unrestrained terror? His answer was that you have a right to kill for political reasons only if you are willing immediately to give up your own life in reparation. You can rightfully sacrifice the life of another in a great political cause only by accepting the sacrifice of your own life at the same time.

Camus's thesis has a look of justice, yet it is not entirely satisfactory. How do you show forth and prove—even for yourself, indeed especially for yourself—your willingness to give up your life? It is easy to think that you are willing to give up your life if you do not actually have to do so, and Camus did not assert that anyone carrying out a political murder must at the same time commit suicide. Moreover, some of the most violent men in politics are fanatics who unhesitatingly sacrifice their own lives. That does not legitimate their terrorism, as Camus well knew. Hence Camus here provided only an inner check for people of conscience but no clear, objective limit on the violence inherent in redemptive politics.

It is not surprising, then, that he went further and repudiated redemptive politics altogether. This meant to repudiate communism, which was widely supported in French intellectual circles in the aftermath of World War II, and Camus was bitterly denounced. Camus did not take a conservative position; on the contrary, his impulses were strongly reformist. He was concerned especially with the poor and the oppressed. But he insisted on our remembering that we are finite. We cannot know society comprehensively and exhaustively, but only portions of it. Therefore, we cannot know the final source of the evils that afflict society. Camus was not tolerant of these evils. He believed that resisting them was necessary to our very humanity. But to discover their ultimate cause and by attacking that cause to eradicate them once and for all is beyond our powers. In short, redemptive politics is impossible. Social evils will always exist, and it is our part as human beings, living in solidarity with one another, to attack these evils unceasingly. Yet we know all the while that we can never completely destroy them.

Camus criticized various aspects of the politics of redemption. For example, it is characteristic of political redeemers to affirm a pattern of history and claim that their own purposes are furthered and made inevitable by historical destiny. This, Camus held, encourages abandonment of moral limits and resort to unrestrained murder. It is, moreover, an illusion; if we cannot comprehend society, neither can we comprehend history. Our minds cannot reach to the beginning or the end. History as a totality, Camus declared, is nonexistent for human beings. It is also characteristic of political redeemers to single out a particular group, such as the working class, as a unique and infallible source of redemptive insight and power. For Camus, human beings are finite without exception. No group is a predestined agent of redemption. Camus attacked Marxist deification of the workers, although he himself came from a working-class family and regarded workers with great sympathy and respect.

Camus was thoroughly political; through politics we struggle against injustice and realize our solidarity as human beings. Yet politics lures us into limitless crime. This is often due, ironically, to redemptive intentions; those who seek the complete eradication of evil become monstrously evil themselves. It is essential, then, to be at once humane and moderate. What Camus offers is an eloquent version of the politics of convenience.

Americans are apt to be easily won over. The politics of convenience, combined with our vast resources, has served most of us fairly well. It may be appropriate to note, therefore, that the politics of convenience is not without weaknesses.

For one thing, the politics of convenience has not served all of us equally well. There are minorities that it has served, and continues to serve, very badly. It was often "convenient" for the colonists in early America to enslave blacks, and it is still "convenient," in the sense of being less expensive and troublesome than a determined effort to bring about racial integration and justice, to abandon the majority of blacks to the squalor and lawlessness of urban ghettos. Also, it has been convenient for men to assign women the tasks of keeping their homes and raising their children while they themselves tended to the affairs of the world at large. Here the convenience involved has had unique force: to raise their children to adulthood is one of the most demanding and inescapable obligations of human societies; and because women must bear the children, and are able to nurse them, it is easy (although perhaps entirely erroneous) to infer that they are best-fitted to raise them. In view of such examples, it is hard not to wonder whether one who concentrates on convenience thereby suffers a deprivation of moral imagination. Is the concern for convenience more or less indifferent, by its very nature, to injustice and suffering? Will it arise primarily among the comfortable and powerful?

This outlook may have another weakness, equally serious. Convenience, even very great convenience, enjoyed equally by all classes and races, and by both men and women, may not long satisfy human beings. A "sensible" person would say that political redemption is a pipe dream and that we should be satisfied if we can merely enhance the ease and comfort of life. Most people are not sensible, however, at least not in the long run. Nor is it obvious that they should be. From the time of Isaiah to that of Marx, people have imagined an era when "the eyes of the blind shall be opened, and the ears of the deaf unstopped," when "the burning sand shall become a pool, and the thirsty ground springs of water."[7] Will we be nobler and better when we cease to have such thoughts? Yet into how much terror and disappointment will they lead us?

Suggested Readings

Plato. *Gorgias*
———. *The Republic*
Aristotle. *Nicomachean Ethics*
Saint Augustine. *The Political Writings of St. Augustine,* ed. Henry Paolucci

[7]Isaiah 35:5 and 7 (Revised Standard Versioin).

Saint Thomas Aquinas on Politics and Ethics, ed. and trans. Paul E. Sigmund
Locke, John. *A Letter Concerning Toleration*
———. *The Second Treatise of Government*
Mill, John Stuart. *On Liberty*
———. *Utilitarianism*
Dostoevsky, Fyodor. *Crime and Punishment*
Green, Thomas Hill. *Lectures on the Principles of Political Obligation*
Troeltsch, Ernst. *The Social Teaching of the Christian Churches,* 2 vols.
Buber, Martin. *Paths in Utopia*
Berdyaev, Nicolas. *The Destiny of Man*
Lippman, Walter. *The Good Society*
Eliot, T. S. *The Idea of a Christian Society*
Schumpeter, Joseph. *Capitalism, Socialism, and Democracy*
Dewey, John. *Liberalism and Social Action*
Niebuhr, H. Richard. *Christ and Culture*
Voegelin, Eric. *The New Science of Politics*
Galbraith, John Kenneth. *The Affluent Society*
Arendt, Hannah. *The Human Condition*
Wolff, Robert Paul. *The Poverty of Liberalism*
MacIntyre, Alasdair. *After Virtue: A Study of Moral Theory*
Kariel, Henry. *The Desperate Politics of Postmodernism*

Chapter **7**

HISTORICAL CHANGE

"To ask earnestly the question of the ultimate meaning of history takes one's breath away; it transports us into a vacuum which only hope and faith can fill."[1] Anyone who tries to think philosophically about history, immediately realizes the truth of this observation by a leading historian of ideas. And it applies not only to questions about the ultimate meaning of history but to many other questions about history—the extent to which humans can control it, the means if any of effective control, and the significance and natural direction of historical change. All philosophical questions can give us the feeling of being on the edge of a precipice, but philosophical questions about history seem particularly dizzying. How can we possibly speak with assurance about the nature and course of the whole stream of human events?

Yet anyone who reflects on politics with seriousness and persistence is inevitably led to try. This is largely, I think, because of the imperfection and failure that attend all political undertakings. Even relatively modest undertakings like Woodrow Wilson's effort to link the United States to a global association of nations are often blocked. Exalted ideals, like those ascendant in France in 1789 and in Russia in 1917, usually lead to violence and tyranny. Are all great political ideals and efforts futile? If not, which ones may bear fruit and under what conditions? If so, is there anything enduring, is

---

[1]Karl Löwith, *Meaning in History* (Chicago: University of Chicago Press, 1949), p. 4.

there any refuge from aimless historical change? Such questions force themselves even on those who would prefer to ignore them.

It is not political failure alone, however, that gives rise to the philosophy of history. Even when prospects of immediate success are good, one may be unexpectedly faced with an insidious little question. What then? Just as the present will give way to the immediate future, so that in turn will give way to the distant future. If world peace and perfect justice are achieved, what then? The answer is that the person asking this question and all of the person's contemporaries will die. Any paradise they create will be left to generations unborn. Finally, too, any such paradise will itself decay and disappear. Ultimately the very earth will become uninhabitable. Many people ignore these certainties, but we cannot with philosophical good conscience suppress the sense of ultimate pointlessness they provoke. Awareness that the human pathway leads to a final abyss has prompted some of the most breathtaking questions about history.

While we reflect on history, we must remember the mystery of things and the ultimate irresolvability of our questions. Asking about the meaning of history "transports us into a vacuum which only faith and hope can fill" because it confronts us forcibly with one of those realities thought cannot grasp. History as whole is not an object before us. This is partly because it is unfinished and partly because what is finished—the past—is made up of human experiences that are not, in their incalculable depths and subtleties, accessible to an outside observer. We cannot speak of history as we can of the chemical composition of water or of the rate at which physical objects fall. Yet thought and speech inevitably objectify the things they touch. Hence we can hardly avoid looking on history *as if* it were an object before us. To speak of something that is not an object as if it were an object, however, is to speak paradoxically.

But suppose we cease to be paradoxical and begin speaking of history as something surely and fully known. Then we may fall prey to serious, and even murderous, illusions. Some of the most majestic and compelling visions human beings have attained concern the goal and meaning of history. This is illustrated by the prophets of ancient Israel and, in the modern world, by Karl Marx. Such is the power of these visions, however, that they are often taken as objectively true. When that happens, they can lead to totalitarianism and violence, for some people then will feel that the secret of all things is in their grasp and the future of the human race under their command. The philosophy of history is a dangerous discipline, and humane and sensible people often urge us to forsake it and confine ourselves to questions not so likely to arouse our arrogance.

To forsake the philosophy of history, however, would be to foresake the effort to understand our possibilities and goals comprehensively. Hence we must think about history and must face the hardest questions it puts before us. We must do this, however, in such a way as to keep alive the consciousness that we are inquiring into a reality our minds cannot encompass. We must think of our questions as ones our humanity compels us to ask, even though they are finally unanswerable. A state of mind so balanced and restrained, yet patient and determined, is not easily attained. It is possible, however, and it is the only way to historical understanding.

We shall restrict ourselves to some of the more manageable queries. Let us begin with one that arises naturally from the disappointments of our time. So much has happened in defiance not merely of our hopes but also of our plans and efforts, that we sometimes feel that history is a fate moving toward its own nonhuman ends regardless of all we can do. We are impelled to ask whether our plans and efforts matter.

27   *Can Human Beings Control the Course of History?*

This is to ask whether politics can be significant, for politics is the activity in which we deliberate and act upon our collective existence. It is the way in which we take part in history. If the course of history is susceptible to human control, then politics can be meaningful. If it is not, we must ask whether the political sphere can be anything more than a stage for puppets, for spectacles that we can watch with interest and amusement but that have no practical effect.

Deeply rooted modern attitudes make our relationship to this question curiously contradictory. Our activism and our confidence that every problem has a solution dispose us to answer in the affirmative. Americans are conscious of having mastered and settled a nearly empty continent and of having made that continent a base of world power. Most of them believe, moreover, that America plays a decisive role in defending civilization and freedom. Thus Americans have felt so sure of their own impact on events that they have scarcely questioned the power of human beings over history.

Nevertheless, it is axiomatic in much of modern scholarship and thought that people are products of society and can be wholly understood in terms of past environing conditions. If so, people are made by history and do not make it. Thus, for example, the major ideas of any past philosopher are often assumed to be called forth by the conditions of the philosopher's historical era and personal life. In similar fashion, political decisions are commonly seen as mirrors of a political situation; if some particular leader had not acted as he did, we are often told, another leader would have done so instead. Politics registers, but does not direct, the forces of history.

An extremely cogent and influential statement of the second view is found in the writings of Marx. In connection with Question 6, we discussed Marx's idea that individuals and societies are shaped primarily by economic relationships. We must look again at this idea to comprehend Marx's concept of history. Marx was acutely conscious of the force of physical needs, for food and shelter, for example. Not that physical needs have greater absolute importance than other needs, like those for companionship and beauty, but they do have the force of biological necessity. Unless they are met, we cannot live. Hence the relationships we enter into in order to meet our physical needs—our economic relationships—are uniquely imperious. They are inescapable and, until they have been met, all-absorbing. They are bound to shape our life and very being. This is the gist of what is often referred to as Marx's "economic determinism." It does not mean that human beings are completely fulfilled by the satisfaction of physical needs, that anyone who is warm, sheltered, and well fed is bound to be happy. It means rather that human beings cannot be fulfilled without the satisfaction of physical needs and are therefore subordinate to the economic system as long as those needs are unsatisfied. To realize our potentialities we must live, and to live we must lead the lives that the economic system requires.

In studying human behavior, consequently, Marxists typically seek explanations in economic circumstances. Activities that many regard as the loftiest expressions of the human spirit—art, philosophy, and religion—are ordinarily analyzed by Marxists in terms of the economic situation from which they have arisen. Politics for Marxists cannot be understood as an autonomous activity. It is a manifestation of economic purposes and tensions. As a historical activity, it is only one of the ways in which we act out the roles economic conditions have allotted us.

The Marxist answer to our question, then, is negative. We cannot control the course of history—not, at least, in most circumstances or in significant measure. To make this a fair generalization, however, two qualifications must be noted. First, "history" will end. The determination of events by economic forces will cease, and indeed that is already coming to pass through the evolution of capitalism. A human entity capable of freely controlling history—the industrial working class, humanity in its full productive and creative potency—will gain ascendancy and human beings will no longer be puppets. This helps to explain why Marxism, in spite of its determinism, has so aroused and inspired many people. It gives them hope.

Further, sophisticated Marxists avoid invoking economic determinism as an invariable law by which everything can be explained without investigation (indeed they often object to the very term "economic determinism"). They use it rather as a methodological postulate, a guide in empirical analysis. Marx himself used the principle with great subtlety and flexibility. Today some of those who consider themselves followers of Marx have granted so much autonomy to noneconomic conditions that the principle has, in their work, been tacitly abandoned.

In orthodox Marxism, nevertheless, the conditioning power of economic forces and relationships remains a methodological axiom. History is seen as much more a product of economic necessities than of human ideals and intentions. Human beings thus have little control over the course of events.

Hardly anyone today would entirely reject the Marxist way of looking at history. Few historians now study any event, cultural, intellectual, or political, without carefully taking into account the economic conditions surrounding it. In this sense, as someone has said, "We are all Marxists now."

But the truth in economic determinism is hard and unpalatable, and perhaps it is dangerous. Much depends on the degree of emphasis given it. So far as it becomes an exclusive or even dominant principle of historical understanding, it does make puppets of us. Our aims and actions are shaped by history and when we deliberate and decide upon something politically, we play a role that economic fate has decided in advance. This, at any rate, is implied. Economic determinism has been widely acceptable only because, as we have seen, it was combined in Marx's thought with the faith that our economic captivity is bound to end. As technology is perfected and nature brought under human control, economic relationships will lose their determining power. Human beings will gain command of their lives and their history.

But hope of this kind has faded, not among Marxists alone, but everywhere. History now seems menacing rather than beneficent. Events since the outbreak of World War I have wantonly violated human wishes and expectations. As a consequence, historical determinism has become a doctrine of doom. To retain hope and to live as human beings and not puppets, it has been necessary to resist philosophies that deny our autonomy and to say, perhaps with qualifications, that history is what we make it.

Followers of Marx have turned toward such voluntarism as consciously and unreservedly as anyone. Lenin, the best-known example, was unwilling to wait for the natural course of events (natural according to Marxist thought) in Russia and in October of 1917 dramatically demonstrated the power of human beings to alter the course of history. A contemporary school of Marxist thought, often referred to as "critical theory," also emphasizes the efficacy of deliberate thought and action. As already noted critical theorists devote much attention to culture as an autonomous sphere of human activity. Although culture does not at present promote freedom, they believe that it can. By deliberately reshaping their culture, humans can rise above the historical forces that have deprived them of dignity and joy.

The voluntarism manifest in Lenin and the critical theorists has been present, often naively, in liberalism all along. Franklin D. Roosevelt and the early New Dealers seldom doubted the power of human beings to shape history. Historical self-confidence was manifest also in Roosevelt's liberal successors, Harry Truman, John F. Kennedy, and Lyndon Johnson.

However, under the last and most commanding of those successors, Lyndon Johnson, history got thoroughly and disastrously out of control. This happened in Vietnam, where America became involved in a war it was unable to withdraw from, win, or justify. That war has provided Americans with a more somber perspective. Now we wonder whether liberal voluntarism has ever been valid. Looking back over the years since World War II, during which strenuous efforts have been made to overcome unemployment, to provide housing for the poor, and in other ways to guarantee everyone a decent level of material welfare, we are not sure that very much has been accomplished. Failures are conspicuous. The notion that we are products rather than makers of our economic circumstances has a new plausibility. Looking further back from our present position of self-doubt, we can see how dubious was the mood of mastery exhibited by Roosevelt and Lenin. Roosevelt's New Deal did not restore prosperity, and Lenin prepared the way, not for the uncoerced harmony he foresaw prior to the Bolshevik Revolution, but for a monstrous tyranny.

As the example of Lenin suggests, the boldest claims of historical mastery are made by modern revolutionaries. There have, of course, always been revolutions. But only in the last few hundred years have revolutions been undertaken by men and women who believed that they were able not merely to replace a government, but to destroy an entire social and political order and build another. Such was the self-confidence that animated both French and Soviet revolutionaries. And it reflected an attitude widespread in modern times and present in many (such as American business people) who are completely uninterested in, or opposed to, political revolution. The self-confidence of revolutionaries is only a dramatic manifestation of the self-confidence of the modern age—a confidence in human power and virtue that arose in the Renaissance, was expressed in the intense activity that peopled and industrialized the North American continent, and was apparently vindicated by the triumphs of science and technology.

The modern ideal of revolution, that of swift and complete reconstruction, provides a convenient focus for reflecting on our power over history. Has the self-assurance of modern revolutionaries any justification? There are good reasons for arguing that it does not, although these reasons do not, as I shall try to show, lay the whole matter to rest.

First of all, it is hard to see how revolutionary self-assurance can be justified in view of the limitations on our ability to know society. We have to beware of letting the triumphs of the physical sciences mislead us. It is highly doubtful that society can be comprehended with the precision and fullness that characterize our knowledge of physical objects. This is not only because society is highly complex, although that is part of it. It is also because we ourselves are elements of society and cannot stand wholly outside it, studying it without prejudice or passion, as we might a mineral. Even if we could, moreover, society is made up of beings who apparently are capable of choosing freely, of choosing in ways that cannot be foreseen and thus cannot be incorporated in any body of knowledge; behaviorists assert that such freedom is an illusion, but a number of distinguished thinkers disagree.

If society is somehow outside the scope of exact and certain knowledge, then we are hardly in a position to transform it at will. We cannot foresee all consequences of our actions and thus must often produce unintended results. It has often been pointed out that both the French revolutionaries of 1789 and the Russian revolutionaries of 1917, rather than transforming society, largely reestablished the old societies they had set out to destroy. In its centralization, its pathologically suspicious authoritarianism, its use of secret police, and its insistence on spiritual as well as political conformity, Stalinist Russia was not unlike Czarist Russia. Such unconscious repetition of the past seemingly testifies to our historical ignorance; if we could understand the past, we would not blindly repeat it.

Another reason for questioning the modern revolutionary élan concerns human character. Belief in the possibility of total and successful revolution presupposes a considerable confidence in ourselves. A revolution can hardly succeed unless its authors are morally good—good enough not only to envision accurately and pursue the welfare of humankind but also good enough not to be corrupted by the use of violence, which as revolutionaries they can hardly avoid. Nor can a revolution succeed unless the populace as a whole is capable of becoming, or of being made, morally good; otherwise the new society will be a house of cards.

It is hardly necessary to say that there is room for doubt that human nature corresponds to these flattering presuppositions. If it does not, if there are serious moral weaknesses both in revolutionary leaders and in the people at large, then a revolutionary situation invites excesses of terror and violence, and the new order, even if better than the old, is bound to provide new opportunities for evil.

Should we be satisfied with a middle position—one that denies that we are either masters of history or mere puppets? Should we assert our power to *influence* history while acknowledging that we cannot entirely *control* it? Such a position would of course be sensible; it would accord with the commonsense impression one is apt to draw from reading history or observing current events. And it would have a certain poignancy. It would envision human beings as denied the unambiguous role either of standing entirely above and governing history or of being so completely immersed in history as never to think of struggling against it.

Probably some position short of either extreme is the true one. However, as I have already observed, anyone who wishes to think and understand would do well to approach middle positions with caution. They encourage us to cease thinking, under the assumption that the question is settled. This is one reason they appeal to us; they promise to lighten the labor of reflection. Often, however, not much has been settled at all; we have decided merely to shun the extremes. The "middle position" may consist, in fact, of numerous different positions—positions the inquirer has not even distinguished, much less chosen among. And deciding, as nonthinkers habitually do, that "the truth lies somewhere in between" two extremes usually provides little light. We go on looking at things as we always have; reflection has not deepened or altered our understanding.

Also, it is not obvious that the middle position is defensible. On the one hand, the case against revolution is so strong that we may wonder whether even limited historical goals can be reached. Is it possible, for example, to maintain stability against the forces of technological change? A great American essayist has remarked that "what actually happens when the steam engine or the dynamo or, for that matter, the automobile, the airplane, and the radio, is invented is simply this: Our hearts lift up and we let out a glad cry, 'Hold on to your hats boys, here we go again.'"[2] Is even moderation historically possible?

On the other hand, the revolutionary ideal has a power and dignity that are not destroyed by rational arguments like the pre-

[2]Joseph Wood Krutch, *Human Nature and the Human Condition* (New York: Random House, 1959), p. 144.

ceding ones. Even if you find good sense in the antirevolutionary argument, you may feel a lingering and inexplicable sympathy for the revolutionary side. As with arguments for direct democracy and for the politics of redemption, they may flout common sense but still say something seemingly in need of being said.

One thing often expressed in revolutionary writing, without which civilization might be far poorer, is a sense of the possible splendor of humanity. Political moderates often assume that human beings are mediocre and life prosaic. The ideal of human glory, expressed for example in the Greek conception of the gods as immortal and powerful human beings, is lost. The potentialities of life come to be identified with the most uninspiring actualities. Revolutionaries refuse to acquiesce in any such identification; they reassert the possibility of splendor.

In doing this, they do more than express a truth about humankind; they also, to use a traditional Christian phrase, bring society "under judgment." They refuse to allow the existing order to define human potentialities. Even those dubious of revolution may feel that the critical perspective on society that revolutionary writings often provide is crucial to our spiritual survival.

Many also will feel that there is at least an intimation of truth in the revolutionary exaltation of man as lord of history. This goes further than mere glorification of life; it asserts that people themselves can bring the potential glory of life into full reality. In the Bible, men and women have "dominion over the fish of the sea, and over the fowl of the air, and over every living thing that moveth upon the earth."[3] In the books of revolutionaries, they have dominion over themselves and their history as well. Some may say that this is an invitation to chaos and violence. That may very well be true. But assuming it is true introduces certain problems that may not be insoluble but are certainly serious. Is the glory of life then purely imaginary and never to be realized? And if we humans are not lords of history, what meaning can history have?

No small part of the demoralization of the present era arises from the fact that we do not know what to think about these matters. Since the beginning of World War I, a series of profound and unforeseen disasters has shaken our confidence. Living in a century that has included two prolonged and ruinous global wars, a pro-

---

[3]Genesis 1:28.

tracted economic depression, and the tyrannies of Hitler and Stalin with their calculated and extravagant violations of human dignity, we doubt that history is under the direction either of human beings or of any beneficent force. A religious civilization might bear such discouragement, for faith in things beyond history would remain. But people today count far less on rising above history than on dominating it, and less on entering another world than on perfecting the one we now inhabit. In these circumstances, to lose confidence in the future is to suffer a basic spiritual disorientation.

Our whole view of ourselves and reality thus is at stake in this question. The revolutionary outlook, although explicitly maintained by only a minority, expresses a humanistic self-confidence that has been shared by the vast majority. For people today to become convinced that they lack the capacity for revolution is not a small matter; it poses a threat to what we might call their "cosmic morale," and it challenges them to revise fundamentally their entire world view.

Having considered the possible extent of human historical mastery, let us consider the means. Here perhaps the most important question has to do with the role of violence.

28 *Can We Guide History Without Using Extensive Violence?*

The two main sides of this question are represented by those we have been calling liberals and radicals. Liberals believe in the possibility of correcting injustice—and in that crucial way guiding history—through persuasion; this belief, indeed, is one of the essential principles of the liberal ideal. Everyone has the right to speak freely and to join with others of like mind in promulgating personal views; by virtue of this right everyone can bring convictions and grievances to the attention of the government and the citizens. The critical point is that one can anticipate a reasonable hearing, which means not only that everything said will be fairly considered but that all necessary actions will be taken. That is one reason why liberty is practical and desirable: it offers a way of peacefully reshaping society. Liberals thus are optimistic as to both ends and means; the most serious injustices can finally be eliminated, and this can be done without violence.

Radicals, on the other hand, typically doubt the effectiveness of persuasion where paramount interests are at stake. Marx, for example, did not expect capitalists to give up their holdings voluntarily. While suggesting that the proletariat might in one or two countries come to power peacefully, he thought that in most countries violence would be unavoidable.

Radicals thus are optimistic as to ends but pessimistic as to means. They believe, like liberals, that injustice will finally be conquered, but they do not expect this to come about through mutual agreement. It is a measure of the seriousness of injustice, at least of economic injustice (if we are speaking of Marx and his followers), that it divides human beings so deeply that they cannot perceive one another's interests or enter into common discussion.

The difference between liberals and radicals arises partly from their differing appraisals of violence. Liberals ordinarily regard violence as a uniquely evil form of power. Not that they rule it out in all circumstances, as do anarchists and pacifists. But they feel it subverts decent relationships more fundamentally than do other forms of power; violence is worse, for example, than propaganda or economic pressure. It must therefore be used only as a last resort.

Radicals usually are more ready than liberals to accept violence as a temporary expedient. In the long run, however, they look forward to a great lessening or even to the total disappearance of violence; and they are likely to condemn vehemently the repressive violence used by the dominant classes. For the typical radical, moreover, the propaganda and economic pressures employed by these classes are morally no better than violence. Effective resistance by those underneath is impossible if violence is barred.

Most radicals go at least this far; some go farther. Some see violence used for revolutionary purposes by oppressed people as a positive good. It is a proof of humanity. Only human beings can violently rebel; doing so, therefore, demonstrates that they are not mere things to be used as others desire.

Something more decisive causes the liberal-radical split over violence, however, than a difference concerning the morality of violence. There is a difference over the nature of human beings. Liberals characteristically see human beings as reasonable. They see them as reasonable both in beliefs and in actions; that is, people not only use reason—and use it competently—in arriving at their beliefs, but they also shape their conduct in the light of these rational beliefs. This is why liberals see persuasion as the best way to attack injustice.

Radicals do not ordinarily dispute the proposition that humans are reasonable in essence; indeed their long-range hopes depend on that assumption. But they usually hold that the realization of this rational essence is thwarted under the conditions created by serious injustice. This is why persuasion cannot work. Marx illustrates this point of view. He believed that human beings were reasonable enough for social and economic life finally, after the consolidation of the communist revolution, to be brought wholly under the governance of reason, with violence disappearing. But he certainly did not believe that capitalists were reasonable, except in the narrow sense of rationally pursuing their selfish interests. They were assuredly not reasonable enough to understand the nature of the common good or the laws of economic development. Why not? Simply because their minds were confined by their circumstances. Capitalists were capable of being rational about their own interests, Marx held, but not about the needs of humanity.

Many radicals adhere to some such determinism as this. They think that serious injustices cannot ordinarily be corrected without violence because these injustices destroy rationality; they establish divisions reason cannot surmount. Guiding history therefore requires extensive use of violence.

In a manner of speaking, the question is whether everyone lives in a single universe—a question touched on earlier in this book. It is hardly too much to say that they do not, as seen by some radicals; at least not for the time being. In Marxism, for example, workers and capitalists live fundamentally different lives. As capitalism enters its death throes, they come to have different philosophies, different emotions, and different ends. As a result, they cannot peacefully communicate with one another; their relations are inescapably violent. Some radicals have placed equally drastic emphasis on the division between blacks and whites. The experiences and interests of blacks and whites are so completely disparate, they claim, that reason cannot deal with the issues that divide them.

Liberals (although not liberals alone) persistently reject such dichotomies. Human beings are never so far apart that they do not still share a single universe of reason, in the liberal view. Hence it can never be taken for granted that discussion is useless and violence inevitable.

The issue is not only the nature of human beings in general but also the nature of reason. I have stated the issue as though reasonableness included concern for the interests of others; I have assumed that a reasonable person can talk with others because of a rational capacity for understanding and respecting their concerns. In short, reason is a moral faculty. To look on reason in this way is in the tradition of liberalism. But there is another concept of reason, and even those who reject it should be prepared to take it into account.

Reason may be nothing more than a faculty for engaging in means-ends calculations, a faculty having nothing to do with morality. A reasonable person may merely be skilled in devising ways of advancing selfish interests, whether or not they coincide with the interests of others. From this point of view reason does not disclose the ideal order within which we should live but is merely, as Hume remarked, the "slave of the passions."

Deciding this particular issue does not decide the question we are discussing, but it does have an important bearing on it. If reason is merely expediential, it may exacerbate rather than moderate historical violence, for it will only make individuals and groups more conscious of their own separate interests.

Help in thinking about the role of violence in history may be gained by considering the doctrine of nonviolence. Some of the most distinguished figures of recent times have defended and practiced nonviolence: for example, Leo Tolstoy (1828–1910), considered by many to be the greatest novelist who ever lived, and Mohandas Gandhi (1869–1948), the architect of Indian independence and at once a great spiritual and political leader. In America, nonviolence is represented by Martin Luther King Jr. (1929–1968), who, like Gandhi, finally lost his life to the violence he stubbornly refused to use in his long struggle against racial domination and injustice.

Fundamental to the view represented by Tolstoy, Gandhi, and King is the distinction between nonviolence and nonresistance. Nonresistance means absolute submission to all injustice and violence; *nonviolence is a form of resistance*. Nonresistance means aban-

doning all means-ends calculations; nonviolence involves sophisticated strategies (it is often associated with civil disobedience, which
was briefly discussed in conjunction with Question 17). Nonresistance is refusal to use power of any kind; nonviolence is refusal to
use *violent* power, but is aimed at swaying people in other ways. It
may seem that nonresistance is absurd, but in fact it can provide a
position of great spiritual purity. It represents a repudiation of politics and of all human devices, with the future entrusted entirely to
God. The great, and perhaps only, exemplar of nonresistance is Jesus. But the spirit of nonresistance—unconditional love for human
beings and limitless trust in God—is present in nonviolence, and
Tolstoy, Gandhi, and King were all inspired by Jesus. The unique
character of nonviolence is captured in the term "nonviolent resistance." Nonviolence is a way of using power and is thoroughly political. Tolstoy sought, in effect, to overthrow the entire social and
political order of Czarist Russia (although he was unable, in his isolation, to seriously threaten it); Gandhi compelled the British imperial government to withdraw from India; and King, although hero-
ically restrained in his ways of resistance, was a revolutionary figure
in American society.

In short, the doctrine of nonviolence offers a powerful affirmative answer to the question before us. We can guide history not
only without using *extensive* violence, but perhaps without using violence at all. Proponents of nonviolence are practically always people in quest of deep and rapid change. They are in that sense radical. Unlike typical radicals, however, they anticipate change
without violence.

It would be misleading, however, to say that proponents of
nonviolence believe in the *possibility* of change without violence;
the proper word is *necessity*. Violence is a corrupting and abortive in-
strumentality. Most radicals exhibit an antipathy to violence—but
mainly in their ends; they envision a world without war and societies without classes or domination. In proponents of nonviolence,
this antipathy covers means as well as ends. Violence is believed to
arise practically always in the company of arrogance and hatred,
and these sinister companions flourish wherever violence rules. Violence is always at enmity with reason and always destroys the possibility of that patient and loving speech, often called dialogue, that

we carry on best with allies and friends but can occasionally enter into with opponents. Violence dissipates our common humanity. This is to say, since our humanity is *essentially* common, simply that it dissipates our humanity.

Nonviolence, on the other hand, opens the way to truly human relationships even in the midst of conflict. It is a way of resisting evil without humiliating and forever alienating the perpetrators of evil. This, at any rate, is the claim of its proponents. The link between nonviolence and dialogue, although implicit in the practice of both Gandhi and King, was strongly emphasized in the writings of Thomas Merton (1915–1968), one of the great spiritual figures of twentieth-century America. Merton was a Trappist monk and hence was unable to participate in nonviolent activities. From his monastery, however, he closely followed the struggle for racial justice led by Martin Luther King Jr., and in his writings he eloquently defended the principle of nonviolence. For Merton, nonviolence differs from violence by arising from humility rather than arrogance and by approaching opponents with respect; it is a victory over hatred in situations where hatred ordinarily is dominant. Nonviolence does not aim to crush those on the other side but to awaken them in their conscience and prepare the way for speaking with them. Nonviolence is patient. Above all, it is intended to create a mood of dialogical openness in circumstances that tempt people to kill one another.

What are the techniques of nonviolence? This is a question without a good theoretical answer. The answer is practical. There are, to be sure, traditional techniques—marches, public meetings, boycotts, and so forth. But the essence of nonviolence is not its techniques, but the spirit animating it—humility and love. Techniques vary with circumstances, and the successful practice of nonviolence requires leaders with not only the skill to devise appropriate techniques, but the charisma to induce multitudes to practice them, without arrogance or hatred, and often in the face of repeated provocation.

Manifestly, there is much here to interest a student of politics. Politics is often unsavory and sometimes brutal; the doctrine of nonviolence is a vision of politics as spiritually noble. Deep historical changes ordinarily involve force and bitter conflict; nonviolence is an ideal of revolution through moral illumination rather than death. Nevertheless, one must ask whether the case for nonviolence is entirely sound.

Unfortunately, it is not—at least, not beyond all doubt. Here we shall take note just of two of the questions to which it is vulnerable. The first is practical. Is the efficacy of nonviolence severely limited by circumstances? Is it limited, for example, by the kind of opponents being faced? It is hard to believe that campaigns of nonviolence could have replaced the invasion of Normandy and the battle of Stalingrad as steps toward the final defeat of Hitler. And is nonviolence dependent for success on leadership of a kind that is rare? A man such as Martin Luther King Jr., for example, is not apt to appear in every generation, and when he was killed, he proved to be irreplaceable. This question does not point toward the complete rejection of nonviolence but rather toward recognizing it as a technique of limited applicability.

The other question is less practical and more philosophical. Does the doctrine of nonviolence obscure, and encourage a refusal to face, the evil in human nature? Proponents of nonviolence seem to assume that the evil in human beings is relatively superficial. Victims can approach their oppressors with love and openness in spite of the wrongs they have suffered; inveterate oppressors can be drawn beyond prejudice and selfish interest into the sphere of dialogue. Is this just another version of the age-old illusion (as some see it) that we discussed near the beginning of this book in connection with Rousseau: the illusion that we are not evil but only unfortunate—unfortunate enough to fall under the influence of circumstances that cause us to behave in evil ways? As we have seen, this view (illusory or not) gives rise to utopian expectations; eventually, by changing circumstances, we shall recreate the human race and bring into existence a transformed world. Is the doctrine of nonviolence a kind of utopianism—a utopianism of historical change?

Now, having reflected on questions concerning both the possible extent and the requisite means of deliberate historical change, let us consider its significance. The question we face here is whether historical change determines the whole framework of human life. Are your relations with other human beings and with the universe totally subject to history? Or is there an immutable structure of right and truth to which a moral and rational being can appeal regardless of what happens in history? It would be reassuring to think that there is, that certain standards and truths, at least, are not engulfed in history. A number of thinkers, however, deny this reassurance. All realities, all principles, all moral rules are mutable, they say. Everything is submerged in the flow of events, and the futility and tragedy of history encompass our world. Is this true?

29　*Do Truth and Right Change in the Course of History?*

We may doubt that all those who answer this question affirmatively—"standards change," they assert—are ready to live in the kind of universe to which they commit themselves. We may doubt, in other words, that they are fully aware of what they are saying. If truth and right really do change in the course of history, then there are no fixed points in relation to which life can be organized and guided. Liberty, democracy, justice, respect for life, honesty—all of the rules you might rely on for conducting your life and appraising your surroundings—give way. And not only right and wrong, but reality itself dissolves and is swept away in the flux of events. You cannot hold to "human nature" or to any other rock. Indeed, if you fully pursue the idea that all basic principles change in the course of history, you will find that idea itself escaping like water through your fingers, for it too must change in the course of time.

Jean-Paul Sartre, the late French writer and thinker, wrote a novel called *Nausea,* in which he depicted with great dramatic force the vertigo and horror felt by a man who begins to perceive the realities around him as completely lacking in firm structure or meaning. Nothing, not even his own hand, has manifest form or purpose. Such a fluid, molten, meaningless universe is literally sickening, hence Sartre's title.

Those for whom "standards change," and for whom that is an absolutely serious and final judgment, live in a universe that is like a ship in heavy seas; the objects around them are unfixed or straining to break away, the deck presses upward beneath their feet or drops away unexpectedly, and even the horizon seems to move.

Such, perhaps, is truly the human situation. If so, it is not something to celebrate; as Sartre saw, what one naturally feels is nausea.

Thus it is not surprising that human beings have always tried to find firm ground above the flood of change, and that political thinkers have sought principles of human relations that will not crumble and disappear in the stream of history. Indeed, it is hardly too much to say that political philosophy began with an effort to find firm ground. Plato as a young man saw the dissolution not only of Athenian political institutions but also of Hellenic moral and religious convictions. Athenian governments were repeatedly overthrown, and the city was filled with people who said, and who acted as though they believed, that there were no fixed standards of morality. Plato's response can be found in *The Republic*, which argued that the basis of political order, and of all valid and fulfilling life, is an understanding of the eternally true and good.

But what *is* eternally true and good? Plato's famous "doctrine of forms" tried to answer this question. Every reality—every person, tree, chair, or rock—is real only because it participates in a universal, changeless form—the form of a person, tree, chair, or rock. These forms, for Plato, were what we might call "ideas" or "essences." They could not be seen or touched, but were absolutely real and could be known intellectually. "The Good," which we have already discussed, may be thought of as the form of all forms and thus as the eternal source of being and of value. What is most important in the present context is that Plato envisioned the forms as neither coming into being nor passing away, as having no history and as unaffected by history.

Philosophers, in Plato's conception of life, dwelt in the world of forms. They had ascended from the things seen and touched to the forms and from the forms to the Good. They had ascended from the changing to the lasting, rising above history. Were philosophers to rule absolutely, then a whole city might be founded on a plane above the violence and confusion of historical change.

Plato's fear of change may have been extreme. His general outlook, however, is not unique and even in his own time was not novel. Plato took up a search that had been initiated by other philosophers and that has continued to our own day, a search for what often is referred to simply as nature. I have already touched on the ancient issue of nature versus convention as the determinant of human character. A notable feature of this controversy is that convention has had so few defenders (although a number have come forward in response to the moral pluralism and doubts of the late twentieth century), while nature has for millennia had a remarkable and rarely questioned authority. One of the principal reasons for this seems to be that nature, that is, the fundamental structure of being, does not change; such at least has been the prevailing belief.

The concept of nature underlies the most durable and powerful idea in the whole history of Western moral and political thought—natural law. This is the idea, noted earlier, that human relations are subject to a law that is discernible by reason and unaffected by historical change. Times and customs may change, but the deepest principles governing human relations remain the same. Some of our most civilized institutions, such as personal liberties, democratic government, and international law and organization, can be traced back to this idea. If this one timber in the structure of our civilization were withdrawn, we might suddenly find ourselves standing in the midst of ruins.

The ancient Hebrews, too, with their profound historical consciousness, sought a standpoint above the flux of history. Granted, they were far less fearful of change and more likely to see it as part of reality than were the ancient Greeks. Even Jehovah (in some ways it would be more accurate to say *particularly* Jehovah) was outside of any fixed and knowable order; divine decisions were free and unforeseeable, and Jehovah is even represented occasionally as repenting of past acts. As for humankind and the rest of creation, here too the Hebrews differed from the Greeks; they did not share the typical Hellenic belief that reality is basically an inalterable rational order.

But even the Hebrews affirmed that some things were beyond historical change. "The mercy of the Lord is from everlasting to everlasting," and one expression of this mercy is the Law, the commandments given to Moses on Mount Sinai. These cannot be touched by any process of historical erosion. In this way the Hebrews, like the Greeks, grounded society on changeless order.

The quest for inalterable realities and rules has been pressed so persistently that one feels in it the expression of a basic imperative of human existence. It seems that we can hardly live if nothing endures. Nevertheless, the last two centuries have witnessed numerous attacks on "nature" and natural law. As for nature (what *is*, as distinguished from what *ought* to be), some of the most profound and persuasive philosophers have argued against the notion that there is a knowable, permanent structure of being. Hume did so, as we have seen, in maintaining the thesis that no necessary connection links cause and effect. When we speak of cause and effect, according to Hume, we merely report recurrent sequences of sensations. We have no way of knowing whether the sequences that held in the past will continue to hold in the future. Hence we can make no assertions concerning the basic order of reality; we cannot even know that there is such an order. A similar view is implicit in the works of Kant, despite his avowed intention of refuting Hume. As already noted, a major theme of his *Critique of Pure Reason* is that the changeless structure people thought they had discovered in nature is imposed by the mind on the sensory data they receive from reality. It does not characterize reality in itself.

The idea that reality is essentially a fixed natural order was challenged from another angle by Henri Bergson (1859–1941), a French philosopher whose popularity has somewhat declined but who was a thinker of great originality and eloquence. According to Bergson, change is not only real, it is the very essence of reality. "There do not exist *things* made, but only things in the making, not *states* that remain fixed, but only states in process of change."[4] This is most obvious in respect to living things and to humankind. Bergson admitted that some realities are relatively fixed, but they are dead and inorganic, not alive and spiritual. He condemned the quest for changeless reality. He saw it as an effort to impose fixity—which the intellect happens to demand—on what is intrinsically "unceasing creation."

A final example of the modern attack on natural order is existentialism. One way of stating the theme uniting the various forms of existentialism is by saying that human nature is not a changeless, transhistorical form. A human being is free, or subjective, and thus

---

[4]Henri Bergson, *The Creative Mind: An Introduction to Metaphysics* (New York: Philosophical Library, 1946), p. 188. The italics are Bergson's.

beyond every fixed, objective principle. Not immutable order, but incalculable freedom, is at the heart of reality.

The question we are considering concerns not only truth but also right. As the views we have just been discussing prevail, the belief in changeless moral principles declines. Kant showed that this is not an invariable rule; although he attacked the traditional concept of nature, he set forth a moral theory with a firm and uncompromising conception of duty. But the traditional ideal of natural law necessarily falls if there is no nature. Hume founded morality on the wants and propensities of the individual, as well as on custom and habit. Bergson thought a good act was a creative act, arising from an intuitive sense of the movement of life; and existentialists have typically argued that choice creates values rather than being subordinated to values. None of these thinkers argued that something was good merely because an individual or a society called it good; they were not total relativists. All, however, reflected the decay of the ancient conviction that moral standards remain despite all historical change.

A good example of the prevalent view that right is relative to time and place is provided by Marx. Much of the force of Marx's writing lay in his apparent demonstration that many realities and standards that had been regarded as part of the inalterable order of nature, such as the profit motive, private property, and government by parliaments, were in actuality merely the beliefs and customs of a particular historical era and were destined to disappear. As a human being, Marx was not without absolute moral standards, as is plain in the bitterness of his denunciations of callous employers. As a thinker, however, he had no such standards: his aim was not to show that capitalist civilization was evil, but that it was temporary. His revolutionary power comes from the skill and thoroughness with which he swept all aspects of the civilization he attacked into the torrent of history.

Is it merely a sign of human weakness that for so many centuries we have tried to ground society on the changeless—on eternal forms, on "nature," or on God? Or is it because of an intuition that relationships without such a foundation have no substance or validity?

What we are asking about, clearly, are the foundations of politics. Was Plato right in his intuition that politics worthy of humanity depended on understanding the changeless, transhistorical structure of reality and building the state thereon? It is not hard to think that he was. The triumph of peace and order represented by the Roman Empire probably could not have come into being without the concept of natural law; it is unlikely that the United States as we know it would exist if the concept of natural law had been forgotten sometime before the New World was settled. On the other hand, some of the most inspiring societies in history, such as Periclean Athens, seem to reflect creativity and novelty much more clearly than they do changeless order (which is part of the reason why Plato was repelled by Periclean Athens and saw Sparta, which was relatively uncreative and unchanging, as morally superior). And one of the most stirring philosophies of modern times is that of Nietzsche, who powerfully attacked the idea of changeless truth and value. For Nietzsche, that idea was one manifestation of the God who had died. Could it be that the concept of immutable truth and right is relatively safe, conducing to peace and lawful order, yet is inglorious? And could it be that the concept of all-encompassing change is dangerous yet provides the only basis on which the heights of human achievement, and the "great politics" Nietzsche envisioned, can be attained?

With questions like these we are groping our way amid the shadows of contemporary despair. We have little confidence in the course of history, and we are afraid that our being and our relationships are wholly at the disposal of a merciless and capricious tide of events.

But is history really so cruel and unreliable? Perhaps it is less malignant and irrational in its ultimate ends than appears on the surface. It may be that the natural and moral order that sometimes seems to be dissolved in history is, in actuality, being created by history and thus may be the innermost logic of the historical process.

These hypotheses define roughly the course of modern thought. Having come to doubt that truth and right are invulnerable to history, thus giving up the ancient and medieval faith that an eternal order of nature underlies historical change, modern thinkers tried to find truth and right in the structure of history itself. This effort produced some ingenious and fascinating conceptions of the historical process. Here we shall confine ourselves to the most general form of the idea, the doctrine of progress. To hold that history tends to produce a good society—not merely increasingly comfortable but also increasingly reasonable and humane—is to hold that history is rational, because it is a process leading toward a desirable end and also, and for the same reason, that it is moral. Truth and right thus regain the primacy that they seemed, for a moment, to have lost; it turns out that they determine the logic of the very historical process that threatened them.

But is the doctrine of progress valid?

30 *Does History Lead Naturally Toward "the Good Society"?*

For some generations modern peoples have answered with an exuberant yes. Progress has been taken to be a natural, if not inevitable, characteristic of human history. A typical and influential representative of this view is the Marquis de Condorcet (1743–1794), an exemplar of the doctrines of the Enlightenment and a victim of the Terror during the French Revolution. The core idea in Condorcet's philosophy of history is the limitless perfectibility of humankind. Condorcet meant not only that humankind *may* become perfect, which Rousseau, an opponent of the doctrine of progress, also believed; he meant that humankind has a strong bent toward perfection and that history, as a result, tends naturally toward the realization of this perfection.

The key to progress, for Condorcet, was rational enlightenment. Science extends and deepens knowledge; printing and education spread it. He assumed, in Socratic fashion, that growth in knowledge must be accompanied by growth in moral excellence. Condorcet admitted that the path of progress might lead through distressing times. He looked back on the Middle Ages, for example, as a period of superstition, intolerance, and priestly oppression. But he seems to have had little fear that we might descend forever into an era of darkness. He saw the human race as moved by a nearly irresistible destiny toward enlightenment, and through enlightenment toward universal freedom and equality.

Well-known exponents of progress in recent times are Hegel and Marx. Both thinkers show the modern inclination to believe in progress regardless of what the determining force of history is thought to be. Neither attributed preponderant influence to conscious will or to knowledge. For Hegel "ideas" (not necessarily held consciously in mind by anyone) and for Marx economic forces, governed the march of affairs. They assumed that these governing forces would eventually be recognized, thus entering into the conscious determination of events, but for long periods of time they might shape events despite the ignorance and resistance of historical participants. Hegel and Marx thought that progress, over the long run, was inevitable. The blindness and inadequacies of human beings might delay it but could not completely block it.

The authority of the idea of progress is particularly evident in the Hegelian and Marxist dialectic. Both thinkers believed that progress comes about, so to speak, in a zigzag fashion rather than a straight line. Progress is not a steady and harmonious forward movement. It occurs through tension and conflict, and the most catastrophic moments may presage the most glorious ones. The fact that human beings are usually backward-looking and confused, therefore, is not an obstruction on the road of history. Far from inhibiting progress, error and conflict are among the devices by which progress is made. Progress could hardly be more emphatically affirmed. Whether through "ideas" or through economic forces, whether by means of the resistance of participants or by means of their cooperation, the law of progress maintains its sway.

But, just as belief in the human power to direct history is counterbalanced by the older conviction that history has its own inalterable laws, so the doctrine of progress, although popular during the last century or two, is matched by far less hopeful views. Indeed, the history of thought reflects a great deal of pessimism about the course of events. For example, the ancient Greeks and Romans generally assumed that history moves through more or less regular cycles; recurrence, rather than progress, was the law of history.

It is easy to understand how such an idea might arise. Recurrence is a pronounced and even awesome characteristic of our environment and life. It occurs in the changing of seasons and the passing of generations. But while the idea of historical cycles is comprehensible, it expresses a mood very far from the hopefulness of Condorcet and other apostles of progress. If history is cyclical, then ultimately nothing is accomplished. There may be achievements within a single cycle, but the long ages of history, comprising many cycles, can be nothing more than the recurrent restoration and decay of what was achieved in the first cycle. A terrible futility reigns in human affairs.

Augustine and other Christian thinkers repudiated the cyclical concept of history. They had to, for otherwise the life of Christ, as well as all other acts of God, would have fallen under the law and so been cursed by the absurdity of endless repetition. However, the alternative view as developed by Christian thinkers also was markedly pessimistic.

Orthodox Christians envisioned history as leading toward a finale of suffering and terror: "For nation shall rise against nation and kingdom against kingdom: and there shall be earthquakes in divers places, and there shall be famines and troubles."[5] With the end of history, of course, God would establish his kingdom, and this climax, to which all the ages since Adam's sin had been leading, would give history a meaning it could not have had were it governed by the law of cyclical recurrence. History was in this way leading toward "the good society." It was not, however, leading toward a good *earthly* society; the kingdom of God was conceived to be, in its perfection, unlike any earthly kingdom. Nor was history leading *naturally* toward a good society; it was leading naturally, that is, under the impetus of iniquitous people, toward catastrophe. Only the intervention of God turned it into a process of redemption.

Thus it is plain that while history has a purpose and meaning for Christians that it cannot have in the classical mind, where it is conceived as cyclical, there is nonetheless an immense chasm between the Christian view of history and the modern doctrine of progress. In the Christian view, the beginning is the moral suicide of humanity; in the doctrine of progress, humanity never loses its fundamental innocence. In the Christian view, the dominant motif is tragedy, and we must anticipate "affliction, such as was not from the beginning of the creation which God created unto this time"[6] ; in the doctrine of progress, the major theme is steady improvement. In the Christian vision, the end is a transfiguration of reality in which the earth, as we know it, vanishes; according to the doctrine of progress, we may look toward increasing harmony and happiness on the earth.

[5]Mark 13:8.
[6]Mark 13:19.

Christianity suggests a deep and little-discussed reason for questioning the doctrine of progress. This is the idea that ultimately nothing is significant except the loss and the redemption of individual souls. "For what is a man profited, if he shall gain the whole world, and lose his own soul?"[7] From this point of view all progress must be spiritual and inward; it becomes questionable whether any historical, as distinguished from personal, development can be progressive or not.

This perspective is not uniquely Christian, although it is suggested by Christianity. In its most general form it is simply the notion that everything must be judged by its effect on individuals—only individuals, never peoples or historical conditions, are ends in themselves. This casts doubt on the idea of progress, even from a materialistic point of view, for the increasing convenience and comfort some nations now enjoy cannot justify the squalor and misery which countless individuals in the past have endured throughout their lives. Are earlier generations to be regarded as mere means to the welfare of later generations?

But the idea of progress is challenged with particular sharpness if the individual is treated as a moral and spiritual entity, as one who is not necessarily better off merely by being more comfortable. On this premise, how can there be historical, as distinguished from personal, progress? If morality is a matter of personal choice and spirituality depends on the soul of the individual, it is not clear how an age, as distinguished from a person, can be morally and spiritually ahead of or behind another age. Can historical conditions place individuals on moral and spiritual levels that they would fall below under other conditions? If so, moral and spiritual greatness are apparently the products of external circumstances, not of personal freedom and moral commitment. Reflection along these lines can lead us to wonder whether the nineteenth and twentieth centuries, with all of their self-satisfaction, have achieved any genuine progress at all.

In other words, when we think of historical progress, we seem to be thinking more of vast multitudes than of individuals. When we think of individuals, the significance of the multitudes that constitute historical eras becomes problematic.

[7]Matthew 16:26.

Today, we do not know what to think about the natural course of history any more than we know what to think about the question of how far history is under human control. Our doubts in both cases are the result of the unexpected disasters that have befallen the human race since 1914. The idea of progress has suddenly come to seem old-fashioned and unrealistic. But what can we put in its place? We do not appear to have the kind of faith that would be required to return to the Christian vision of history, although many have sensed the apocalypse in the nuclear cloud. The cyclical concept of history strikes us as no less implausible, and as intolerable as well. It is implausible because for two millennia we have been taught that history had a direction and a purpose and because in the past two centuries we have seen events, like industrialization, that we know have never happened before, which seems to disprove any theory of cyclical recurrence. The cyclical view is intolerable because, after believing for so long that history is purposeful, we are crushed by the thought that it is merely endless, useless repetition.

In James Joyce's novel *Ulysses,* a character says that history is a nightmare from which he is trying to awake.[8] This remark expresses the mood of historical insecurity and fear that half a century of disorder and violence has engendered in many people today. It expresses the mood of those who have confidence neither in their own control of history nor in the beneficence of its natural tendencies. If we cannot direct or trust the course of events, it is difficult not to feel that the universe is like a capricious despot who may at any time disrupt our existence and lay waste our future. Personal life is burdened by the impression that the surrounding universe is senseless; political life is demoralized by the feeling that the consequences of any action are incalculable and menacing.

Thus we are pretty much forced to face the question of whether history has meaning—a question that may paralyze modest and cautious inquirers while inducing reckless inquirers to indulge in grandiose and undemonstrable generalizations. Moreover, so sweeping is the question that it drives us beyond all observable realities. It forces us to ask whether there is any such being as God, or transcendence, or any such reality as eternity, which might give meaning to history and which even, perhaps, is essential if history is

[8]James Joyce, *Ulysses* (New York: Modern Library, 1914), p. 35.

to have any meaning. At the outset of this book, I warned that thinking is not always fun. Questions about the meaning of history succinctly illustrate the point. They "take one's breath away." I do not deny that we scarcely know what we mean when we ask such questions. On the other hand, I do not see how we can responsibly avoid them.

SUGGESTED READINGS

Saint Augustine. *The City of God*
Burke, Edmund. *Reflections on the French Revolution*
Hegel, G. W. F. *The Philosophy of History*
Tocqueville, Alexis de. *The Old Regime and the French Revolution*
Marx, Karl, and Engels, Friedrich. *The Communist Manifesto*
Dostoevsky, Fyodor. *The Possessed*
Sorel, Georges. *Reflections on Violence*
Bury, J. B. *The Idea of Progress*
Berdyaev, Nicolas. *The Meaning of History*
Malraux, André. *Man's Fate*
Buber, Martin. *The Prophetic Faith*
Popper, Karl. *The Open Society and Its Enemies*, 2 vols.
Löwith, Karl. *Meaning in History*
Niehbur, Reinhold. *The Nature and Destiny of Man*, Vol. II
———. *Faith and History*
———. *The Irony of American History*
Strauss, Leo. *Natural Right and History*
Camus, Albert. *The Rebel*
Bultmann, Rudolf. *History and Eschatology: The Presence of Eternity*
Fanon, Frantz. *The Wretched of the Earth*
Arendt, Hannah. *On Revolution*
Ellul, Jacques. *Autopsy of Revolution*
Didion, Joan. *The Book of Common Prayer*

EPILOGUE: THE IDEA OF HUMANE UNCERTAINTY

In the face of questions that for twenty-five centuries have defied the efforts of philosophers to find demonstrable answers, how can we avoid intellectual despair? To show that there are perennial questions about politics may rebut heedless votaries of religion or science, dogmatists who assume that no great questions remain unanswered. However, it may only fortify those who shun political speculation, not because they assume the great questions have already been answered, but because they assume they can never be answered.

The major premise of this book may be phrased as a response to such threatened despair. Although our answers are never adequate, we encounter being in questioning itself. Truth is found in the act of thought but can never be embodied in universally compelling principles. The value of paradoxes is that they forcefully remind us of the inadequacy of our verbal formulas. They impel us to continue thinking. This is why, according to the epigraph, "the thinker without a paradox is like a lover without feeling."

Why this troublesome discontinuity between our understanding and our answers, between reality and words? To respond to this query even briefly and tentatively is not easy. In order to clarify the groundwork of this book and the value of thought, however, it is perhaps worth trying. Certain ideas of Kant's may help.

According to Kant, knowledge in the strictest sense of the word, knowledge that can be embodied in unequivocal and universally compelling scientific propositions, pertains to objects. This may at first seem obvious because it may seem that all genuine realities must be objects. But according to Kant an object is only a particular form of being, and objective being is not being in itself. What, then, is an object? Greatly simplifying Kant's analysis, an object is an entity existing in space and time, characterized by qualities like unity and plurality, and resulting from certain causes and causing certain effects. It is of the essence of an object that its location in space and time, its general nature, and its relation to other objects can be rationally specified.

Is this not true of being itself rather than merely of objective being? Not according to Kant. An object can be rationally located and defined not because it happens to have just those qualities that correspond with the categories, like unity and plurality, and cause and effect, that structure our minds. It is rather because objects are created and given those qualities by our minds. All that being itself provides is a chaos of sensations. We must organize those sensations if we are to have a coherent experience. Space and time, and concepts like cause and effect, are the forms by means of which we do this. An object can be rationally located and defined because its essence is bestowed upon it by mind in the very act of understanding it. An object is an intellectual artifact and not a thing in itself; it cannot exist without mind.

This is not to say that we create only such objects as we please, however. Gaining understanding is governed by processes inherent in the human mind as such. Personal volition and inspiration play no role, and the objects in my mind are necessarily the same as those in the minds of everyone. Although space and time, for example, are not "out there," existing independently of my mind, neither can I call them into existence nor abolish them at will. As a human being, possessed of the rational faculties that characterize the human essence, I necessarily arrange reality in a spatiotemporal framework.

Much in Kant's analysis is debatable. How, for example, can we say that being in itself causes our sense perceptions if causation is only an intellectual device for interrelating those perceptions? How can we even speak of being in itself if we can know nothing about it? Such questions have been discussed in countless volumes. We cannot debate them here, nor have we any need to do so. The important thing is to see how Kant opens the way to insight and vision.

The study of Kant can bring liberation—liberation from the materialistic assumption that every reality must be an object and the universe as a whole merely a vast collection of objects. Many people think this assumption is forced upon us by common sense. For those who accept it, the consequences are drastic. Being loses its mystery; persons turn into mechanisms; religious ideas become absurd. We live within, and are mere elements of, an inhuman and ultimately meaningless causal order. Kant unlocks the doors of this cosmic prison. Without denying the reality of objects or questioning the authority of science, he opens the way to a more human and hospitable universe beyond the world of things.

The study of Kant can liberate us not only from the world of things but also from the dispassionate, precise, and systematic knowledge through which that world is understood. Science of the kind that attains its greatest perfection in physics and chemistry ceases to be our one sure means of access to reality. Room is made for intuition, wisdom, and faith. Not that science is discarded; within its own realm it retains unshakable authority. But its realm does not comprise the whole of being.

If we adopt the Kantian perspective, our minds are no longer confined by preconceptions mistaken for ultimate realities. Ideas like world, God, and humanity are recast and our range of vision is immeasurably enlarged. The world, which we automatically envision as a kind of all-inclusive object that we ought to be able to know in its entirety just as we know every other object, turns out to be simply the way in which we organize experience. The world is the context of objects but not itself an object; it is a way of looking at reality. We cannot know the world as a whole because no such thing exists, and we need not think of it as a totality that encloses and determines our lives.

As for God, we are no longer compelled either to imagine the divine as some stupendous but strangely insubstantial—because "spiritual"—physical entity, or to deny the very idea of God as a manifest absurdity. A major difficulty met in religious discourse is the assumption that every reality must be some kind of object. If this assumption were valid, atheism would be inevitable, for it is plain that no object—nothing within space and time, and thus finite, and nothing causally determined from without—can be God. In challenging the identification of being and objectivity, Kant reopens for the modern age the whole question of divine reality. In limiting reason, Kant asserted, he made room for faith.

Finally, the Kantian revolution enables us to look with new eyes at ourselves. It would be impossible in a few lines to do justice to Kant's obscure and complex theory concerning our knowledge of human beings. Suffice it to say that a human being is not only more than an object of knowledge but is the source of the whole world of objects. A person is not completely unknowable, for each one has a body and a psychic mechanism that can be studied through science. These are only appearances of the person, however, not full and authentic personal being. We are no longer burdened with the notion that a human being is merely a thing. We are not forced to dismiss as illusions the mysteries we sense in ourselves and in those we love.

"Everything that is an object for us," wrote the twentieth-century Kantian philosopher Karl Jaspers, "even though it be the greatest, is still always within another, is not yet all."[1] This is one way of expressing Kant's overall vision. An object is something that our minds carve out of being in itself, and even the world in its totality is carved out of being in itself. Thus every reality we can know is encompassed by being in its fundamental mystery. Encompassing being is not only the environment of every knowable reality, however, but also comprises the true "inner" being of every such reality. I discover myself and my friends not only in what a psychologist may tell me but also in the encompassing mystery. None of this is easy to express or understand, but that is primarily because we are trying to get in touch with things that "thought cannot think."

How does this relate to the question with which we began, that concerning the discontinuity between words and reality? How is this discontinuity to be explained? We have to recall that words are fitted primarily for dealing with objects and hence are inadequate, even misleading, when applied to being in itself. "Words" is shorthand for the knowledge in which words are combined in unambiguous, demonstrable propositions, and propositions in turn are combined in systems explaining whole areas of reality. Kant enables us to see why we are able, through science, to gain unassailable knowledge of the things around us, whereas in trying to understand ourselves and others, as we have been doing in this book, we end in uncertainty.

What does Kant tell us about the possibility of somehow gaining insight into the encompassing mystery? Although we can gain no knowledge of being as it is in itself, we can, according to Kant, become aware of it. We become aware of it in defining the boundaries of knowledge; we become aware of it in moral life, in discerning and acting upon our duties; and we become aware of it in contemplating the beautiful and the sublime. We do not attain knowl-

---

[1]Karl Jaspers, *Reason and Existenz: Five Lectures,* trans. William Earle (Noonday Press, 1955), pp. 51–52.

edge, in the proper sense of the term, in any of these ways. We do, however, become conscious of realities that transcend knowledge.

Let us note here that far from everyone is persuaded by such views, in spite of the consensus among philosophers that Kant belongs among the few greatest thinkers of all time. Feminists, for example, are almost uniformly suspicious of Kantian philosophy. There are Marxist feminists and Freudian feminists but, to my knowledge, no Kantian feminists. This may be partly because Kant appears to be an exemplar of the rationalism and legalism of which many feminists are so dubious. In his *Critique of Pure Reason* Kant defended, as we have already noted, the possibility of formulating absolutely certain and universal laws pertaining to the physical universe; and in his *Critique of Practical Reason* he argued that personal conduct was under the command of sure and unconditional laws of reason, laws he called, forbiddingly, "categorical imperatives." Thus, both in epistemology and ethics, he seems to represent the epitome of rationalism. And there is no doubt that rationalism was an important and conspicuous aspect of Kant's philosophy, even though, as my preceding remarks suggest, it was not all of Kant's philosophy.

It is an error, however, to interpret Kant's philosophy as a form of unqualified rationalism. As I have said, Kant defended reason but at the same time drew boundaries around it. In doing this he made room for superrational forms of insight, such as empathy. He made it possible to claim authority not only for science but also for intuitive understanding, for an immediate grasp of persons and situations that in their uniqueness surpass the grasp of science. As we have seen, feminism is linked with a modern revolt against one-sided rationalism. The signal point here is that Kant, for all of his rationalism, laid the foundations for this revolt. His philosophy offers suitable grounds for the richer, more intuitive conceptions of human understanding foreshadowed in many feminist writings.

Noteworthy too is that Kant's moral philosophy embodies a claim that feminists cannot find uninteresting. Every person, for Kant, possesses ultimate and inviolable moral authority; to be human is to have the capacity for judging right and wrong. This implies, first of all, the autonomy many women have felt driven to claim for themselves. Every person is a kind of legislator, able to formulate categorical imperatives, and thus to live by laws that are both universal in scope and riveted to the innermost center of one's reason and conscience. And Kant's moral theory implies not only autonomy but equality as well. *All* persons are competent when it comes to moral judgments. Setting aside casual utterances outside his major treatises, Kant introduces no qualifications concerning gender. In these ways, Kant's ethics displays a spirit that is liberating and egalitarian.

From the standpoint of this book, one of the most interesting parts of *The Critique of Pure Reason,* Kant's major work, is his development of the "antinomies of pure reason." An antinomy is a pair of propositions that are mutually contradictory even though both propositions are rationally defensible. For example, to say that some things happen because they are freely chosen and to say that everything happens according to the laws of nature is to voice an antinomy, one formulated by Kant himself. Whenever we speak of being in itself as though it were a set of objects laid out before us we necessarily fall into antinomies. But we can only speak, and only reason, as though we were speaking and reasoning about objects. Thus the desire for ultimate truth involves us inevitably in the formulation of antinomies. Kant does not conclude that we should restrain our desire for truth in order to avoid antinomies, but only that we should anticipate the contradictions into which the quest for truth will lead us. If we do this, the antinomies can become indirect disclosures of being in itself.

Antinomies, of course, are what we have been calling paradoxes. That is why Kant's theory of antinomies is interesting in the context of this book. It clarifies and supports the main premise of the book, that thinking provides no certain and unequivocal answers but nevertheless opens the way to understanding. Although Kant always expressed himself with a sobriety and care that is often not evident in Kierkegaard's highly flavored prose, his basic view does not conflict with the epigraph of this book. Kant believed that reason drives us toward being in itself and toward ultimate truth. In doing this it drives us toward antinomies through which being in itself is indirectly disclosed. Thus we strive toward the antinomies. In this sense, Kant would agree, "the paradox is the source of the thinker's passion."

Kant and Kierkegaard alike thus suggest that wisdom is not gained by answering questions once and for all but in establishing a thoughtful and continuing relationship to questions. They suggest that wisdom is a thinking state. But to think is to be uncertain; like-wise, to entertain antinomies or paradoxes is to be uncertain. We are led in this way to the idea that wisdom lies in uncertainty. To ac-knowledge this and to maintain a stance not of absolute assurance but of inquiring openness is what I mean by "humane uncertainty."

We have been speaking of the inner life of the individual and humane uncertainty seems like a very personal, rather than institu-tional or public, matter. But the concept is not without political meaning. For one thing, from awareness of my power of asking questions arises an intuition that any organization or authority that attempts to suppress my questions and to make me an automatic part in some monolithic group, as a totalitarian state does, violates my essential being. An act of thought is a declaration of freedom; to be serious about reflection is to be incapable of subservience.

Moreover, humane uncertainty contains an intuition not only of freedom but also of equality. One person may know more about mathematics or automobile engines than another, but in the face of the perennial questions, we are all, in our lack of definite, demon-strable answers, equal. The wise stand above others, it would seem, only in their consciousness of this primal equality.

Finally, in humane uncertainty are seeds of community. To ac-cept uncertainty as the sphere of truth is to repudiate the ideologies that objectify and degrade us. An ideology is a political creed de-signed as a guide to action for masses of human beings. Seeking mobilization rather than thought, and a new order rather than communication, an ideology claims to be the whole and final truth. There is no such thing as a paradoxical ideology. Moreover, an os-tensibly total truth, intended to activate multitudes of people and transform society, must have interpreters and enforcers. Every ide-ology in this way is implicitly dictatorial. Anyone who shares Jasper's sense that human beings are always more than we can know or say about them stands apart from all ideologies and is ready, not for action and the exercise of power, but for communica-tion.

Have we now reached the ultimate premise of political think-ing? The question is important because, while wisdom may be a thinking state, the converse is not true: a thinking state is not al-ways wisdom. Uncertainty is not necessarily humane. It may be a state of enervating doubt and a source of nihilistic rage, provoked by the feeling that nothing on earth is worthy of devotion or respect. Does humane uncertainty depend on principles that we have failed to notice? Two such principles suggest themselves.

The first is that truth is good. "Truth" is one of those words we often capitalize, taking it to represent something so obviously sublime that no question of its value could conceivably arise. But it is possible, after all, that the ultimate truth might prove to be uninteresting, useless, or even harmful. If the structure of reality were fundamentally antithetical to human interests, illusion might be not only pleasanter than truth but also essential to keep human beings from suffocating under a blanket of hopelessness. Serious inquiry requires that such possibilities be rejected. Truth must be assigned great value.

The second premise is that the truth must be sought through public dialogue, with no one excluded. This premise is not required for thinking as such, but for thinking in the only way most of us would find acceptable—in a way open to participation by all and not merely by a privileged few. That inquiry should be open to all, however, is no more self-evident than that truth is good. Granted, we are all equal in our inability to answer definitively the perennial questions. It may be argued, nevertheless, that the ability to reflect fruitfully on these questions is confined to a few. Or in the absence of any countervailing moral imperative, one may simply prefer to work within some exclusive circle of inquirers—one confined, for example, to members of a certain nationality or social class. To commit oneself to truly public dialogue, dialogue open to all, one must repudiate elitist strategies of inquiry such as these. One must have respect for all human beings, for there is no greater sign of respect for a person than the willingness to speak with or listen to that person.

In sum, to engage in serious and fully human inquiry it is necessary to hold in high regard both the truth and every human being. On what assumptions—on what view of the universe and humanity—does such an attitude rest? Many would say that it rests on no assumptions at all. The value of truth and the dignity of every person are self-evident. But is this really the case?

To begin with, why should we look on truth as an ultimate value regardless of the nature of reality? Why should we care about truth if it neither interests us nor has any practical value? In the history of thought truth has usually, albeit not invariably, been a religious value; reverence for truth has expressed reverence for being, which has been regarded as either divine in itself or expressive of the divine. Such a view is logical and understandable, even though someone may dispute its religious presuppositions. But is it logical or understandable to retain reverence for truth after denying the divine?

And why should we respect every individual, regardless of character and intellect? The idea of a dignity inherent in every person can be regarded as no less religious in its presuppositions than the idea that truth is good. In Western thought that idea is derived historically from the faith that every person is of concern to God. If this faith is rejected and reliance is placed solely on dispassionate empirical analysis, someone could argue that every human being no more deserves respect than does every horse or every automobile.

The question before us can be summarily restated. To enter seriously into inquiry that is open to all expresses substantial faith in the universe. One must believe that truth is good and that all persons have the potentiality and right to share in the search for it. Does this faith make sense if its final object is only what we can see and objectively know, rather than God?

This question also arises from an assumption underlying every page of this book and made every day by all of us: in one way or another truth is accessible. I have been arguing that some kinds of truth can be gained through reflection; scientists believe that other kinds are reached through empirical analysis. But how can we be sure that such processes do not occur within the boundaries of some all-encompassing illusion to which we are inescapably confined by the very nature of reality and our minds? And even if we are not confined by any such illusion, and truth is accessible to us, how can we have the courage to seek it in the face of the total and everlasting oblivion that death, according to all appearances, will bring upon every seeker of the truth long before the whole truth has been found?

Summing up, we begin to see that serious reflection, such as that carried on in political thinking, is not a mere matter-of-fact activity that anyone, with any sort of view of things, can enter into. It involves assumptions, and these assumptions seem to be broadly religious. Truth must be good; all persons without exception must be worthy of the respect shown them when they are included in the search for truth; and, finally, truth must be accessible and in some sense invulnerable even to death. How can these things be true if there is no divine ground that makes reality worth knowing; that gives dignity to every person—even to persons of little intelligence and poor character; that warrants our assuming that truth is accessible to us and has a value that is invulnerable even to death?

Someone might object that to speak of "religion" in this fashion is far too vague. What sort of religion? There is apparently more than one possibility. For example, the Jewish faith can readily be the faith of an inquirer. The God of the Jewish scriptures (what Christians call "The Old Testament") is often thought of as overbearing and doctrinaire, necessarily an enemy of free thought and open inquiry. We might do well, however, to remember the charge often made by atheists—that we create God in our own image. No doubt we often do. This reflection may lead us, however, to question not the reality of God but the validity of our images of God. It is not clear that the divine despot of human imagination is anywhere to be found in the Old Testament. If one had to offer a concise characterization, it would be hard to improve on the statement that the God of the Old Testament is one who speaks and listens. Granted, sometimes God commands or condemns and no human answer is possible. But in Genesis we encounter a Creator who has placed humankind in a universe that is good and knowable and has given men and women natural powers, such as reason, to enable them together to inhabit that universe and to understand and exercise dominion over the realities within it. And very often, and in some of the greatest Biblical passages, God pleads for attention and free assent. In sum, God is frequently, and perhaps fundamentally always, dialogical.

Some suppose that in turning from the Old Testament to the New you confront a more dogmatic faith. No doubt Christianity has often been dogmatic. But again we must ask what is inherent in faith and what human beings, in their weakness and perversity, have read into faith. The Gospels present not a doctrine but a story, an account of the life of Jesus. The central event of that story, the Crucifixion, can be seen as a symbol of the necessary defeat of every human truth, a symbol of a truth that lies beyond every truth we can state and possess. Søren Kierkegaard, the source of the epigraph to this book, was a Christian and at the same time an indefatigable and uninhibited thinker. The ultimate paradox he had in mind was Christ, the presence of eternity in time. Both by his inquiring life and undogmatic theology, he suggests the possibility of interpreting Christianity not as a final disclosure of the truth but as an act of divine liberation, enabling us to search for the truth. The author of this book adheres to an inquiring and communal Christianity of the kind exemplified in the figure of Kierkegaard.

No human example of the life of inquiry or of the faith on which inquiry rests, however, is more instructive than that of a man who lived several centuries prior to Christ. Let us end these reflections by briefly considering Socrates, the homely, amiable, and disturbingly intelligent Athenian who was put to death on account of his uncompromising pursuit of rational inquiry. Apparently Socrates did not expound a complete and definite doctrine but devoted himself to asking questions; these concerned matters of ultimate import, such as friendship, justice, and truth. Socrates devoted his whole mature life to such questions. Although he sought out people reputed for their wisdom, he seems always gladly to have entered into conversation with anyone he happened to meet who was willing seriously to talk. He concluded at the end of his life that no one could answer his questions and that those reputed to be wise were in reality ignorant. It was this conclusion, expressed in conversations that resulted in publicly humiliating some of the most eminent men in Athens, that led ultimately to his trial and execution.

Two aspects of Socrates' life are particularly noteworthy in relation to the ideal of humane uncertainty. First, Socrates concluded not only that all others were ignorant but that he himself was ignorant. He was superior to others, he held, only in his awareness of his ignorance. Thus on the face of things Socrates was a failure. A lifetime of questioning had led him to no answers, had indeed led him to a death sentence, imposed by his fellow Athenians, for sowing spiritual and intellectual confusion in the city.

Yet Socrates lived the last days of a life that had brought him to intellectual uncertainty and a shameful death with triumphant composure, as though, in his long intellectual struggle, he had magnificently succeeded. At his trial his defense was characterized, as his conversation always had been, by a calm but disconcerting irony. In prison he refused to save his life by escaping, although this could have been readily arranged, because a voice, murmuring in his ears "like the sound of the flute in the ears of the mystic," warned him that in escaping he would betray the laws under which he had always lived. He devoted his final hours to discussing the immortality of the soul, apparently approaching the question with complete openness of mind. At the end he calmed his weeping friends and "readily and cheerfully" drank the poison brought by the executioner.[2] Socrates did not act as though thinking had brought him only to a state of total perplexity. His "ignorance" seemed to be the paradoxical sign of an awareness that was inexpressible but so sustaining that even the imminence of death did not affect his tranquillity.

We have no certain knowledge of Socrates' political outlook. He was probably as unwilling to identify himself with definite political principles as with principles of any other kind. But it is not difficult to discern certain broad political ideals in the outlines of his life. To begin with, his whole career was a moving enactment of freedom. He was ridiculed by his fellow citizens and threatened with exile and death by the government but imperturbably continued to live and speak according to the unutterable but irresistible imperatives that governed his life.

Further, although Socrates may have had elitist leanings (having been, perhaps, the original source of Plato's concept of the philosopher-ruler), his manner of life was in some ways egalitarian. He did not claim special authority, except for that implicit in his mission of demonstrating the universal ignorance in which he shared, and was apparently willing to talk with anyone willing to talk with him. In one of Plato's dialogues, he is depicted as showing that significant knowledge can be elicited from an uneducated young slave.

Finally, Socrates was a thoroughly communal man. Loyalty to the very city-state that had sentenced him to death kept him from escaping prison, and his stubborn questioning represented an indefeasible openness to communication. Whatever the truth that

---

[2]These events are recounted, on the basis no doubt of firsthand reports, in three works by Plato: the *Apology, Crito,* and *Phaedo.*

Socrates had discovered, it was not a truth that could be embodied in a definite set of propositions and securely possessed. Nor could it be imposed on others. It was a truth that could be found only in dialogue.

Socrates displayed that difficult balance between personal independence and social responsibility, between uncertainty and the capacity for action, that we may call civility. He was apparently interested in all ideas and wholly free of fanaticism. In his openness, however, he was committed to the most serious of all tasks, the search for truth. Through a similar paradox, he was "ignorant"—unable to pronounce finally on the truth or falsity of the ideas he discussed—yet he was capable of rare decisiveness and courage in the performance of civil functions, on one occasion risking death by defying, on grounds of illegality, an order from a governing clique.

Today we scarcely even aspire to such a stance. We assume that the test of political seriousness is dedication to practical results. Many respect above all else impassioned and uncompromising action. Yet history has been heedless of our demands. After striving for two centuries to command events (dating modern activism from the time of the French Revolution), the human race is nearly overwhelmed with misfortune. Could it be that what is required, rather than the sometimes complacent and sometimes desperate assertiveness of the modern age, is Socratic civility?

For most of us, doubt is unsettling, and we avoid serious discussion because we are afraid of doubt. But Socrates seems to tell us that doubt can be a source of health and hope and that the confidence of a free and communal person may be born, strangely, of uncertainty.

We are living today in a period of uncertainty, but it is an anxious and debilitating uncertainty, not the serene and luminous uncertainty of Socrates. Not only traditional religious faith, but even confidence in science, is weak. Vast multitudes of people crowding the earth have no clear and stable concept of what is real or how we ought to live. Our spiritual situation could hardly be more ominous.

If the idea of humane uncertainty is valid, however, our situation is not hopeless, and we should not try totally to eradicate our doubts. They may provide a pathway to understanding. When we try to replace doubts with objective principles that cannot be shaken or destroyed, we turn aside from this pathway. We turn aside not only from possibilities of deeper understanding but also from one another. So fundamental a diversion can be disastrous. The totalitarianism and violence of our time result in some measure from the efforts of men and women to escape from uncertainty. Those who cannot live with doubt cannot live with human beings who are thoughtful and independent enough to be sources of doubt.

Thus, for the sake both of understanding and of community, we may hope that our age of anxious uncertainty does not give way to one of perfect certainty. The greatest achievement of political thinking today would not be to overcome our doubts but to help us live with them in a state of freedom and civility.

I_{NDEX}